Preschool Education in America

Preschool Education in America

*The Culture of Young Children
from the Colonial Era to the Present*

Barbara Beatty

Yale University Press   New Haven and London

Designed by Sonia L. Scanlon.

Set in Fournier type by Clarinda, Clarinda, Iowa.

Printed in the United States of America by Vail-Ballou Press,
Binghamton, New York.

Library of Congress Cataloging-in-Publication Data

Beatty, Barbara, 1946–

    Preschool education in America : the culture of young
children from the colonial era to the present / Barbara
Beatty.

      p. cm.

    Includes bibliographical references and index.

    ISBN 0-300-06027-0 (alk. paper)

    1. Education, Preschool—United States—
History.   I. Title.

LB1140.23.B43   1995

372.21'0973—dc20   94-41347

        CIP

A catalogue record for this book is available from the British
Library.

For Shelton and Caroline Beatty and Douglas and Lucy Meyer,
and to the memory of Abigail Adams Eliot

Contents

Preface

This is the story of how Americans came to think that young children should have access to preschool education outside the home. (By young children, I mean three-, four-, and five-year-olds, not infants and toddlers, though their needs are equally important.) More specifically, this is a history of policy and pedagogy in American preschool education. I began by asking why, when there is mounting evidence of the importance and cost-effectiveness of early education and when more than half of mothers of preschool-age children in America work outside the home, is no provision made for universal preschool education in the United States today. To answer this question, I have studied why and how Americans have educated their young children since institutionalized preschool programs were begun in this country a century and a half ago.[1]

Americans have used different forms of extrafamilial preschool education since the colonists arrived on this continent in the early seventeenth century. Families often employed neighborhood women to run informal dame schools. Private and public infant schools were started in the early nineteenth century. Around the turn of the century, in what I argue was one of the greatest changes in modern American educational policy, kindergartens gained sufficient acceptance to become part of most major public school systems, making the education of five-year-olds a public responsibility. Private nursery schools for three- and four-year-olds started up in the early twentieth century, and the federal government sponsored public preschools for poor and needy children during the Depression, World War II, and the War on Poverty of the 1960s. But preschool programs for poor children became stigmatized and have not become universal. Most American children under the age of five do not have access to publicly supported education, and there have never been enough preschools to meet the needs of all needy children.

This book traces and analyzes preschool educators' answers to the following questions: Should the education of young children be a public or a private responsibility? Should the public be responsible for the education of all young children or only for children in need or "at risk"? What is the purpose of preschool education? What should young children be taught, and when? What are appropriate educational environments for young children, where should programs for young children be housed, and for how many hours a day should they operate? Who should control, administer, and teach in programs for young children?

I attempt to portray the American preschool movement in a balanced fashion, showing both the help it provided to young children and families, as well as its potential for harm. Preschool programs function in the contested and shifting space at the intersection of the private family and public life. During the early nineteenth century, when my narrative begins, the permeable, preindustrial family was becoming more private and closed. Institutionalized preschool education was one of the first of many movements to begin helping families and, in the process, opening them up again. But this help could also be weakening and intrusive, although of course preschool educators did not see it this way. In their view, they were part of a tireless and selfless crusade for the betterment of young children.[2]

By founding homelike schools and educating parents to be teachers at home, preschool educators combined aspects of private and public life in novel ways. They resisted state control at the same time they sought state support. This desire to mediate and meld private and public functions and domains yet retain separateness is, I think, one of the reasons there is still no universal public preschool education in this country. Even public kindergartens show traces of this ambivalence in that attendance is generally not compulsory.

Though preschool education was pedagogically more diverse than public elementary and secondary education, the ideas and institutions described in this book nevertheless show a certain uniformity. It would be an oversimplification to say that young children from upper-class backgrounds were educated in private preschools where they were protected from academic pressure and encouraged to be autonomous, express themselves, and play, while poor children were institutionalized in charity or public preschools where they were prepared for school and socialized to conform to societal norms. But social class did affect preschool pedagogy, while at the same time a canon evolved that prescribed the educational activities all young children were supposed to experience. This orthodoxy was promoted by a large body of prescriptive literature written primarily by middle- and upper-class women. Addressed to a national audience, this literature helped create a national culture of young children in which, as in the larger culture, the ideas and values of the majority were overrepresented.

Because of the dominance of this literature, the diverse methods of home education employed by families from differing social, economic, cultural, religious, ethnic, and regional backgrounds are largely missing from this history. Yet focusing on the upper and middle classes is problematic, not only because of whom and what it excludes, but also because social class is difficult to define. Historians use various background factors as proxies for social class and sometimes fail to specify clearly what these proxies are. I argue that the acquisition of the mores, attitudes, values, and patterns of speech and behavior that kindergarten and nursery school educators tried to teach young children and mothers became class markers. This book describes how preschool educators developed and promoted practices that aided the process of class formation and socialization and established a normative paradigm for American parents and children.[3]

Another omission is that this book does not deal with the parallel history of child care in America. Some young children were educated and cared for in day nurseries or other programs that were identified or identified themselves as child-care centers rather than preschools. Although the distinction between preschool education and child care is often artificial, it represents a very real historical division. Until recently, preschools and day nurseries were thought of as very different kinds of institutions, with different purposes and clienteles, staffed by people with different occupational identities, allegiances, and training. It is thus historically, if not politically or pedagogically, correct to discuss preschool education separately from child care.[4]

The final theme woven through this book is the relationship of children's culture to women's culture. The culture of young children existed within "woman's sphere," the domain within which nineteenth-century women worked and lived and by which their lives were defined. Women's culture and woman's sphere can be seen as liberating or limiting constructs, depending on the perspective of the historian. In my view, the culture of young children was both. Preschool educators established new kinds of institutions and vocations that crossed public-private boundaries and enlarged public responsibility for young children. The physical spaces in which preschool education took place extended beyond the home and expanded woman's sphere outside the family. The kindergarten in particular attempted to combine and address the interests of both women and children, and some preschool educators advocated children's liberation and led very untraditional, liberated lives. Most preschool educators, however, advocated women's adherence to traditional roles of motherhood and child nurture, and in general it seems wrong to associate preschool education with feminism. Kindergarten and nursery educators were primarily concerned with the well-being of young children, not women. *Maternalism,* the term Seth Koven and Sonya Michel use to describe political movements to advance the social welfare of mothers and children, would seem a better theoretical umbrella for the preschool movement than *feminism.*[5]

Though the culture of young children was coterminous with women's culture, little boys also attended kindergartens and nursery schools. Indeed, unlike other forms of education, most preschools were initially coeducational, rather than being provided only for boys. Men, too, were involved in early childhood education. The founders of the infant school and the kindergarten and authors of some of the key preschool texts were male, and male psychologists were influential in the nursery school movement. Even so, it was primarily women who promoted, started, directed, and taught in programs for young children; who published the teaching guides and journals; and who established and ran the training schools and professional organizations. Examining preschool education provides an opportunity to see a field in which women had almost complete autonomy to create an alternative professional model, establish occupational norms and practices, and make internal policy decisions. The price of this autonomy was marginalization. Women were left alone with young children because most men were not interested in or felt uncomfortable working with young children or considered young children to be within the province of women.

Female preschool educators communicated ideas about educating young children to mothers, who, by the mid–nineteenth century, were mainly responsible for the education of young children at home. Whether because of lack of time, desire, or other constraints, fathers played a much smaller role in child rearing. They are thus largely absent from the literature. This should not be taken to imply, however, that the presence of fathers was not considered important in young children's lives. In fact, many preschool educators exhorted mothers to get fathers more involved in their children's education.

Omissions such as this constitute only one of the problems of relying on prescriptive sources. It is difficult to estimate how many mothers and teachers actually read books on preschool education or how many young children experienced the activities they describe. But unlike most other writers of advice literature, preschool educators were in direct communication with mothers. Most of the authors of these texts worked, or had worked, with mothers and children on a regular basis. Unlike pediatricians who treated sick children sporadically or psychologists who studied samples of children in laboratories, preschool educators daily saw a wide range of children and mothers. They mediated between academia and real life in a two-way interchange through which mothers' questions and concerns affected scholarly research and experts' advice influenced mothering.[6]

This book describes the physical and social environments in which the young have been and are educated, as well as the educational practices directed at them. I have tried to interpret the meaning of these environments and practices for young children, but this is very hard to do. Though adults often complain about their noisiness, young children are the most silent and silenced of historical actors. They rarely participate in the formal discourse that goes on over their heads, except on the most basic level and then in an inarticulate or obstructionist manner. Consequently, historians are left to describe adults' ideas about children and the institutions designed for them. We can analyze the contexts of children's lives and how those contexts change over time, but we cannot truly capture children's own experiences and culture. This book tells part of the story of the construction of children's culture and poses the question, To what extent does modern American society value the culture of young children?[7]

Acknowledgments

I began research for this book twenty-five years ago when I became a kindergarten teacher in the Boston public school system. Because I've been working on this project for such a long time, I have many people to thank. I learned an enormous amount from the children, families, and teachers at the Farragut, Jefferson, and Hennigan schools in the Mission Hill and Roxbury sections of Boston where I taught for three years. I also learned a great deal from the children, families, and wonderful staff of the Lesley Ellis School in Cambridge, Massachusetts, Lesley College's laboratory preschool, which I directed for five years.

Because of these experiences, this is an "insider" history, but it is written with the perspective of an outsider. I gained objectivity from studying social policy and history of education at the Harvard Graduate School of Education, where this book originated as my doctoral dissertation. I want to thank my advisers and professors, whose knowledge, wisdom, and thoughtfulness aided immeasurably in my work (its shortcomings, of course, are my own). I am especially grateful for the guidance of Sheldon H. White of the Harvard Department of Psychology, whose generosity to students and understanding of the inner workings of psychology and education are legendary. I am indebted to Joseph Featherstone, now of Michigan State University, for introducing me to the "long conversation" of educational history, and to Mary Jo Bane, now of the Kennedy School of Government at Harvard and the U.S. Department of Health and Human Services, for teaching me about policy concerning families and children and for showing me that activism and scholarship can go hand in hand. I am also grateful for Patricia Albjerg Graham's scholarly and career advice, along with that of Courtney Cazden and others.

Another reason this book took so long is that I enjoy spending time in libraries and archives and kept unearthing more treasures

I wanted to include. I am grateful to the librarians and archivists who made my work possible and pleasant. In particular, I want to thank Bob Rogers of the Gutman Library at the Harvard Graduate School of Education, Lauren R. Brown at the Special Collections Division of University of Maryland College Park, Dorothy Mosakowski of the Clark University Archives, Margery Sly of the Smith College Archives, and Wilma Slaight of the Wellesley College Archives. I am also grateful to the Radcliffe Scholars Program of the Schlesinger Library, which provided me with a research grant, to the Alumnae Office of Wheelock College, and to Margaret Dollar, who assisted me in one phase of this research. Thanks are also due to Abigail Adams Eliot, Rhoda Case Brown, and Eleanor Tilden Jefferson, who graciously allowed me to interview them and gave me invaluable insights about the history of preschool eduction.

My ideas were influenced by conversations with colleagues and by reading and hearing about their research. I want to thank Barbara Brenzel, Barry Bull, Ken Hawes, and Linda Eisenmann, with all of whom I have worked in the Education Department at Wellesley College. I am also grateful to our departmental secretaries, Ethel Brown, Faye Stylianopoulos, and Adele Rosenthal, and to Wellesley College's support for my research. The work and encouragement of colleagues from other institutions, especially Ann Taylor Allen, Joyce Antler, Emily Cahan, Geraldine Clifford, David Labaree, Ellen Lagemann, Marvin Lazerson, Sonya Michel, Sally Schwager, David Tyack, and Roberta Wollons, have been most helpful. I am also appreciative of the support and good judgment of Gladys Topkis of Yale University Press, an editor whose enthusiasm about education is buoying. In addition, I want to thank the people who worked on the production of this volume. Sarah St. Onge's elegant copyediting helped my ideas come through more clearly. John Cook's photographic skill made it possible to see more of what early preschools were like, and Suzanne Greenberg was able to capture what I look like. The staff at Yale University Press were delightful to work with and unfailingly helpful.

I am lucky to have many friends whose company and kindness have seen me through this long process. I am especially grateful to Carolynn Maltas and Marti Katz and for the support of Barbara Coleman and Douglas Hughes. Finally, and most important, I am grateful to my family: to my husband, Michael Meyer, to my parents, Shelton and Caroline Beatty, to my brother, John Lee Beatty, and to my children, Douglas and Lucy Meyer. My mother and father gave my brother and me a wonderful childhood filled with stories, books, travel, education, and love and provided expert proofreading and editorial suggestions. I am most in debt to my children, for all they have taught me and for cheering me on as I wrote a book about "other people's children."

On May 24, 1952, the *Boston Herald* quoted Abigail Eliot, the founder of America's first nursery school, as saying, "The most important thing is to enjoy your children, to love them, be fair and just with them. If you do that they're pretty likely to come out all right."

Preschool Education in America

Chapter 1   "The School of Infancy"

European Origins of the American

Preschool Movement

The ideological origins of the American preschool movement
can be traced to the religious, philosophical, political, industrial,
scientific, and technological revolutions that transformed Europe
in the seventeenth and eighteenth centuries. From this ferment
came new ideas about education, including the notion that young
children could benefit from education outside the home and
needed to be educated differently from older children. Though
the Greeks, Romans, and other ancient civilizations had concepts
of "ages of man," Philippe Ariès and other modern scholars
argue that only in the seventeenth century was childhood "discovered" as a unique life stage requiring special care and treatment. (Difficult to document, the recognition of *childhood* probably occurred at different times in different places, cultures, and
ethnic and religious groups.) Beginning in the seventeenth century such Protestant ministers as Johann Amos Comenius and
such Enlightenment and romantic philosophers as John Locke
and, later, Jean-Jacques Rousseau wrote treatises advocating
more child-centered, naturalistic approaches to education and
child rearing. In the late eighteenth century the teaching methods
of the Swiss educator Johann Heinrich Pestalozzi in particular
provided the basis for a nonacademic pedagogy that came to be
seen as appropriate for the education of young children.[1]

The first institutionalized extrafamilial educational programs
for young children grew out of communitarian social reform
efforts. In the early nineteenth century the British industrial-
ist and social reformer Robert Owen organized infant schools
for the young children of workers in his utopian, socialist

communities in New Lanark, Scotland, and New Harmony, Indiana. Evangelical Protestant reformers opened similar schools for the poor in London and elsewhere. Though infant schools were intended for and first used with children from the lower classes, upper-class European parents soon began to think that extrafamilial education might benefit their children, too, and a few private infant schools for affluent children were opened.

At the same time, however, affluent parents were being encouraged to become more involved in educating their young children at home. Comenius, Locke, and Rousseau all advocated private, home-based education for young children, as did Maria Edgeworth and her father, Richard Edgeworth, who produced a technical manual for improving home education. Thus there was general acceptance of the notion that young children from poor families should be educated outside the home, but no consensus that similar experiences were good for children from higher-class backgrounds. These ambivalent, class-biased European attitudes greatly influenced ideas about the education of young children in America, set the precedent for separate preschools for rich and poor, and sowed tenacious doubts about the effects and value of early educational programs.

Johann Amos Comenius's School of Infancy

The work of the seventeenth-century Moravian bishop Johann Amos Comenius (1592–1670), whose *Great Didactic* provided the first outline of a modern system of universal education, reveals the increasing attention of philosophers and educators to very young children. Born in what is now the Czech Republic, Comenius was deeply affected by the violence of the Thirty Years' War and spent his life working to achieve peace. He hoped that universal education would end political violence and promote social harmony, thus preparing the way for the Lord. Comenius believed all children should be educated together because God had made all persons in His image. As traditional, classical methods of education had obviously failed to make men and women pious and capable of living together in harmony, he also thought new educational methods were necessary.[2]

Like later Enlightenment and romantic philosophers, Comenius looked to nature to provide the guidelines for a new pedagogy. He envisioned a special "school of life" with appropriate pedagogical methods and content for each of the classical seven ages of man and used the naturalistic imagery of plants and horticulture to describe "gardens of delight" where large numbers of children were to grow, play, and learn together joyfully and harmoniously.[3]

But despite his millennialist faith in schooling and his advocacy of universal institutionalized education, Comenius was opposed to formal schooling for children under the age of six, whom he thought should be educated at home by their mothers. Written between 1628 and 1635 and first published in English in 1650, Comenius's *The School of Infancy* prescribed in detail how mothers should educate their young children at home. After the "school of birth," which involved mothers' thinking healthy, happy thoughts while pregnant (a common recommendation), children were to be breast-fed, raised in a healthy home environment, and educated in a naturalistic manner.

Comenius described a full curriculum of educational activities divided into three areas: things young children should know, things they should be able to do, and things they should be able to say. He thought children under six should acquire knowledge in eight fields: "natural things," "optics," astronomy, geography, "chronology," history, "household affairs," and "politics." And for each of these fields Comenius provided examples of content appropriate for young children. Optics, for instance, meant knowing the difference between light and dark and the names of common colors; geography was knowing where one was born.[1]

Comenius also thought young children should acquire skills in five different fields: dialectics, arithmetic, geometry, music, and manual activities. Young children should know what a question and an answer were and "be able to reply distinctly to a question proposed, not talking about onions when the question is garlic"; they should "be able to count to twenty, or even all the way to sixty," "understand what is an even and what an odd number," and be able to do simple addition; they should know "small, large, short or long, narrow or broad, thin or thick" and what an inch, a foot, and a yard were; they should be able "to sing from memory some little verses from the Psalms or hymns"; and they should be able "to cut, to split, to carve, to arrange, to tie, to untie, to roll up, and to unroll" (20–21).

Comenius further thought that by age six children should be able to express themselves understandably, if not correctly. They should be able to use natural rhetoric, to repeat common figures of speech, and to memorize a few verses of poetry. Other experiences in the school of infancy included a long list of activities concerning health, cleanliness, justice, patience, industriousness, and so on. Importantly, Comenius also noted that instruction in the school of infancy should be individualized both because homes were not orderly places like schools and because young children achieved speech and other developmental milestones at very different ages (21–22).

Comenius took particular pains to explain why he felt children under six should be educated at home instead of with other children in a school, noting especially the unhealthy effects of large classes and the tendency of external schooling to weaken young children both physically and mentally. Young children needed "more watchfulness and care than a teacher, having a number of children under him," was able to provide. And, Comenius thought, because young children's brains were "not consolidated before the fifth or sixth year," they learned better "spontaneously, imperceptibly in play, so much as is convenient in the domestic circle" (80).

Comenius worried most about the potentially harmful effects of excessively early education. Using naturalistic tropes that would become recurrent themes, he described how a young shoot taken out to be planted "while too tender, grows feebly and slowly, whereas the firmer one grows strongly and quickly." Young horses "prematurely put to the carriage" became weak, but if given more time to grow they pulled "more strongly, and more than repay you for the delay." After age six, however, group schooling was preferable to private tutoring because "young trees when transplanted always grow tall, and garden fruit has always a richer flavor than forest fruit." Older children needed group socialization, or they would become wild (80–81).

Similar analogies to horticulture and animal husbandry filled later literature on early education. To a society that believed in the great chain of being, young children were closer to animals and plants than adults were. For seventeenth- and eighteenth-century Europeans, nature was the great text on human development. They had first-hand knowledge of gardening, farming, and animal care and saw what happened to plants and animals that had been badly or carelessly treated. That young children too might suffer permanent damage from being exposed prematurely to the elements, overworked, or allowed insufficient time to ripen seemed incontrovertible, and to ignore such dangers was to court certain disaster. Comenius introduced the possibility of a new, naturalistic form of education that was appropriate and even beneficial for young children—that might produce better, healthier fruit.

John Locke's Thoughts on Education

John Locke's little book of advice on education, *Some Thoughts Concerning Education* (1693), was to have far greater impact in America than *The School of Infancy*, which was little known until the late nineteenth century. Though unmarried, John Locke (1632–1704) was a medical doctor and had considerable experience educating the sons of British aristocrats. Like Comenius, he opposed schooling young children outside the home. In fact, he was opposed to school-based education of children of any age and recommended that, if possible, they be educated at home, by their parents and a tutor. Schools were incubators of "roughness and ill breeding." For Locke, social isolation of children was preferable to the risk of their acquiring rude and immoral habits from schoolmates. Virtue, he asserted, was "harder to be got, than a knowledge of the world; and if lost in a young man is seldom recovered."[5]

Although the principles of home education Locke advocated could be applied universally, his work was explicitly intended for the education of sons of gentlemen. Though he conceptualized children as "white paper, or wax to be moulded as one pleases," Locke did not think all children were the same and was not proposing that all children be molded in the same way or together. "Each Man's Mind has some peculiarity," he stated, and "besides that I think a Prince, a Nobleman, and an ordinary Gentleman's son should have different ways of Breeding."[6]

Written as a series of letters on the education of the son of his cousin Mary Jepp Clarke and her husband, Edward Clarke, Locke's *Some Thoughts Concerning Education* was both a philosophical treatise on education and a practical manual on good breeding. Like the physician he was, Locke began with sections on health, recommending that children's feet be washed frequently in cold water to lessen the danger of exposure to colds from wet shoes and that they play in the open air, wear loose clothing, and eat simple food. Locke thought character training was the most important part of good breeding and encouraged parents to establish their authority as soon as possible. Opposed to physical punishment, he suggested instead that parents teach by force of will and personal example and use children's desire for "esteem" and wish to avoid "disgrace" as forms of control (153). He particularly recommended the efficacy of developing and utilizing children's feelings of internal guilt to make them self-governing. "If you can once get into Children a Love of Credit, and an Apprehension of Shame and Disgrace," Locke wrote, "you have put into them the true Principle, which will constantly work, and incline them to the right" (155).[7]

Though *Some Thoughts Concerning Education* was not especially about young children (the Clarkes' son was eight when Locke began writing letters to them in 1684), it contained a great deal of advice about educating preschool-age children. Locke was criticized for treating children too much like little adults because he told parents to reason with their offspring whenever possible. But he was aware that it was not always possible to reason effectively with young children. "No Body can think a Boy of Three, or Seven Years old, should be argued with as a grown Man," he wrote. "Long discourses, and Philosophical reasoning, at best, amaze and confound, but do not instruct Children" (181). Setting the right personal example was the best way to deal with young children. Locke also advised parents to let children play on their own as much as possible. "Childish Actions, are to be perfectly free and unrestrained," he stated, "as far as they can consist with Respect due to those present" (157).

But though young children were to have plenty of time to play, Locke recommended beginning formal instruction in reading very early, as soon as they could talk (173–74). Locke thought learning should be like play, not like business or work (235, 236). Young children should want to learn to read books, naturally. If they did not, Locke described various games with lettered dice to help them learn the alphabet and to trick them into early academics without their knowing what they were doing (238).

The Clarkes also had a daughter Elizabeth, whom Locke liked very much, and Locke wrote to Mrs. Clarke separately about Elizabeth's education. In general, he did not think girls should be educated very differently from boys, except for some of their early physical experiences. Women were the "softer sex" and therefore should not have "rough usage." But, Locke wrote Mrs. Clarke, "I acknowledge no difference of sex in your mind relating . . . to truth, virtue, and obedience." Girls were to get exercise and play outdoors like boys, but, to protect their beauty and their complexions, they should play in the shade and go for walks in the early morning, when the "busy sunbeams" were less "hot and piercing." And girls' discipline should be in the hands of their mothers, not their fathers.[8]

The first American edition of *Some Thoughts on Education* was published in Boston in 1830, and, by the end of the nineteenth century, the book had appeared in some thirty-five English-language editions. Though Locke's vision of childhood was more cerebral, austere, guilt-ridden, and adult-oriented than that of the romantics who were to follow, his ideas nevertheless did much to counter Calvinist views of infant depravity and contributed to the growth of freer, more playful, and more experimental attitudes toward education and child rearing. Transitional in some of his views, Locke was deeply modern in that he wanted parents to break with the past and trust their own ideas about what was good for their children. He concluded his brief treatise by encouraging parents "to consult their own Reason, in the Education of their Children, rather than wholly to rely upon Old Custom."[9]

Jean-Jacques Rousseau's Natural Children

If anyone broke with "Old Custom," it was the philosopher Jean-Jacques Rousseau (1712–1778), whose *Emile* is one of the most radical books ever written on education and child rearing. The bible of the "New Education," as the European pedagogical reform movement was called, *Emile* is a romantic portrayal of a child growing up in nature. In a reversal of traditional educational practices, Rousseau advocated treating young children as children rather than as potential adults. Childhood was to be prolonged and protected rather than rushed and exploited for adult purposes. "The chief thing," Rousseau advised parents, was to "prevent anything being done" rather than to instill adult ideas, behaviors, and skills. "Childhood has its place in the sequence of human life," he wrote; "the man must be treated as a man and the child as a child."[10]

Rousseau's own happy but brief childhood may have influenced his views on child rearing and education. The son of a Protestant watchmaker, he lost his mother shortly after his birth and was raised by an aunt and his indulgent but mournful father until the age of ten, when he was sent to a boarding school. Like Locke, Rousseau had experience educating children, but his stint as a tutor was unhappy and apparently unsuccessful. Unlike Locke, Rousseau was a father himself, but he rejected paternity and his progeny and forced his mistress, Thérèse Lavasseur, to give their five babies to a foundling home in Paris. Rousseau later appeared to regret abandoning his children, and this may have been part of the motivation behind his writing *Emile*, the story of an imaginary child and child-rearing experience.[11]

Published in 1762, *Emile* was an idealized description of education based on children's supposedly natural development rather than on traditional didactic teaching and schooling. But nature to Rousseau was a negative concept, defined as something not touched by society or man, whereas man himself and man-made things were unnatural. Education was also negative: it consisted of not doing anything unnatural more than doing something positive.

Rousseau was obsessed with the dangers of precocity, which he saw as resulting from early exposure to "unnatural" social experiences. Such exposure could cause corruption and permanent deformity, for man "mutilates his dog, his horse, and his slave. He destroys and defaces all things . . . he will have nothing as nature made it" (5).

Like Locke, Rousseau thought schools were unhealthy for children, but he also saw the home as an unnatural environment. Deprecating mothers, he criticized the results of the stultifying, arbitrary way he thought women educated their young children at home. He proposed instead that mothers give their children up to male tutors, who would educate them in a safe, natural environment away from society. (He was even ambivalent about breast-feeding because it would distance children from their tutors.) Like Locke, he recommended loose clothing, simple food, cold baths, going barefoot, and lots of time for play. Some of his ideas, however, sound even more controlling and manipulative than Locke's. For example, Emile was to be forced to sleep in an uncomfortable bed, tricked into running foot races he could not win, and obliged to undergo other contrived experiences from which he was to learn particular lessons.

But unlike Locke, Rousseau was opposed to teaching young children to read, which he called "the curse of childhood" (80). He postponed Emile's formal reading instruction until the age of twelve, ridiculed contrived methods such as using little letter cards or games, as Locke had suggested, and insisted that parents should wait until children showed signs of wanting to read on their own (81). Rousseau was also critical of Locke's overall approach to reasoning with young children. Excessive reasoning, he said, made children "exceedingly silly," "argumentative and rebellious," and, worst of all, precocious and old before their time (53). Reasoning, he argued, should be the end result of education, not the beginning or the means. Childhood had "its own ways of seeing, thinking, and feeling," Rousseau wrote in a direct reference to Locke, and "nothing [was] more foolish than to try to substitute our ways" (54).

And also unlike Locke, Rousseau thought girls should be educated very differently from boys. Though he was in some ways a member of the Enlightenment, his ideas on the education of girls reflected the essentialist, biological determinism of newer, romantic views on women. For Rousseau, men were by nature "strong and active" while women were "weak and passive" (322). Dependent, docile, and subject to authority, Sophie, Emile's wife and helpmate, was to be educated for the sole purpose of meeting Emile's needs for company and eventual socialization. She was to be responsible for child care and trained to remain in her place.[12]

Rousseau's condemnation of traditional school curricula and pedagogy in *Emile* was an impetus for the creation of new teaching techniques. In place of formal instruction in reading or book learning, he prescribed informal learning experiences in which children explored the physical environment, observed objects in nature, and played games designed to enhance their sensory abilities (except for smell, which Rousseau thought too sophisticated a sense for young children).

Though some of Rousseau's pedagogical ideas were extreme and impractical to implement, they were enormously influential. Both Rousseau's and Locke's books were models: Locke's for the raising of a civilized, rational English gentleman and Rousseau's for the rearing of an unfettered, natural citizen. Neither recommended group schooling for children of any age; neither had much use for women. And both expected adults to devote an unrealistic, even inordinate amount of time to the education of an individual child. But despite this impracticality, *Some Thoughts Concerning Education* and *Emile* were widely read, and European parents and educators began trying to implement Locke's and Rousseau's ideas with real children.

Papa Pestalozzi's Home-Style Pedagogy and Programs for Young Children
Johann Heinrich Pestalozzi (1746–1827) was the first European educator to develop pedagogical methods consciously derived from experimentation with real children. Born to middle-class parents in Zurich, Pestalozzi became interested in education as a means of ameliorating the living conditions of the poor. He named his first son, born in 1770, Jean-Jacques and attempted to raise him in a Rousseauean manner. Pestalozzi was "seized," he wrote in his journal, by Rousseau's "visionary and highly speculative book" *Emile*. He described going on a walk with his three-year-old boy and pointing out natural occurrences, such as the fact that water ran downhill, which appar-

ently delighted the child. Pestalozzi raved about this new, natural approach to education and recommended that other parents lead their children "out into Nature" and teach them "on the hilltops and in the valleys" so that they, too, would know that nature was "the real teacher and that you, with your art, do nothing more than walk quietly at her side."[13]

The results of Pestalozzi's Rousseauean experiments with his son were less than wholly satisfactory, however. By the age of eleven, the boy could not read or write, though some of his difficulty may have been due to a sickly constitution and rheumatic condition. Pestalozzi professed to be untroubled by the boy's learning problems, but, like many other parents, he came to doubt the applicability of Rousseau to academic learning and later sent his son to boarding school.[14]

Concerned about the effects of economic and industrial change on Swiss society, Pestalozzi began experimenting with pedagogical methods designed especially to educate poor children. More a benevolent paternalist than an egalitarian, he aimed not to raise the social-class status of the poor but to make them independent. "The poor," he wrote, "must be educated for poverty"; educating them required "detailed knowledge of the probable situation in which they will spend their lives." The children at Neuhof, the experimental farm school he opened in 1774, worked in the fields, did domestic tasks such as spinning, weaving, and household chores, and engaged in group lessons and other activities designed to be educational and uplifting. But Neuhof proved costly to run, and it closed after a few years. To support himself, Pestalozzi turned to writing.[15]

Like Rousseau, Pestalozzi thought true education should be based on nature. But he saw the family and home, not the wilds of nature, as the most natural environment for children. In his first literary work, *The Evening Hours of a Hermit* (1780), he stated that domestic relationships were "the earliest and most excellent of the relationships of Nature. . . . Hence the home is the place where the educational process runs its course"[16]

In his widely read novel *Leonard and Gertrude* (1781), Pestalozzi introduced a new model for the teacher: a peasant mother. Gertrude's home-teaching techniques are responsible for the rejuvenation of the village of Bonnal, in which the novel is set. She teaches her children "to count the number of steps from one end of the room to the other" and uses the ten panes in her cottage's windows "to unfold the decimal relations of numbers." She makes the children "count their threads while spinning, and the number of turns on the reel, when they wound the yarn into skeins." And "in every occupation of life she taught them an accurate and intelligent observation of common objects and the forces of nature."[17]

Pestalozzi's Gertrude moved the new education from Rousseau's outdoor Eden into a warm and cozy peasant home. But both were idealized, artificial environments, what Joseph Featherstone calls "institutionalized naturalism." Rousseau rigged Emile's supposedly natural experiences, and Pestalozzi created model schools and stylized educational set pieces, like Gertrude's conveniently numbered window panes. This consciously constructed naturalism, which idealized an older bucolic era in which children supposedly frolicked in the fields and whistled while they worked, was to become the hallmark of early childhood education and the source of much of its enduring, sentimental popular appeal.[18]

Pestalozzi thought schools were artificial institutions where children were unhappy and learned little of real value. In *Christopher and Alice* (1782), a sequel to *Leonard and Gertrude*, Pestalozzi explicitly criticized traditional schooling and the parent "who, having plenty at home, runs about begging; and that is the very thing which our village folks do, by forgetting all the good lessons which they might teach their children at home, and, instead thereof, sending them every day to gather up the dry crumbs which are to be got in our miserable schools." What parents taught their children at home was much more important than anything a teacher might teach them at school. "The parents' teaching is the kernel of wisdom, and the schoolmaster's business is only to make a husk over it," Pestalozzi concluded. Through his book *How Gertrude Teaches Her Children* (1801), he tried to "make home instruction possible again for people neglected in this respect." The goal of this early attempt at introducing parent education to the poor, Pestalozzi asserted, was "to raise every mother whose heart beats for her children, step by step, till at last she can follow my elementary exercises by herself, and be able to use them with her children."[19]

But Pestalozzi did think older children needed schools, though as much like a home as possible; indeed, he organized such homelike schools for children who lacked good homes. As he wrote to the British educational reformer James Pierrepont Greaves, schools needed to be more student- and learner-centered, places "in which the pupils are taught to act as teachers and educated to act as educators." Schools needed especially to be infused with what kindergarten originator Friedrich Froebel would later call the "mother spirit." "Above all," Pestalozzi wrote Greaves, a school needed to be a place "in which the *female character* is at an early period developed in that direction which enables it to take so prominent a part in early education."[20]

What Pestalozzi hoped to do was revive the kinds of home-style educational methods he thought peasant mothers had lost through industrialization. In fact, though his pedagogical practices were not designed or intended for young children, he provided a model that made extrafamilial schooling seem appropriate even for them. Like Rousseau, he thought children should sense and touch things rather than just reading or being told about them. Though this method, which became known as "object teaching," was later reduced to simplistic lessons in which children were shown concrete things and then parroted answers to set questions, it opened the way for the myriad "manipulatives" such as puzzles and blocks that fill preschool classrooms today.

Affection was another central theme in Pestalozzi's pedagogy. From all accounts, he enjoyed being around children and spent as much time with them as possible. In a letter describing his school at Stanz, he recounted how he and the children ate, drank, and even slept together in an intimate, familylike environment. He emphasized the importance of maintaining a loving, emotionally supportive atmosphere and encouraged the children and his staff to call him Papa Pestalozzi.[21]

Pestalozzi's views on education became very well known during his lifetime. After the success of his books, he was able to attract government backing and return to his practical educational work. In the late 1790s and early 1800s, he founded a succession of homelike model schools at Stanz (1798–1799), Burgdorf (1800–1803), and Yverdun (1804–1825). Followers and assistants came to live and work with him, and numerous visitors from Europe and the United States visited to observe his educational techniques. Though his schools eventually closed, and Pestalozzi died destitute in 1827, his pedagogical ideas and methods would influence educational practice for many years to come.

Ironically, though Pestalozzi's pedagogy was expressly designed for poor children, it became especially popular with wealthy parents. Private Pestalozzian schools were started for upper-class children in England, Spain, and Russia in the first decades of the nineteenth century. Pestalozzi's ideas also affected the authors of English advice manuals on home education, which were widely read by American parents. And Pestalozzianism was introduced directly to the United States, where Pestalozzian infant schools were founded for rich and poor children in major Eastern cities in the 1830s.[22]

The Edgeworths' Practical Home Education Methods

Maria and Richard Edgeworth's home education manual, *Practical Education* (1798), reflected the practical, technological spirit that was changing the human and natural landscape of the late eighteenth and early nineteenth centuries. Richard Lovell Edgeworth (1744–1817) was a member of the Lunar Group, the society of Birmingham intellectuals, scientists, inventors, and businessmen that originated much of the technology of the British industrial revolution. It is not surprising that one of this extraordinary group would focus on the problem of how to develop human capital through the use of more effective child-rearing and educational methods.

Like Pestalozzi, by whose work he was initially much influenced, Richard Edgeworth raised his first son in a Rousseauean fashion. In his memoirs, he attributed the boy's early ability in mechanics to Rousseau's emphasis on things and described him as having "a ready and keen use of all his senses and of his judgment." But Edgeworth also found his son "not disposed to *obey*" and thought he "showed an invincible dislike to control," which soon became problematic. Though Rousseau, who met the boy in 1771, apparently approved of the child, Edgeworth became involved in a new project, left his son in a Catholic seminary, and eventually disowned him. As with Pestalozzi, however, this initial lack of success did not dim Edgeworth's enthusiasm for experimental child rearing.[23]

The germ for *Practical Education* came from a plan for an educational system that Richard Edgeworth and his second wife, Honora Sneyd, developed for their own children. The author of a guide to road and carriage making, Edgeworth applied this same sober, engineering mentality to child rearing and education. More like an animal husbandry or technical manual than a philosophical treatise, *Practical Education* was a family effort. Edgeworth's oldest daughter, Maria, did most of the writing and is properly listed as the principal author. Edgeworth himself wrote the chapters on the teaching of reading and subjects for older children. The chapter on obedience was based on Honora Edgeworth's notes, and, according to the preface, "the whole manuscript was submitted to her judgement" and revised by her before her death. Maria Edgeworth's brother Lovell sketched the section on teaching chemistry, and her brother-in-law, Thomas Beddoes, a medical researcher, provided ideas for the sections on "Toys" and "Tasks."[24]

Maria Edgeworth (1767–1849) was well qualified to write a practical manual on child rearing and home education. Single, she lived at home with various of her fourteen brothers and sisters by her father's four marriages and knew a great deal about the realities of dealing with young children. One of her first literary projects was the translation of Madame de Genlis's *Adèle et Théodore; ou, Lettres sur l'éducation,* a Rousseauean account of a noblewoman's experiments with domestic education. Maria also began writing children's stories based on simple, daily events. Some of these stories were designed to teach children lessons in specific subjects such as chemistry and mechanics; others had a moral purpose. Maria later became a best-selling writer of popular novels.[25]

The Edgeworths' *Practical Education* offered parents specific information and suggestions on a wide range of topics, including such key pedagogical themes as play and playthings, when and how to begin reading instruction, children's literature, and socialization for self-control. The overall effect of the book was to underscore the importance of childhood experiences in shaping adult character and to impress on parents the gravity of their task as educators. The wealth of detail and attention the Edgeworths devoted to what had previously seemed trivial or entertaining aspects of children's lives and behavior, such as play and toys, emphasized the potentially permanent effects of early experience and the serious way in which parents should examine all aspects of what they did or did not do for their children.

In good Rousseauean fashion, Maria Edgeworth began by warning parents to leave their children alone, as "the danger of doing too much in education" was "greater even than the danger of doing too little." She went on to introduce the scientific, laboratory-for-learning method that would lead to educational toys and modern, cognitive approaches to child-rearing and early education. A child's room, as she depicted it, should be like a workshop, fitted with functional toys and "pieces of wood of various shapes and sizes, which they may build up and pull down, and put in a variety of different forms and positions; balls, pulleys, wheels, strings, and strong little carts, proportioned to their age, and to the things which they want to carry in them." Instead of fanciful playthings such as furnished doll houses and wind-up animals, she recommended that children be supplied with a "rational toy-shop . . . with all manner of carpenter's tools, with wood properly prepared for the young workman, and with screws, nails, glue, emery-paper" and other such materials. The book also included lengthy descriptions of chemical and optical experiments for young children.[26]

On the issue of when and how young children should be taught to read, the Edgeworths compromised at four as the age when reading instruction should begin, recommending neither Rousseau's counsel of leaving reading until very late nor the advice of popular manual writers like Mrs. Barbauld or Locke, who encouraged parents to start as soon as possible. As to reading methods, the Edgeworths described a very modern-seeming phonetic scheme of their own invention, with special diacritical marks under and over letters to regularize the inconsistencies of English spelling and pronunciation (1:34).

Nowhere was Maria Edgeworth's practicality more apparent than in her opinions on children's literature, which placed her squarely in the Platonic tradition of valuing virtue and morality over fantasy. She condoned censorship "to preserve children from the knowledge of any vice, or any folly, of which the idea has never yet entered their minds" (1:289) and advised mothers to read children's books themselves first and, if necessary, to mutilate them, as "few books can safely be given to children without the previous use of the pen, the pencil, and the scissors" (1:288).

In Lockean fashion, Maria Edgeworth argued that children should read or have read to them books that cultivated the "habit of reasoning" (1:299). She warned against overimaginative works and dismissed fairy stories as "not now much read" (1:294). She especially cautioned parents against allowing their daughters to develop a taste for sentimental literature, as the exaggerated emotions and overblown prose of these works cultivated "what is called the heart prematurely," lowered "the tone of the mind," and were incompatible with "sound sense, or with simple reality," so important in the education of women (1:297). For similar reasons, she also thought adventure stories were bad for boys; even *Robinson Crusoe,* the only book Rousseau allowed Emile to read, was proscribed. For girls, however, who "must very soon perceive the impossibility of their rambling about the world in quest of adventures," this type of reading would not "torment the imagination" and was not problematic (1:300). Not surprisingly, the kind of literature Edgeworth particularly recommended for children was "the history of realities" (1:302): natural history books and stories with moral and scientific lessons such as those she had begun to produce prolifically herself.

The Edgeworths took a balanced view on discipline. Like many other British reformers of their time, they were utilitarians who espoused efficiency. Though they did not explicitly condemn physical punishment, they recommended that parents use the least amount of such punishment possible and make sure it was intelligible to children by being "not only immediately, but repeatedly, and uniformly, associated with the actions which we wish them to avoid" (1:154).

Above all, the Edgeworths counseled consistency. Parents needed to be sure that children could actually do what was being asked of them and then had to make sure that what had been asked was done. Unlike Locke, they advised against using guilt and the "delicate secret influence of conscience" (1:305). Instead, they emphasized the importance of self-control, which they thought children should be taught directly, through practical experience or by parental admonition and example, not by being shamed or disgraced.

Maria Edgeworth's views on girls' education also emphasized self-control. A far cry from Rousseau's portrayal of Emile's simpering, manipulative wife, Sophie, her ideas were also a long way from those of her contemporary, women's rights advocate Mary Wollstonecraft. Learning to control their temper was particularly important for girls, Edgeworth stated, "because much of the effect of their powers of reasoning, and of their wit, when they grow up" would "depend upon the gentleness and good humor with which they conduct themselves." Unlike Rousseau, who recommended what she termed "debasing cunning" as the principal mode of female interaction with men, she thought women should "support the cause of reason with all the graces of female gentleness" and learn to speak and act simply and straightforwardly.[27]

Like Comenius, Locke, Rousseau, and Pestalozzi, the Edgeworths thought parents should teach their own young children at home, if at all possible. Likening schools to prisons and insane asylums, they condemned them as morally unhealthy environments in which young children acquired bad habits. To "a public school, as to a general infirmary for mental disease, all desperate subjects are sent," they declared, and once there, children picked up contagious vices (2:100).[28]

Though the Edgeworths advocated what today would be called home schooling, they did not focus especially on the role of the mother in child rearing and education, as later domestic education and preschool advocates would do. Indeed, they thought fathers should be much involved in their children's education. The father "who has time, talents, and temper, to educate his family" was "certainly the best preceptor," they stated. In this respect, *Practical Education* was a transitional book. Rather than the paeans to mothers found in Pestalozzi's work, the Edgeworths supplied a wealth of practical information about materials and activities. This practicality made their guide enormously popular in England, and in the United States it became a model for American domestic education manuals and reinforced the idea that young children should be educated at home.[29]

Robert Owen and the British Infant School Movement

It took the visionary radicalism and millennialist zeal of a communitarian social reformer to initiate a movement to educate young children outside the home. Robert Owen (1771–1858) wanted very young children—the younger the better—to be educated together, in groups, outside their homes, so that they would be more influenced by the social pressures of a school environment than by their families. Owen advocated school for young children for precisely the reason other theorists did not: to counter their individualism. A futurist, not a naturalist, he saw the model for the school as the factory, and his high-tech visions included larger, cleaner, more efficient institutions, not smaller, warmer, cozier communities. Owen's idea was to institutionalize social relationships as humankind's natural state. To achieve this aim required creating a new institution, an infant school, where young children's characters could be shaped to form a new generation of transformed adults.[30]

Like Pestalozzi, some of whose methods he appropriated, Owen became involved in education because of his concerns about the effects of industrialization on the lower classes, effects with which Owen had a great deal of firsthand experience. Born in Wales into a craftsman's family, Owen left home at the age of ten to apprentice with merchants in various parts of England. He became a factory superintendent in Manchester and in 1793 was invited to join the Manchester Literary and Philosophical Society, where he met industrial innovators such as James Dalton and Robert Fulton and honed his increasingly radical social views. In 1800 he became the manager of his father-in-law's cotton mill in New Lanark, Scotland. Using income from his successful political essays and contributions from other radicals like Jeremy

Bentham, Owen purchased New Lanark and turned it into an experimental utopian community.[31]

In 1816 Owen opened the Institution for the Formation of Character at New Lanark, which included an infant school for children just walking through age five. For a small fee, the infant school cared for and educated the children of mothers who worked in the cotton mill. Children aged six to ten attended classes for about five-and-a-half hours a day, with breaks for recess and lunch. The younger children had a half-day of organized activities, such as marching, clapping, and dancing, and informal instruction and for the rest of the school day played freely in a paved outdoor area under the supervision of a female assistant.

Like Pestalozzi, Owen thought young children should be taught with tangible objects rather than books and treated tenderly rather than harshly. The infant school at New Lanark was "furnished with paintings, chiefly of animals, with maps, and often supplied with natural objects from the gardens, fields, and woods." Owen opposed any harsh or hurtful disciplinary methods and exhorted teachers to act kindly at all times.[32]

Like Rousseau and Pestalozzi, Owen thought traditional academic education made children unhappy. As he said in his autobiography, the children at New Lanark "were while in school the happiest human beings I have ever seen." They were "not to be annoyed by books," and their teachers were taught how to instruct them "for their amusement, for with these infants everything was to be amusement." The only exception Owen recommended to this rule, according to his son, Robert Dale Owen, was Maria Edgeworth's "little works," which Owen nonetheless thought contained "too much of praise and blame."[33]

For all this emphasis on children's happiness, the large class sizes and monolithic architecture at New Lanark, along with Owen's bent toward utilitarianism and efficiency, created an impersonal, factorylike atmosphere. For Owen, the main reason for following the pedagogical principles he outlined was that they were conducive to the creation of a new moral order. This new moral order could come about only through group education. Hence, unlike Pestalozzi, Robert Owen did not see mothers as perfect teachers for young children. As his daughter, Jane Dale Owen, explained, mothers' affection for their children was "apt to warp the judgment." Children of all ages and sexes needed to be educated in groups (though not necessarily coeducational groups) in "public schools, but diametrically opposed in nature and tendency to the public schools of the present day."[34]

Owen's ideas on infant education influenced British educational and social reformers whose political views were less radical than his own. A group of London philanthropists and politicians headed by Lord Brougham hired James Buchanan, the teacher at New Lanark, to begin an infant school in Westminster, and other infant schools also were started, notably one in Spitalfields taught by Samuel Wilderspin, who promoted his own pedagogical methods in competition with Owen's. Wilderspin was a schoolmaster, not a socialist. Where Owen envisioned a new moral order and attempted to foster attitudes of cooperation and social harmony, Wilderspin was interested in teaching reading, writing, and the Scriptures to large numbers of children. Instead of trying to ameliorate the effects of industrialization, he employed mechanical methods in the classroom. Above all, Wilderspin was interested in efficiency and cost-effectiveness, as evidenced by the title of one of his popular books: *On the Importance of Educating the Infant Children of the Poor, Showing How Three Hundred Children from Eighteen Months to Seven Years of Age, May Be Managed by One Master and Mistress* (London: T. Goyder, 1823).

Wilderspin was especially interested in infant schools as a means of combating petty thievery and other urban crime, although he seemed more concerned with protecting society from the problems caused by cripples and beggars than with protecting young children from bodily harm and poverty. Wilderspin also stressed the importance of moral and religious instruction, especially for girls. Citing the widely accepted fact that "females are naturally more inclined to devote themselves to religious observances than the other sex because their feelings are more easily wrought upon" (216), he suggested that this emotionality and religiosity made women better teachers for young children because they could shape their moral character. This connection among women, religion, and the teaching of young children would become very salient in America, where Wilderspin's more conventional pedagogy predominated over Owen's utopianism, especially among female evangelicals, who were the main force behind the infant school movement in the United States.

Chapter 2   "Too Large an Undertaking

for a Few Ladies"

The Infant School and the

Family School in America

During the first third of the nineteenth century Americans began
experimenting with educating young children outside the home.
Pestalozzi's pedagogy influenced educators in New England;
Robert Owen helped organize an infant school as part of a
communitarian experiment in Indiana; and women's groups in
major cities along the Eastern seaboard started infant school
societies. Some public primary schools enrolled children aged
four or younger and used infant school methods. Americans also
read European home education manuals such as the Edgeworths'
Practical Education, and an indigenous American child-rearing
literature developed, emphasizing the role of the mother as the
teacher in the "family school."

During the late 1820s and 1830s the infant school and the
family school competed as models for the education of young
children in America. Understanding the outcome of this competition requires some background on the historical, economic,
social, political, and educational context in which the two movements took place in America. The late eighteenth and early
nineteenth centuries were a period of rapid transition and dis-
location in American society. Changes in family life began to al-
ter the roles of men, women, and children even before the transformation known as industrialization. Although most of America
remained agrarian, families were becoming less self-sufficient economically but otherwise more isolated and private. Fathers
were becoming wage earners who worked outside the home,

mothers were becoming homemakers and consumers rather than producers, and children were becoming dependents, drains on family income rather than contributors to it.[1]

These changes in economic roles were accompanied by shifts in internal relations within families, what Steven Mintz and Susan Kellogg describe as a "domestic revolution." Fathers' authority declined with the evolution of more democratic family relationships in which emotional support became the focus of family life. As the family retreated from the community and public life, the values of the home were increasingly held up as a counterbalance to those of the marketplace, birth rates dropped, fewer children were boarded out, and mothers began investing more time in child rearing. Political changes affected family life as well. After the American Revolution, for example, women were exhorted to become educators of a new generation of American citizens. In Jacksonian America "womanhood" became a cult, and domesticity was elevated to the status of a national ideal.[2]

American mothers began relying on a new advice literature for information about their domestic "empire." Advances in printing technology, publishing, bookselling, and transportation made this literature more readily available to women in urban areas and in the Northeast. Yet, although domestic literature was meant for a national audience and began to minimize regional, ethnic, and sectarian differences in child rearing and early education, some areas of the country—particularly rural areas and the South—remained beyond its reach.[3]

The central theme of the new American child-rearing literature was that mothers should learn more about and spend more time educating their young children at home. For indigent mothers, however, the message was different. They were encouraged to send their children to charity infant schools where they could be socialized and educated communally and saved from the supposedly harmful influence of their families.

Most American parents probably were not aware of these new child-rearing and educational ideas, nor were very many young children in the United States enrolled in the new programs. Young children who were cared for outside the home attended private schools or dame schools or were looked after informally by relatives or neighbors. Some attended public primary schools with their older brothers and sisters. Institutionalized preschool education was a rarity in nineteenth-century America.

The Education of Young Children in the Colonial and Early National Eras
The discovery of childhood appears to have been well under way in seventeenth- and eighteenth-century America. Children from birth to age six, called "infants," were dressed and treated differently from older children and youths. Despite horrendously high rates of infant mortality and Calvinist beliefs in infant damnation, colonists appear to have been much attached to their children and concerned about their upbringing and education. As Anne Bradstreet's poetic expressions of affection for her children and Cotton Mather's ambivalent, intense involvement in child rearing attest, young children were an important focus of adult attention in colonial New England.[4]

Most young children in colonial America were cared for by their own mothers, though as the eighteenth century progressed the urban upper classes began using wet nurses, as was the custom in England. Weaning generally began around the age of one. Some children were boarded out at an early age, but usually for relatively short periods until they were older. Physical punishment was common, but even Cotton Mather advised parents not to strike their children in anger. Locke's *Some Thoughts Concerning Education* was widely read, and many Puritan parents tried reasoning with their children rather than whipping them.[5]

The colonists thought children were capable of early intellectual development and began didactic instruction at a very young age. Early education consisted primarily of teaching children, especially boys, to recite the catechism and to read the Scriptures. (Fathers were initially responsible for these important tasks, in part because more men than women were literate in seventeenth- and eighteenth-century America, although increasing evidence suggests that many American women could read even though they could not write.) What would be termed "the disease of precocity" in the 1830s was thought normal and good in the 1700s. In her diary Esther Burr described disciplining her infant daughter, Sally, commenting that "although she is not quite ten months old, yet when she knows so much I think 'tis time she should be taught."[6]

Though most families may have handled quite well the job of teaching children to read, there was growing uncertainty in colonial America about their ability to manage such a critical religious, educative function. Colonists increasingly transferred responsibility for education to schools. In New England cities and towns began passing laws stipulating that children be taught to read and requiring the provision of schools. The well-known Massachusetts statute of 1642 charging parents to educate their children referred to "the great neglect of many parents and masters in training up their children in learning and labor." A series of laws passed in Massachusetts beginning in 1647 went even further, requiring towns of fifty families or more to appoint a schoolmaster and towns of a hundred or more families to set up a grammar school. Though at first these schools were only for older boys, once instituted, public responsibility for education gradually expanded to include girls and younger children of both sexes.[7]

Children were educated in a variety of private settings before they began attending public grammar school around the age of seven. Some were taught at home by their parents or by governesses; others in the homes of relatives or friends if they were boarded out or in their masters' homes if they were apprenticed. Increasingly, however, both little boys and little girls were taught in schools, either in petty or dame schools run by neighborhood women or in private schools run by schoolmasters, who charged relatively low fees and accepted children from a range of social-class backgrounds. Dame school teachers, often widows, taught very young children how to read the Bible and cared for them much as their mothers would have.[8]

Gradually, dame schools became more public. Cities and towns began paying the teachers a small salary, although teachers continued to be very poorly paid. In 1641 in Woburn, Massachusetts, for instance, Mrs. Walker, a widow, received only one shilling and three pence for her annual teaching efforts after the town had deducted taxes and other fees. But salaries slowly increased, as did public control. In 1789, for example, Massachusetts required licensing for dame school teachers.[9]

The new system of public primary schools, or "common schools," begun by evangelicals, Sunday school supporters, socially conscious Quakers, and other religious groups in America in the early 1800s was not created out of whole cloth. In many cities and towns, dame school teachers became the core of the primary school teaching staff. For a while, younger and older children attended primary school together, as they had done in private dame schools. An estimated 40 percent of three-year-olds were enrolled in public schools in Massachusetts in 1839–40, for instance. In the early nineteenth century, then, some young children in America went to public primary schools, some to private dame schools, and a few attended a new type of educational institution.[10]

The American Infant School Movement

The infant school movement was in some ways part of the larger common school campaign. Infant school advocates argued that programs for younger children should be a public responsibility as well. Some primary school advocates agreed, and some appropriated infant school methods, programs, and personnel. In fact, this overlap of functions may have caused the public to overlook the distinctions between the two types of schools, thereby depleting support for infant schools.

The idea that education for young children should differ from preparation for grammar school was introduced to America at the beginning of the nineteenth century. In 1806 the Scottish-born geologist and social reformer William Maclure arranged for one of Pestalozzi's assistants, Joseph Neef, to go to Philadelphia to direct a Pestalozzian school. Neef spent three years studying English, wrote a short book entitled *Sketch Plan and Method of Education*, and in 1809 opened a school. In 1819 and 1824 Maclure arranged for two other Pestalozzian teachers, Marie Duclos Fretageot and Guillaume Sylvan Casimir Phiquepal, to come to the United States. This small group worked at various schools in the Philadelphia area.[11]

Robert Owen took a personal interest in encouraging infant schools in America. During a visit in 1825 he gave speeches to Congress, met with American reformers and educators, and purchased Harmonie, a Rappite religious community on the banks of the Wabash River in southern Indiana. Volunteers soon began arriving at the community, rechristened New Harmony, and a school was promptly started. In January 1826 Maclure, Neef, Fretageot (whom Owen had already met), Phiquepal, and others landed in New Harmony in the so-called Boatload of Knowledge and reorganized the school into an educational society. But there was to be little harmony in New Harmony. About four hundred children were enrolled in different schools, including about one hundred two- to five-year-olds in an infant school run by Fretageot and Mrs. Neef. Soon financial disputes erupted between Owen and Maclure, and pedagogical tensions developed between the Neefs and Fretageot. Owen departed, leaving his sons, Maclure, the Neefs, and Fretageot to manage the educational experiments, which limped along for some years after the communitarian project ended.[12]

Despite this inauspicious beginning, infant schools enjoyed a period of popularity in America in the late 1820s and 1830s. In March 1825 John

Griscom opened an introductory department for very young children as part of his private school for paying students in New York. Griscom's school was apparently very successful and drew the attention of prominent New Yorkers to the infant school idea. Other American educators also became advocates of infant schools and Pestalozzianism. William Russell, the Scottish-born, Boston-based editor of the newly founded *American Journal of Education,* devoted himself to the cause of establishing infant schools for children from all social classes, published descriptions of the movement's progress, and heralded the founding of infant school societies in New York and Philadelphia in 1826, Hartford in 1827, Boston and Providence in 1828, and elsewhere in the eastern United States and Canada.

The promotion of public infant schools in New York began in 1826 when De Witt Clinton, a member of the Public School Society and governor of the state, encouraged Mrs. Joanna Bethune to found an infant school society. Bethune, the recent widow of Divie Bethune, a wealthy supporter of the Public School Society, had helped operate Sunday schools and an industrial school and had organized both the Female Union for Promoting Sabbath Schools and the Penny Society, later the Society for the Relief of the Destitute Sick.[13]

Though the Infant School Society of the City of New York had a board of male advisers, most of whom were members of the men's public school group, the women's group was more than just an auxiliary of the men's education society. While both groups focused on religious and moral instruction, the women concentrated on the education of very young children and claimed to espouse Pestalozzian methods, though an 1827 infant school manual published by Joanna Bethune under the pen name "A Friend of the Poor" appears to have been more influenced by Wilderspin than by Pestalozzi.[14]

Bethune's society began a campaign to gain public financing for infant schools. It met resistance from members of the Public School Society and others who were concerned that the expense would detract from educational efforts for older children. Some opponents also argued that young children should stay home with their mothers. After various experiments, petitions, and reports, these objections were overcome in 1830, when the New York legislature approved public support for infant schools. But rather than allow the women's infant school group to receive public funding directly, the men's society decided to open infant schools and to incorporate those the women had started.

In Philadelphia, as in New York, infant schools were incorporated into the public system, where they eventually became lower grades of the primary schools. Prominent male infant school supporters in Philadelphia included Swedenborgian minister Maskell Carll, the millennialist Sylvester Graham, wealthy Quaker philanthropist Roberts Vaux, and the Irish Catholic publisher and activist Mathew Carey. In 1828 Carey successfully lobbied the legislature to pass a bill approving public funding of education for children under five. The controllers of the public schools moved slowly, however, and in the ten years before infant schools were finally incorporated into the public system, female infant school societies started some sixty schools, and private infant schools, including a Quaker infant school, were also begun for middle- and upper-class children. Finally, in 1838, after much pressure from Carey, infant schools were incorporated into the Philadelphia public schools. As in New York, however, they soon lost their special character as programs for very young children.[15]

The influence of evangelicalism and the interplay of class, gender, pedagogy, and educational reform were particularly apparent in the brief history of the Infant School Society of the City of Boston (ISSCB). Encouraged by William Russell, on August 8, 1828, a group of "about ninety ladies" met at the house of Mrs. William Thurston, the wife of a prominent Congregationalist leader, to found an infant school society. The members of the ISSCB came from somewhat lower social-class backgrounds than did Boston's Unitarian elite. A number of women in the group were wives or relatives of well-to-do male evangelicals in the Society for the Religious and Moral Instruction of the Poor, the Sunday school association that had been the moving force behind the institution of public primary schools in Boston a decade earlier. The ISSCB was also advised by a "council of gentlemen," many of whom were members of the men's education group.[16]

The ISSCB and the men's group shared the same primary goal—moral instruction of poor children—but the women focused on educating very young children. As an article in the *Ladies' Magazine* stated, the education of young children was "entirely in the province of Ladies; Men are apt to regard children under four years of age, either as plagues or playthings." The women's society also expanded its responsibility to include moral reform of poor families. Infant school teachers instructed their young charges to teach their parents new behaviors and mores. As this glowing account from one of the ISSCB's annual reports illustrates, infant school teachers were proud of their ability to transform and reform the lives of their young students' parents.

> On Saturday I talked to the children about keeping the Sabbath. One little girl said, "I am going to ride tomorrow with my mother!" I gave them such instruction as I thought the occasion required. On Monday the little girl came to me and said, "I did not go to ride yesterday!" I asked her why?
>
> "My mother did not go!"
>
> "And why did not your mother go?"
>
> "Because I told her it was wicked to ride Sunday." The same child came to me about three months since and told me her father said he would not drink any more rum. I asked her why?
>
> She replied, "I told him the Bible said, drunkards cannot go to heaven!" She has told me since that he has not drunk any.[17]

The ISSCB's reports also provide clues as to why and how poor and lower-class parents used infant schools to further their own goals, despite such proselytization. The few mothers who worked outside the home in antebellum America and the many more who worked inside the home may have thought their children would be happier and better educated in infant schools. The society's *Sixth Annual Report* cited the thanks of a "grateful working mother" who wrote of the "vast advantages" of infant schools to "such parents as have to work, as many do, from twelve to sixteen hours a day for their support."[18]

Wealthier families became interested in the benefits of infant education for their own children. The author of an 1829 article in the *Ladies' Magazine* asked, "Why should a plan which promises so many advantages, independent of merely relieving the mother from her charge, be confined to the children of the indigent?" Even well-to-do mothers might have trouble meeting their young children's needs. "It is nearly, if not quite impossible, to teach such little ones at home, with the facility they are taught in an infant school," the author stated. "If a convenient room is prepared, and faithful and discreet agents employed, parents may feel secure that their darlings are not only safe, but improving." Though little is known about private infant schools for wealthy children in Boston, these arguments appear to have been compelling, as several such schools were started.[19]

Infant schools enjoyed a brief heyday in Boston in the late 1820s and early 1830s. The ISSCB opened as many as five schools at various locations between 1828 and 1835, and the movement spread to other cities and towns in Massachusetts. Another infant school society, started in Boston in 1828, began a school on Salem Street that enrolled large numbers of young children. At the peak of the movement in the early 1830s, thirteen or more infant schools were in operation in the city.[20]

Encouraged by their success, the women of the ISSCB put pressure on the men of Boston's Primary School Committee to incorporate infant schools into the public schools. The School Committee studied the matter and conducted a survey, but primary school teachers, many of whom were former dame school teachers, disparaged their erstwhile charges. Infant school graduates, they reported, had a "sing-song style which it was subsequently found almost impossible to eradicate," were "the cause of restlessness and disorder among the other children," and were "intractable and troublesome, restless from want of constant excitement, and their attention with difficulty fixed upon their studies." The ISSCB countered the teachers' criticisms, but the School Committee remained unconvinced. In 1830 the proposal to incorporate infant schools into the public school system was rejected.[21]

An influential factor in this defeat was the flowering of romantic ideas about children, education, and women. Like the British romantic William Wordsworth, whose "Ode on Intimations of Immortality in Childhood" was their anthem, transcendentalists, as some American romantics called themselves, worshiped children as godlike beings through whom adults could experience rejuvenation, a second childhood. In his first book, *Nature* (1836), Ralph Waldo Emerson called infancy the "perpetual messiah, which comes into the arms of fallen men and pleads with them to return to paradise." Bronson Alcott was even more ecstatic: "Childhood hath Saved me!" he once exclaimed.[22]

It was Alcott who introduced romantic educational philosophy to Boston. Born in 1799, Amos Bronson Alcott was a Yankee peddler and schoolteacher who had discovered the ideas of Pestalozzi, Owen, Goethe, and Wordsworth while experimenting with teaching practices in his classroom in Connecticut. In 1828 Abba May, a member of an infant school society in Boston, visited

Alcott's school and, impressed by what she saw, invited him to teach at the Salem Street infant school.[23]

Alcott had visited infant schools in New York and Philadelphia. He found Joanna Bethune's infant schools "too mechanical and sectarian" and characterized the program he saw in Philadelphia as "an engine of orthodoxy." For Alcott, true education was centered on children, not adults. Alcott outlined his romantic approach in a pamphlet, *Observations on the Principles and Methods of Infant Instruction* (1830). "Every infant," he wrote, was "already in possession of the faculties and apparatus required for his instruction, and . . . by a law of his constitution" used "these to a great extent himself." The teacher's role, Alcott explained, was to "facilitate" the child's development, to "accompany the child in his progress, rather than to drive or even lead him." And the key to children's development, according to Alcott, was play, which he called "the appointed dispensation of childhood."[24]

Alcott's views were indicative of a radical shift in ideas about children and education taking place in Boston and other urban centers in the late 1820s and 1830s. Early schooling was not seen as problematic in Boston even as late as the mid-1820s. By the 1830s, however, the romantic vision of childhood had led to a reversal in attitudes about preschool education. Where precocity and early academic instruction were once seen as good and necessary, they were now thought to be bad and harmful.

These new attitudes about precocity were greatly affected by Amariah Brigham's *Remarks on the Influence of Mental Cultivation and Mental Excitement upon Health* (1832). Brigham, who was director of the Hartford Insane Asylum, saw precocity as a "disease," not as just a developmental problem. Echoing Rousseau, he warned that early mental excitement would "only serve to bring forth beautiful, but premature flowers, which are destined to wither away, without producing fruits." Other American advice givers repeated Brigham's concerns, including the Rousseaucan trope on premature fruit. In her popular book *Letters to Mothers* (1838), Lydia Sigourney wrote, "I once admired precocity, and viewed it as the breath of Deity, quickening to ripe and rare excellence. But I have since learned to fear it."[25]

These rapidly changing views on children and education were coupled with another development that probably more than anything else contributed to the decline of infant schools in Boston and elsewhere: the adoption of the romantic ideal of womanhood. In the doctrine of separate spheres that took hold in Jacksonian America, a period of social unrest during which gender roles became more rigid and sharply divergent, women were supposed to stay at home as goddesses of the hearth and nurturing wives and mothers. The growth of this romantic ideology of domesticity led to a new emphasis on home education and new fears about the effects of separating young children from their mothers. Popular magazines and education journals were flooded with concerns about mother-child relationships. In 1828, the same year the ISSCB started, an article in the *American Journal of Education* criticized infant schools because they provided "occasion for remissness in the discharge of parental duties, by devolving the care of infancy on teachers, instead of leaving with the mother the full weight and responsibility of her natural relation. The strength of domestic attachment in the child is also said to be weakened, by removing him for a considerable part of the day from the home, and furnishing him with enjoyment of a higher kind than he could experience there." And in 1830 William Russell turned over publication of the *American Journal of Education* to home education advocate William Woodbridge, who immediately began questioning the quality of Boston's infant schools and promoting Pestalozzian-style domestic education.[26]

Even female supporters began rejecting infant schools because they took young children out of the home. The *Ladies' Magazine* disclaimed its earlier support for infant schools, stating "We have never urged their adoption, by those who have the means to provide for their infants." And the women of the ISSCB admitted that the concept of *school* for young children was problematic, saying in their final annual report, in 1835, that the term had "probably done much to incite prejudice against them. . . . They may more properly be termed neighborhood nurseries or infant asylums."[27]

Gender also figured saliently in the reasons the women of the ISSCB gave for their lack of success. They blamed men's lack of attention to the infant school cause, and their own inability as women to accomplish a task of such magnitude. The society's final report accused "clergymen and other gentlemen" of paying attention to Sunday schools but not to infant schools. Aware of the men's education society's successful efforts to promote primary schools in Boston, the women were "anxious to place" their "institutions in the hands of gentlemen" and expected support from the male society for their cause. In 1835, however, Boston was in the midst of an economic depression, and the men's evangelical society was in financial difficulty. Donations from private contributors declined. No longer able to support its schools, the Infant School Society of the City of Boston abandoned its efforts, and the movement to establish infant schools in Boston ended in failure. Daunted, the women declared instituting infant schools to be "quite too large an undertaking for a few ladies."[28]

The American Family School

In the 1830s promotion of extrafamilial infant school education was supplanted by the advancement of the "family school," in which mothers were to take on the role of teachers. Like the American home schooling movement of today, the nineteenth-century home education movement combined conservative reactions against the perceived immorality of public schools with liberal concerns about the supposed harmful effects of didactic teaching on young children. Traditionalists and romantics alike weighed in with advice on different methods of educating young children, bringing the question more to the fore in the minds of American parents. The decade between 1830 and 1840 saw the publication of numerous American manuals both on child rearing and on home education, a prodigious output capped in 1841 with what became the bible of American domestic advice generally: Catharine Beecher's *Treatise on Domestic Economy*. Numerous pamphlets and articles in popular periodicals such as the *Ladies' Magazine, Mother's Assistant*, and the *Family Magazine* added to this wealth of prescriptive information on child rearing and family life.[29]

Though they differed somewhat in tone and content, all these sources emphasized the paramount importance of moral education in the home. Parents from a diverse spectrum of political, religious, and class backgrounds hoped that providing their children with a strong sense of moral character would keep them safe from the unrest and social problems endemic in Jacksonian America and supply a compass for navigating the increasing uncertainties of life. This search for some sort of permanence, however illusory, contributed to the maintenance of traditional Christian values that characterized most of this advice literature. In fact, reliance on moral education and character training as a hedge against the future remained a constant in American child-rearing and child-teaching literature for many years to come.[30]

The other main theme in this literature was the key role of the mother in home education. In this period, the patriarchal bonds between husbands and wives were being superseded by the ties between women and children.

This shift came about gradually, however. Many of the earlier guides were written by men, particularly ministers. Some of these, such as Heman Humphrey's *Domestic Education* (1840) and Theodore Dwight's *The Father's Book* (1834), attempted to restore the father as the principal home educator. But as men came to dominate in the marketplace and women at the fireside, domestic advice literature written by women for women focused almost exclusively on the responsibilities of mothers in home education.[31]

Mothers were particularly suited to be home educators, the guides stated or implied, because they were innately more emotional than men and thus better at the education of the heart, on which moral education depended. Unlike parent educators in the early twentieth century, who worried about excessive mother love and permissiveness, early nineteenth-century advice givers advocated increasing displays of affection and loosening the reins and seemed relatively unconcerned about spoiling children. Lydia Sigourney, for instance, encouraged mothers to infuse their teaching "with smiles, and the dialect of love." This affectionate, romantic-maternal educational mode did not renounce parental authority; the controls were simply subtle and emotional rather than physical and rational. As advice giver Samuel Goodrich put it, the "mother holds the reins of the soul."[32]

Guides also recommended motherly, informal teaching techniques in order to avoid the dangers of precocity. Like Amariah Brigham, the writers were worried about the ill effects of early academic instruction on children's health. Samuel Goodrich expressed these concerns succinctly: "To require these little creatures to sit down upon benches, to bend studiously over a book, to restrain their tongues, and keep their legs and arms motionless, which Heaven impels them to keep in constant exercise," was "violating nature, injuring the health, and disgusting the young pupil with the whole business of school education." Precocity remained a danger even when children were taught at home by their mothers. Goodrich gave a horrific example of a mother whose "insane ambition" caused her to push her son's mental development prematurely, thus creating a monster whose "head grew rapidly, and at last became enormous" while "his limbs became shrunken, and almost useless."[33]

In view of these anxieties about health and precocity, early nineteenth-century home education guides recommended that mothers wait until their children were six or so before teaching them reading and other academic skills. Some guides suggested that allowance be made for individual differences—instruction for some children, for example, might begin as early as age four—but in general six was the new norm. As the author of an early advice manual who identified herself only as "A Mother" put it, the "precise age children can be taught their alphabet . . . is not easy to determine; but, by six years old, every child can be made to read with facility, and that age is soon enough. . . ." Instruction in writing and arithmetic should also wait until age six, she advised. Heman Humphrey, president of Amherst College, commented in 1840 on this rapid change in ideas about early reading instruction: "Had some older friend said to us, some four and twenty years ago, when we were arranging our lettered blocks, and showing our Reuben or Simeon, that h-a-t spells hat, 'You are quite too early for the advantage and safety of your child, you had better leave the little fellow to his cob-houses and his antics till nature has had time to do her part,' I dare say we should have gone on, without giving much heed to the advice, believing it to be a loss of precious time to withhold instruction for a single week."[34]

The new sense of relaxation was probably due in part to economic and technological developments that had made American life more comfortable and materially secure by the 1830s. In his book *The Little Philosopher; or, The Infant School at Home* (1830), Jacob Abbott described a mother introducing the concept of philosophy to her older child by letting her infant play with and, in the process, tear the pages of a new book. Unlike a colonial mother, for whom a book would have been a relatively rare, precious object, this romantic mother answers her older child's concern that the baby's tearing of the book's pages is "mischief" by saying, "It is not for mischief. A piece of paper is something new and curious to him; and he likes to shake it about and to see how it will move; and to pull it, to see how strong it is, and how easily it will tear. In that way he is learning the nature of it."[35]

Manuals described independent, inquisitive, noisy children whose mothers encouraged them to ask questions constantly. There was much emphasis on Pestalozzian-like teaching with objects and exploring the natural environment. Lydia Maria Child exhorted mothers to go beyond "pat a cake" and teach their children to observe their surroundings and question "the why and wherefore of everything." In what sounds like a Pestalozzian object lesson, she described a mother telling her child, "This ball is *round*; this little tea table is *square.*" Mothers sometimes forgot, Child stated, "that things long familiar to us are entirely unknown to an infant."[36]

Americans in the early nineteenth century were discovering early childhood and finding that infancy, as this period of life was still called, was a critically important stage for education, though of a kind different from traditional schooling. Infancy was particularly important, manual writers argued, because it was the period when moral character was established. Young children's consciences were still "plastic," receptive to instruction about moral discipline. Unlike the case with reading instruction, later was too late for character training. On this key point of timing all authors of American advice manuals agreed. The job of the parent was gently to guide the development of the child's conscience as soon as possible so that it would not have the chance to stray from the straight and narrow. But the task of moral education was no longer simple; children were now believed to have free will, which introduced new twists and turns into the processes of development and parenting. Moral education was "a fearful responsibility," Samuel Goodrich wrote, from which parents could not shrink because they "usually decide the character of their offspring."[37]

Because moral education was best carried on in the home, early nineteenth-century American advice givers were convinced that the family school was superior to the infant school or the primary school as an environment for young children. Thus Lydia Sigourney asked why any mother who did not need to would expose her child "to the influence of evil example? . . . Why yield it to the excitement of promiscuous association, when it has a parent's house, where its innocence may be shielded, and its intellect aided to expand?" Domestic advice givers like Sigourney were reacting against both mass schooling and schooling for the masses. With considerable accuracy, they saw classrooms as crowded, underventilated, unhealthy places where teachers lacked the time or knowledge to educate young children appropriately or well. Most homes seemed healthier, more moral, and more educational environments than schools were, and most mothers seemed to be better teachers for little children than the professionals were. Bronson Alcott's cousin, William Alcott, wrote in an 1843 article in the journal *Mother's Assistant* that the "*family school*" could "do more towards teaching the young what they ought to know, than is now done by our whole array of processes and instruments of instruction." And that same year Charles Holden wrote that no school could be as good for young children as "the schoolhouse at home, with the tender mother as the mistress."[38]

As with all prescriptive literature, it is impossible to know how many mothers heeded this advice and actually employed the pedagogical methods the manuals prescribed. Most mothers did not keep records of how they taught their children, but Bronson Alcott was one parent who did. Though Alcott was nothing if not unique and thus is not representative, his extensive journals document the growing influence of romantic educational ideas on someone who was both a producer and consumer of advice. Alcott, later the model for the noticeably absent father in the most popular and widely read novel of the American family, *Little Women,* was a very present father with his own family. After the birth of his first child, Anna, in 1831, he immediately set to work on a new project, a baby biography in which he recorded the daily lives of his first three daughters in minute detail. Alcott also practiced the new educational techniques on other peoples' children, assisted in his efforts by Elizabeth Peabody, another charter member of the transcendentalist group.[39]

Born in Billerica, Massachusetts, in 1804, Elizabeth Palmer Peabody once said she felt she had been "pre-natally educated" for the occupation that was to be the "passionate pursuit" of her life: children's education. Her father, Nathaniel Peabody, had been a teacher before becoming a physician and then a dentist. Her mother was a teacher who managed and taught at a number of schools in addition to teaching her own children. When Peabody moved to Boston in 1825, she served as a tutor to the children of the famed Unitarian minister William Ellery Channing and became acquainted with others who shared her interest in education. In 1827 infant school advocate William Russell collaborated with Peabody and her sister Mary in operating a school in Russell's home, where the sisters were living at the time. Russell then introduced Elizabeth Peabody to his close friend Bronson Alcott.[40]

Peabody collaborated with Alcott in founding the Temple School in 1834, one of the most notorious and radically romantic of American educational experiments. Her *Record of a School* (1835) provided her side of the argument over Alcott's controversial dialectic teaching techniques, in which he asked children about, among other things, Christ's conception. Peabody's book also gives a glimpse of her own "maternalist" educational philosophy. In the introduction she stated her view that everything in education had "its germ in the maternal sentiment." And though "metaphysical thought" was required to understand the principles of education, Peabody was certain that every intelligent woman would find "on analyzing her own mind," that she knew "more of metaphysics" than she did of "anything else."[41]

After her falling out with Alcott over the Temple School, which soon closed, Peabody decided to try her hand at giving advice on home education. In 1836 she began the journal *The Family School,* which furnished information about domestic education along with literary selections for both parents and children. Peabody explained that she hoped to provide something of interest and value to the entire family and promised everything from original poetry, literary criticism, and essays on "moral and intellectual self-culture" to Sunday school lessons and obituaries.[42]

Peabody promised to devote special attention to the new journal's "Religious and Moral Department." Her first contribution was an account of the divine origins of a child's soul and body, designed "to give a very little child a spiritual view of himself." Entitled "The History of Goodness," the story demonstrated how to introduce this topic without exposing young children to premature knowledge of sexuality, as Peabody felt Bronson Alcott had. It also displayed the relative relaxation of limits on other forms of personal freedom characteristic of transcendentalist child-rearing and educational practices. In Peabody's rather saccharine account, "Goodness" asks God's permission to come down from heaven "to live inside of a dear little baby" whose "dear mother . . . wants a little baby very much." The "dear little baby" comes down to earth, but "Love" informs the mother that "Goodness" has "wings to fly back on" and that she must let him "fly about a little" whenever he wants to.[43]

Among its wide variety of selections, the second issue of *The Family School* contained a continuation of "The History of Goodness" and a defense of the first installment, which had elicited some criticism. One mother had written that the story was too imaginative, and thus children could not be told that its account of their origins was true. Citing "no less authority than that of Matthew and Luke," Peabody responded that she would say the story was true, even the part about the angel of love. When asked about the passage directing the mother to allow the child to "fly about a little," Peabody responded that she meant this "to indicate a liberal mode of education." But in case anyone might think her too liberal in matters sexual, she added that her "very first principle of education" was "that the Imagination make the senses her servants, and thus delivered from their bondage, becomes herself the handmaid of Reason and Conscience."[44]

Though a short-lived publication, *The Family School* is fascinating evidence of the inroads romanticism had made in the child-rearing and educational ideas of America's intellectual vanguard. Vestiges of Calvinism remained, but parents were encouraged to let their children's souls "fly about a little." Rationality and morality still reigned supreme, but sensory experiences and imagination had made important, if shackled, appearances. Peabody's equation of education with flying was a radical departure from the rigidity of the past and a harbinger of the even more romantic pedagogy of a new institution for young children beginning in Germany at this time, which Peabody herself would soon help introduce to America.

Chapter 3   "Come, Let Us Live with Our Children"

Friedrich Froebel and the

German Kindergarten Movement

Just as Americans were turning against the idea of extrafamilial education for young children, a new pedagogy was developing in Germany that would eventually lead to the permanent establishment of programs for young children in American public schools. Friedrich Froebel's kindergarten succeeded where the infant school failed for two main reasons: it was perceived as a supplement to rather than a replacement for familial child rearing, and it was seen as a new environment appropriate for young children, not a school. Froebelianism was a romantic reconstruction of supposedly traditional modes of child nurture, not an attempt to take children away from their families and force-feed them academics. But at the same time the kindergarten was a force for modernization within the family and in education, legitimizing extrafamilial education and new pedagogical methods and modifying relationships among young children, women, families, schools, and the state.

Froebel's romantic pedagogical innovation overcame fears about precocity by providing an appealing alternative to academic instruction. He developed elaborate new educational methods and materials intended especially for young children. His comprehensive curriculum of play and handwork activities furnished teachers with a script for what to do with young children instead of teaching them to read, write, and count. And Froebel used play as a teaching medium, creating games and songs designed to inculcate attitudes of cooperation and voluntary self-control. This social curriculum attracted a wide range of reformers who saw the kindergarten as a means of fostering social harmony and preventing class conflict.

Social-class identification was an important variable in the progress of the kindergarten movement in Europe and America. Unlike his predecessors, Froebel envisioned the kindergarten as a program for all children. In Germany, however, the kindergarten became segregated on the basis of social class. Such divisions existed in the American kindergarten movement as well, and class socialization was a motive in the promotion of educational programs for young children; even so, the kindergarten succeeded in becoming more universalized.

Froebel's female followers made the kindergarten one of the first and most popular of modern women's movements. Like Pestalozzi, Froebel based his model for the teacher on the peasant mother and derived many of his educational methods from folk child-rearing practices. But kindergarten teachers were real women, not idealized female role models, and kindergarten teaching and advocacy provided new occupations for women outside the home. Froebel also stressed educating women to be better children's educators inside the home and focused on women's and children's joint interests, thus assuaging concerns about the separation of young children from their mothers.

Friedrich Froebel and the Invention of the Kindergarten

Like so many other nineteenth-century European and American educators, Froebel's ideas were deeply influenced by his religious background. Born in a small town in Thuringia, Friedrich Froebel (1782–1852) was the son of a Lutheran minister. Estranged from his stern, pious, busy father, Froebel was raised by a stepmother he did not like and led a lonely, isolated childhood. He did live happily for a while with a maternal uncle who became his guardian, and then, at the age of fifteen, he was apprenticed to a forester.[1]

During the two years he spent studying plants and trees, Froebel became very interested in organic growth and acquired the sense of order and harmony in nature that would permeate his educational philosophy. After his apprenticeship, he studied for two years at the University of Jena, where he particularly enjoyed biology and botany and became more grounded in the organic principles of natural development. He was introduced to the ideas of Kant, Goethe, Schiller, and other German rationalist and romantic thinkers and writers and began reading broadly in philosophy, science, and literature. He was particularly impressed by the work of Johann Gottlieb Fichte, who advocated Pestalozzianism as a means of German national regeneration through education. Froebel also was "profoundly moved" by Friedrich von Schelling's *Bruno; or, The Over-Soul,* from which he derived a more theoretical underpinning for his views on nature and the interconnectedness of all things.[2]

Having inherited some money after the deaths of his father and uncle, Froebel decided to embark on a new vocation. He met Anton Gruener, the headmaster of the Frankfurt Model School, who suggested that he become a teacher. Gruener had been a disciple of Pestalozzi's, and in 1805 Froebel went to Yverdun to study for two weeks at Pestalozzi's model school. Though much taken with Pestalozzi's emphasis on concrete experience, learning by discovery, and play, Froebel criticized the "incompleteness" and "one-sidedness" of Pestalozzi's curriculum and teaching methods, which he found to be "superficially worked out" and "mechanical."[3]

In an attempt to correct this imbalance, Froebel tried a Rousseauean educational experiment during which he briefly lived with three pupils in an isolated natural setting. He then returned to Yverdun to study for two more years, attended university for a while at Göttingen and Berlin, and then joined Lützow's infantry corps in 1813. Following his stint in the military, he worked as a mineralogist in the Royal Museum in Berlin where the rocks and crystals offered him yet more evidence that "under all kinds of various modifications [there was] one law of development": unity.[4]

Finally, in 1816, at the age of thirty-four, Froebel had the opportunity to put his eclectic educational ideas into practice. When his older brother died, his widow offered to pay Froebel to teach her three sons. Two of Froebel's other nephews also attended the small school, which Froebel boldly called the "Universal German Educational Institute." Froebel was joined by two army friends, Wilhelm Middendorff and Heinrich Langenthal, who were to become life-long associates. He also married Henrietta Wilhelmine Hoffmeister, who supported him in his educational work. Froebel set up his model school in the backward but beautiful village of Keilhau, in the mountains of Thuringia. In this sylvan setting Froebel, his associates, and a growing number of students engaged in a form of naturalistic education consisting largely of physical labor and long walks through the woods.[5]

After fourteen years at Keilhau, Froebel moved to Switzerland, where he became concerned about children's lack of appropriate preparation for school and mothers' lack of training in how to nurture and educate their children. In 1836 he returned to Blankenburg, near Keilhau, and in 1837 opened the first kindergarten. He called his invention "Anstalt fur Kleinkinderpflege" (institution for fostering small children). The new institution attracted attention, and teachers began coming to the school to study with Froebel, who eventually opened two other kindergartens in Frankfurt.[6]

But Froebel was dissatisfied with the name of his new creation. As the story goes, one day as he was walking over the Steiger Pass to Blankenburg, he kept repeating, "Oh, if I could only think of a good name for my youngest born!" Then, according to one of Froebel's associates, "Suddenly he stood still as if fettered fast to the spot, and his eyes assumed a wonderful, almost refulgent, brilliancy. Then he shouted to the mountains so that it echoed to the four winds of heaven, '*Eureka!* I have found it! KINDER-GARTEN shall be the name of the new institution!'"[7]

The name *kindergarten*—child garden—was the perfect romantic metaphor to describe Froebel's new educational institution for young children, and it helped gain acceptance and support for his ideas. "As in a garden, under God's favor, and by the care of a skilled, intelligent gardener," Froebel wrote in an 1840 address to German women, "growing plants are cultivated in accordance with Nature's laws, so here in our child garden, our kindergarten, shall the noblest of all growing things, men (that is children, the germs and shoots of humanity) be cultivated in accordance with the laws of their own being, of God and of Nature."[8]

Froebel's Educational Philosophy and Methods

Underlying Froebel's educational philosophy was his conception of unity, which he thought children experienced through play. Froebel believed in the unity and connectedness of inner states and external actions. The key to this inner-outer connectedness was self-activity, through which the inner was made outer. Human beings, he thought, became "truly godlike in diligence and industry, in working and doing, which are accompanied by the clear perception or even by the vaguest feeling that thereby we represent the inner in the outer." For children, play was "the purest, most spiritual activity of man at this stage, and, at the same time, typical of human life as a whole—of the inner, hidden natural life in man and all things." Above all else, Froebel thought, mothers should be taught to "cultivate," "foster," "protect," and "guard" play because "the plays of childhood" were "the germinal leaves of all later life."[9]

For all its biological metaphors, Froebel's educational philosophy was pre-scientific in its account of human evolution and its positing of absolute rather than empirically derived principles of development and learning. Froebel believed unquestioningly in the divine origins of nature. His 1826 book *The Education of Man* begins with the statement that there is "an eternal law . . . based on an all-pervading, energetic, living, self-conscious, and hence eternal Unity, and this Unity is God." His later works are filled with similar statements of transcendental religious faith.[10]

Despite this quasi mysticism, Froebel was a naturalist and a developmentalist. Believing in the organic inevitability of human physical growth and mental development, he thought that education should be "passive and following" of natural development rather than "categorical and prescriptive." In good Rousseauean fashion, he was opposed to hurrying children through life. "The child, boy, man indeed, should know no other endeavor but to be at every stage of development wholly what this stage calls for."[11]

Froebel's educational system was based on supposedly natural laws: the law of unity, the law of self-activity, the law of connectedness, and the law of opposites, which, simply put, states that human beings learn best by perceiving things in context with their opposites. This last law Froebel thought particularly important for teaching. When an intellectually disputatious young man once challenged it as being the same as Hegel's dialectics and questioned its usefulness, Froebel responded that while he had not had time to study Hegel's system, he felt that "the whole meaning" of his own educational method rested "upon this law alone." "Everything else," he stated, was "mere material, the working of which proceeds according to the law, and without that law would not be practicable."[12]

Despite this insistence on the importance of theory, the materials and activities Froebel invented between 1835 and 1850 became the heart of his educational system. Specified play with these gifts and occupations, as he called them, would lead children to experience symbolically the unity of the universe, the connectedness of inner and outer states, part-whole relationships, and other of his educational principles. His materials and activities were also carefully sequenced according to the law of opposites to maximize the educational potential of teaching through contrasts. Whether they accomplished these educational objectives became immaterial as they took on almost magical significance in the minds and hands of his followers. They were the tangible basis of material kindergarten culture and occupied the attention of kindergarten teachers and children for many hours a day.

There were some twenty gifts and occupations, each based on geometrical concepts or folk craft activities. The first six gifts involved solid shapes; gifts seven through thirteen were based on flat shapes; and the ten or so occupations consisted of various types of handwork activities. The first gift—six small woolen balls of different colors—was designed to be the very first plaything of an infant or very young child. By manipulating these fuzzy balls, Froebel theorized, the child would learn the concept of unity by symbolically experiencing the quality of roundness. The first gift was also supposed to teach the child to abstract and analyze through comparing contrasting colors and distinguishing between color and form and to sense the essential properties of mobility, motion, direction, and position. Detailed directions, complete with diagrams, explained what the kindergarten teacher or mother was to say when introducing the first gift—how the balls were to be held, moved, suspended from a string, swung, and so on. Later kindergarten guides even supplied edifying anthropological information such as the history of the ball in the Stone Age and in Egyptian, Aztec, and Greek and Roman cultures.[13]

Froebel provided lengthy directions for the use of the other solid gifts as well. Gifts two through six were a wooden cube, a cylinder, and a small ball, along with a frame in which to suspend them; a two-inch wooden cube divided into eight one-inch cubes; a two-inch wooden cube divided into eight oblongs; a three-inch wooden cube divided into twenty-seven one-inch cubes, three of which divided into halves and three into quarters; and a three-inch wooden cube divided into twenty-seven solid oblongs, three of which divided into halves to form prisms and six of which divided into halves to form square half-cubes.

The activities and rationales for each gift were quite complex and advanced by modern standards. The fourth gift, for example, according to a guide by American kindergartners Kate Douglas Wiggin and Nora Archibald Smith, was to illustrate "the law of Equilibrium or Balance, and the law of Transmitted Motion or Propagation of Force." Children were to use the fifth gift to make twenty geometrical forms: "Cube, Rectangular Parallelopiped, Square Prism, Triangular Prism, Rhomboidal Prism, Trapezoidal Prism, Pentagonal Prism, Hexagonal Prism, Heptagonal Prism, Octagonal Prism, Square, Oblong, Right Isosceles Triangle, Rhomboid, Trapezium,

Trapezoid, Pentagon, Hexagon, Heptagon, Octagon." Clearly, in Froebel's methodology, romantic notions of childhood abilities had not fully replaced older conceptions of young children's intellectual capacity.[14]

The other gifts, based on flat objects and planar relationships, were even more complicated in their rationales and use. Gifts seven through ten consisted of small and large variously colored squares, isosceles triangles, right-angled isosceles and scalene triangles, and obtuse-angled triangles. Other kindergarten materials included connected and disconnected slats of varying lengths; round and square wooden sticks of different lengths and colors; whole and half wire rings of different diameters; colored threads; and "points," seeds, shells, beans, or pebbles with which young children were to construct hundreds of precise formal figures and designs. The directions for the seventh gift in a later Froebelian guide, for example, ran to 92 pages and included 554 specific steps.[15]

Derived in part from traditional peasant activities such as weaving and sewing, Froebel's occupations were intended to help young children apply what they had learned from the gifts by making things with different materials. Kindergarten children were to occupy themselves by pricking designs into premarked paper; sewing designs with colored threads on premarked cardboard; drawing geometric networks on special slates grooved with quarter-inch squares; painting on paper ruled with one-inch squares; weaving mats out of small strips of colored paper; stringing colored wooden beads, papers, and straws; interlacing small strips of colored paper; folding paper in origamilike designs; cutting and mounting precise paper silhouettes; constructing designs out of cardboard; and modeling in wax or clay. Most of the occupations required intellectual and fine motor skills that modern psychologists and educators would think inappropriate for young children.

In addition to these gifts and occupations, Froebel also made up finger plays, games, songs, and poetry, as well as gardening and nature study activities. He got many of his ideas from watching real children play. In fact, observing, learning from, and being with children was the hallmark of Froebel's method. His primary aim was to strengthen popular culture and enhance young children's development and learning by encouraging and expanding the earliest intimate play relationships of adults and children, getting mothers and teachers to participate actively in children's play and games rather than standing apart from them as adult authority figures. This was the meaning of his motto "Come, let us live with our children," which appeared on the frontispiece of many of his works and became the slogan for the Froebelian kindergarten movement.[16]

Froebel conceptualized children's play as quite a structured activity and was ambivalent about the value of spontaneous free play. According to Froebel, play was "not trivial" but "highly serious." It gave "joy, freedom, contentment, inner and outer rest, peace with the world." Undirected play, in Froebel's view, was a waste of time. "Without rational conscious guidance," he wrote, "childish activity degenerates into aimless play, instead of preparing for those tasks of life to which it is destined to lead."[17]

Mutter- und Koselieder (1843), the book that Froebel thought contained his most important educational ideas, was about play. Though intended for use in home education, *Mother Play* became very popular with kindergarten teachers, many of whom declared it to be Froebel's best work and the key to understanding and implementing his pedagogical system. Froebel initially tested the games and songs in the book on the children of his associate Middendorff and circulated them widely for use and comment before publishing them. Another associate, Robert Kohl, wrote the music for the songs, which were later published in a separate volume. The book also featured quaint woodcuts of children, baby animals, farm scenes, and medieval life, along with diagrams illustrating how to perform the finger plays.[18]

Mother Play begins with "Mother Communings," poems designed to encourage what today would be called "bonding," which included rhymes on observing, playing with, talking to, and breast-feeding babies. The first group of finger plays and songs, intended to promote infants' sensory perception, included body awareness, movement, sensory discrimination, and imitation activities such as "Play with the Limbs," "The Weather Vane," and "Tick Tack." The next set of games and songs was meant to teach concepts of classification, number, size, and form to somewhat older children and included such finger plays as "The Nest," "The Pigeon House," and "Naming the Fingers." The third set, known as "light songs," was meant to lead the child's attention to more distant objects and abstract knowledge such as awareness of the moon and stars and the play of light and shadow. The final set of games dealt with social relationships and introduced moral themes such as the concepts of good and evil.

Much of the success of *Mother Play*, and of the kindergarten movement, was due to Froebel's realization that mothers and women who lived and worked with young children on a daily basis would welcome a guide for interpreting the behavior of the often mysterious creatures who inhabited their houses and classrooms. A quotation from Schiller, "Deep meaning oft lies hid in childish play," was printed on the frontispiece and cited frequently by Froebel's followers. American kindergartner Susan Blow analogized in her translation of *Mother Play* that it was as if Froebel had unlocked an ancient and secret code. "In this precious volume," she wrote, "he deciphers all that the child feels in cipher, and translates for mothers the hieroglyphic of their own instinctive play."[9]

In addition to its pedagogical aims, *Mother Play* reflects Froebel's interest in preserving the oral culture of child rearing and children's play. Like Pestalozzi, he worried that mothers were no longer nurturing their infants as naturally as in the past and that centuries of stories, songs, and games were in danger of extinction. Like his contemporaries Richard Wagner and Jakob and Wilhelm Grimm, he mined German culture to create cultural archetypes for children's behavior, light operas to be played out in nurseries or classrooms. In the process, he invented a new culture of child nurture and education in which older child-rearing methods were renovated and put to modern uses.

Worried that modernization and urbanization prevented young children from playing as much or as "naturally" as they used to, Froebel thought it especially important for city children to be introduced to country life and nature. To this end, he made up numerous poems, songs, and games relating to animals, plants, farming, and gardening, a nostalgic, bucolic imagery that proved enormously attractive to educated, middle- and upper-class parents and educators. Froebel thus contributed to the creation of a new artistic style and literary genre, children's kitsch, a combination of idealized folk culture and artificial naturalism that was to become the hallmark of popular commercial culture for young children.

For Froebel, who as a child had not enjoyed a happy family life, the family was the key social and socializing unit in which the basic principles of children's characters were formed. Mothers' behavior was particularly important, he thought, and it was their responsibility to establish the loving and morally elevated home atmosphere on which children's successful social development depended. Positive sibling relationships were part of good family life, too, as the finger play "Happy Brothers and Sisters" symbolized.

Though Froebel thought the most important social learning was relational, learning a sense of individuality was critical, too. He believed that each child should develop "as much as possible in accordance with his own individuality and personality." The great value of play was that it fostered both individual and social development. While playing, children had opportunities for self-expression but also learned cooperation. For Froebel, reciprocity—taking turns—was the essence of social harmony. In his description of "The Snail Game," for example, he wrote, "Each member of the circle should have a chance to lead, for it is especially developing to a child to recognize himself on the one hand in his own independent activity, and on the other as the member of a well-ordered totality."[20]

Though simplistic and patronizing, by having middle- and upper-class children imitate the activities of laborers and artisans, *Mother Play* also taught children to respect the importance of this work. Froebel believed in the possibility of harmonious human development and harmonious human relationships and saw the kindergarten as a means of promoting congenial, respectful, and potentially equitable relations among people from different social-class backgrounds. This naive but appealing belief in the possibility of achieving social harmony without loss of individual freedom attracted reformers from various political backgrounds and contributed to the success of the kindergarten as a mainstream social and educational movement.[21]

Maternalism, Liberalism, and the Spread of the Kindergarten Movement

The kindergarten was linked with political liberalism and with social policies promoting the welfare of mothers and children. Though Froebel's primary concern was education, he was greatly concerned about the role of women in German society. Women and children, he stated, were "the most oppressed and neglected of all" classes in society. His plan for their emancipation was to join their needs and interests and elevate the status of child rearing and education. Though his call for a return to women's traditionally "nurturing mission" seems reactionary today, in the mid–nineteenth century it was perceived as progressive by many. Well-to-do German women with liberal political leanings began espousing Froebelianism and supporting kindergartens in increasing numbers.[22]

It is debatable whether Froebel's views should be termed feminist. As historians disaggregate the various women's movements of the nineteenth century, more distinct strains of feminism and maternalism are beginning to appear. Ann Taylor Allen characterizes the kindergarten as a form of feminism and focuses on some of the more politically radical members of the kindergarten movement in Germany. Seth Koven and Sonya Michel define movements more concerned with the protection and social welfare of women and children than with women's political enfranchisement as maternalist rather than feminist. Though women and men from quite different ends of the political spectrum, including advocates of women's and children's rights, supported kindergartens in both Germany and the United States, in my view, Froebel's essentialist definition of women's biologically determined nature and role in society and his linkage of women's and children's welfare better fit the maternalist model.[23]

Froebel thought the root of all social problems, particularly those of women and children, was society's undervaluation of women's maternal function. Divisions within the family caused by industrialization and the change from an agricultural family-production economy to a modern wage economy had created a rift between women and children and devalued women's natural role as mothers. Affluent women were leaving child rearing and education to servants, nurses, and governesses while they participated in leisure or social activities, while laboring women left their children to go to work. Modern society, Froebel argued, "often acting against the feelings of the mother, and in opposition to the womanly soul in general, as well as to the contradiction of the needs of child-life" had brought about "an unnatural separation between childhood and woman's life, between womanliness and child-life." All who were "true friends of humanity" and desired the "honorable appreciation of woman's soul" must seek to do away with this separation.[24]

Equally concerned with the effects of industrialization on wealthy and poor women, Froebel addressed his proposal for universal kindergartens to German women generally. In an open letter to the "Wives and Maidens of Germany" written in Blankenburg in 1840, he asserted that kindergarten training was "applicable to all classes of society" and to "all kinds of women engaged in minding children." To reunite women and children, Froebel proposed the founding of a new comprehensive entity, a "General institution for the complete culture of child-life up to school-age," which he envisioned as a training center for mothers and teachers as well as an educational program for young children (161).

It seems ironic that Froebel's remedy for the separation between women and children was to create an institution that involved separating children from their mothers for at least part of the day. This apparent contradiction was intentional. Like many other maternalists, despite his concern on their behalf, Froebel did not fully trust mothers to gauge and do what was best for their own offspring. The "primordial union of womanly life and motherly life with childhood," Froebel argued, could "only be won back again by a carefully planned mediation between the external relations of women's lives, the civic and social demands upon them, and the claim of the child's being" (158). Distrust in mothers' abilities to do what was right for their children was to grow much larger as the preschool movement progressed.

Though consciously concerned with elevating the status of women and children, Froebel was not a political radical. The kindergarten became associated with German liberalism because political reformers saw preschool education as a means of fostering noncoercive social change. Kindergartens appealed to different groups for different reasons. Some Germans stressed the potential of the kindergarten primarily as a means of preventing anarchy and civil disorder, arguing that properly raised and educated children would want to cooperate in socially constructive ways rather than disrupting the state and society. Other Germans saw in the kindergarten seeds of more radical political and social transformations. These differing visions made the transition to America along with the kindergarten itself.[25]

Interest in kindergartens increased enormously in Germany in 1848, a year of revolution and change in which forty-four kindergartens were opened. In 1849 a Hamburg women's group, the *Frauen-Bildungsverein,* or Hamburg Women's Education Society, asked Froebel to begin a women's kindergarten training course, and in 1850 the group began a school run by Froebel's politically more radical nephew, Karl Froebel, and his wife, Johanna. In the period of repression following the failure of the revolution, the radicalism of the training school provoked censure from political authorities that resulted in an 1851 government decree prohibiting the kindergarten as an agency of atheism and subversion. Soon thereafter, in 1852, reportedly in a state of depression, Friedrich Froebel died. Shortly before his death he sent inquiries to a nephew who lived in the United States about the possibility of beginning kindergartens in America, where Froebel pinned his last hopes for the realization of his educational plans.[26]

After Froebel's death German women continued to be very active in the kindergarten cause. The Baroness Bertha von Marenholtz-Bulow was particularly influential in promoting Froebel's ideas in Germany and America. The mother of a son to whose care and education she was devoted, the baroness was captivated by Froebel's concept of the role of women in society and used her influence to raise financial resources and public awareness for his educational ideas.[27]

Marenholtz saw kindergartens as a form of benevolent social control. Unlike most Froebelians, who supported universal kindergartens, she advocated the institution of separate schools for children from different social-class backgrounds. Children from lower-class backgrounds should not be given a high-culture education, the baroness explained, because it would falsely raise their expectations, and "there might be no more unhappy beings than learned men, on the joiners bench, and the artist as a chimney sweep." Instead, she thought working-class and poor children should attend *Volkskindergartens*. Arguing that the mothers of these children were incapable of practicing Froebelian techniques "because their work does not permit it and because at any rate they do not have the time," she felt that upper-class women should take it upon themselves to educate lower-class children in the tradition of noblesse oblige. "Until the mothers of the lower classes are a better educated race," she asserted, "the education of their children must be in the care of the educated class." Marenholtz also stressed the usefulness of Froebel's occupations in teaching vocational skills to lower-class children rather than their value as a pedagogical innovation for the intellectual and spiritual education of all children.[28]

Like many other indefatigable female kindergarten advocates, Marenholtz made promoting the kindergarten her life mission, devoting her considerable resources to the advancement of the Froebelian cause in Germany and elsewhere. She worked to have the ban on kindergartens lifted, finally succeeding in 1860; wrote numerous books on the kindergarten, including *Reminiscences of Froebel*; traveled and lectured widely; founded a kindergarten training school and *Volkskindergartens;* and started various kindergarten societies. She was also influential in convincing German Froebelians to emigrate to America, where they formed the initial cadre of kindergarten experts.[29]

Others in the German kindergarten movement espoused more democratic political views, among them, Froebel's niece, Henriette Breymann, who became the leader of liberal kindergartners who remained in Germany. Intelligent, single, and looking for something to do with her life, Breymann studied with her uncle at Keilhau, where she found companionship and commitment in the kindergarten cause. After marrying the liberal politician Karl Schrader in 1871, she began implementing her own ideas about Froebelianism and women's rights and reorganized the Society for Family and Popular Education started by Marenholtz. Under Schrader-Breymann's direction, the Pestalozzi-Froebel Haus, which she founded in Berlin in 1880, became a center of curricular innovation and reform and was visited by numerous influential Americans interested in childhood education.[30]

The diaspora of liberal freethinkers from Germany after 1848 helped make the kindergarten an international movement. Beginning in the 1850s, Froebelian kindergartens were opened in England, India, and other parts of the British Empire, as well as in Belgium, France, Italy, Russia, Sweden, Japan, and elsewhere throughout the world. In the United States, the kindergarten catalyzed a second round of preschool advocacy. Froebel's emphasis on combining women's and children's interests helped overcome resistance to the idea of young children being educated outside the home. His romantic pedagogy and elaborate educational materials provided an alternative to academic instruction that seemed appropriate for young children. His focus on voluntary self-control and socialization fit well with evolving models of moral education and character training. The generality and sentimentality of his ideas enhanced the kindergarten's popular appeal and permitted people with a wide variety of political beliefs to join the movement. Froebel's reliance on women as teachers and advocates was especially important because it harnessed a new and powerful interest group, putting the force of the growing numbers of educated American women behind the kindergarten.[31]

Chapter 4   "Paradise of Childhood"

Early Private and Public

Kindergartens in America

Unlike the infant school, the kindergarten was not initially promoted in the United States as a compensatory program for poor children. There was no negative stigma attached to attending a kindergarten; American parents paid for private kindergarten education for their young children as a positive good. This identification of the kindergarten as a voluntary supplement to upper- and middle-class child rearing rather than a remedial intrusion into lower-class family life had much to do with its acceptance in this country. The kindergarten became the successor to the domestic education movement that won out over the infant school. Some of the same liberal parents and educators who, thirty years earlier, had supported Bronson Alcott's romantic version of infant education but rejected the rigid academics of the infant school now promoted the kindergarten.

Froebelianism began in the United States as a German cultural movement. Americans then took up the kindergarten as an educational reform. Froebelian pedagogy dominated American kindergartning during the first decades of the private kindergarten movement. Maintaining orthodoxy was emphasized, in part to ensure quality and to control entry into the new occupation and also out of belief that pure, German-style Froebelianism was the correct approach to educating young children.

Americanization of the kindergarten began when Elizabeth Peabody, Susan Blow, and other American educators joined the kindergarten cause. In Boston, Peabody meshed Froebelianism with transcendentalist philosophy and domestic ideology and promoted kindergarten teaching as a vocation for American women. In St. Louis, the other early center of the kindergarten movement, Susan Blow collaborated with William Torrey Harris, leader of American Hegelianism and superintendent of the St. Louis schools, to introduce kindergartens to the public system. Blow became a very influential kindergarten trainer whose dogmatic advocacy of Froebelianism and resistance to change shaped the discourse on the education of young children in America through the end of the nineteenth century.

In the late 1870s the American kindergarten movement began to take on momentum, spurred by publicity from kindergarten exhibits at the 1876 Centennial Exposition in Philadelphia and by the growth of a commercial kindergarten supply industry. As kindergartens became more popular, the wisdom of educating young children outside the home, in what Edward Wiebe, author of a well-known kindergarten guide, called the "paradise of childhood," seemed uncontroversial. Yet, though few expressed concern about the potential ill effects of private kindergartens on young children, there was resistance to incorporating kindergartens into the public schools. Americans were ready to accept the idea of privately controlled extrafamilial education for young children but not the extension of public schooling to children under the age of six.[1]

German-American Kindergartens and Kindergarten Guides

The first kindergartens in the United States were begun by German immigrants for their own children. Conducted in German, these early kindergartens were intended in part to preserve German language and culture for second-generation German-Americans. For some German émigrés, they were also meant to promote liberal political ideology and to find a new home for Froebel's educational ideas.

The first kindergarten in the United States was begun in 1856 in Watertown, Wisconsin, by Margarethe Meyer Schurz. Born in 1832 in Hamburg, Margarethe Meyer belonged to a wealthy, politically liberal Jewish family that supported many educational and cultural causes and was educated in kindergarten methods by Friedrich Froebel, who was apparently very impressed by her work. In 1852 she moved to London to aid her ailing sister, Bertha, who was married to radical German Catholic religious dissident and kindergarten advocate Johann Ronge. The Ronges had started the first kindergarten in England, in which Margarethe taught. Johann Ronge introduced Margarethe to Carl Schurz, a young, university-educated Christian freethinker who had been exiled from Germany for his involvement with the revolution. Margarethe Meyer and Carl Schurz were married in 1852 and emigrated to the United States, where they eventually settled in Wisconsin.[2]

In the fall of 1856 Margarethe Schurz started a small kindergarten in her home, using the Froebelian pedagogy of gifts and occupations. Six children, including her three-year-old daughter, Agathe, four of Agathe's cousins, and another little boy, attended Schurz's private, German-speaking kindergarten. Though Schurz herself taught kindergarten only briefly—her husband's advancing career as a general in the Union Army and Republican politician caused the family to move frequently—relatives maintained the program for a number of years.[3]

There are records of nine or ten other German-speaking kindergartens in the United States in the late 1850s, 1860s, and early 1870s. Caroline Louise Frankenburg, another of Froebel's students, began a small private kindergarten in Columbus, Ohio, in 1858. Many early kindergartens were founded in connection with the bilingual German-English academies that opened in cities such as Louisville, New York, Detroit, and Milwaukee. Adolph Douai began a kindergarten in 1861 as part of the German-American academy he directed in Newark, New Jersey, and another opened in a similar school in Hoboken at about the same time. In 1865 William N. Hailmann added a kindergarten to the German-American academy he directed in Louisville, Kentucky. And there were presentations on the kindergarten at conventions of the German American Teachers Union held in Cincinnati, Ohio, in 1871 and in Hoboken, New Jersey, in 1872.[4]

The German-American kindergarten movement made its most lasting impact via the various German-American kindergarten guides written in English and published in America in the 1860s and 1870s. One of the most popular of these early works was Edward Wiebe's *The Paradise of Childhood* (1869). Wiebe, who had trained in Germany under Froebel's second wife and widow, Luise Froebel, emigrated to Springfield, Massachusetts, in the 1860s, where he became well known as a music teacher. Wiebe tried—unsuccessfully, at first—to interest Milton Bradley in publishing a manual of Froebel's songs and games. A New Englander, Bradley had made his fortune selling kits of games for Union soldiers in the Civil War. In the summer of 1869, after hearing a lecture on the kindergarten by Elizabeth Peabody, Bradley experienced what he later described as an "awakening" and began producing Froebelian materials.[5]

Against the advice of his business associates, Bradley decided to publish Wiebe's *The Paradise of Childhood*, which initially sold for three dollars. Wiebe's guide provided a lengthy "script" detailing exactly what kindergarten teachers and mothers should say and do. He instructed kindergartners always to use the same terms to avoid producing "any ambiguity in the mind of the child" and stated that everything must be done "with a great deal of precision" as "order and regularity in all the performances" were "of utmost importance."[6]

This Germanic insistence on order was also evident in Adolph Douai's guide *The Kindergarten*, published in 1871 in New York by Ernst Steiger. Douai was a socialist who advocated collective child rearing and universal public kindergartens to counter individualism and foster egalitarianism. His radical, anti-private-family, antiprivatism critique was not apparent in his kindergarten manual, however. In it, Douai explained that what distinguished his guide from earlier works was its adaptation for large kindergartens and normal school training and the inclusion of German as well as English text. He recommended using a platoon-style plan in which large numbers of children were divided into groups that could thus participate simultaneously in different Froebelian activities under the supervision of one teacher. In addition, he described bilingual kindergartens with two teachers, one speaking English and one speaking German.[7]

In 1872 Steiger published another German-American kindergarten guide, *The Child*, an interpretation and translation of Baroness Marenholtz's ideas by Matilda Kriege. Kriege, who was Marenholtz's protégé, had tried unsuccessfully to start an English-speaking kindergarten in New York and then in Boston in 1868. Apparently in both instances American parents perceived her kindergartens as too German for American children, even though they were taught in English. Kriege and her daughter Alma then offered a seven-month version of the traditional two-year Froebelian training program, drawing the ire of other German kindergarten trainers who thought proficiency in Froebelian methodology required more time. Kriege never compromised Froebel's prescription regarding which learning activities were appropriate for young children, however. In her interpretation of Marenholtz's work, she took pains to answer Americans' questions about early reading and insisted that parents must wait until age seven to introduce formal instruction, adding that waiting would result in increased academic achievement later on.[8]

Condemnation of early academics was even more apparent in William N. Hailmann's *Kindergarten Culture* (1873). Hailmann, who was born in Switzerland in 1836, came to the United States in 1852 and, after teaching high school in Louisville, Kentucky, began investigating elementary schools. During a trip to Zurich in 1860 he visited Swiss kindergartens and immediately became a kindergarten advocate. On returning to the United States he became director of the German-American Academy in Louisville and later directed a similar academy in Milwaukee. With his wife, Eudora, Hailmann was very active in promoting kindergartens throughout the Midwest. He presented a paper on "The Adaptation of Froebel's System to American Institutions" at a meeting of the National Education Association in 1872 and chaired the NEA's special kindergarten committee. In 1883 Hailmann became superintendent of schools in Laporte, Indiana, where he started public kindergartens.[9]

Hailmann's kindergarten guide stressed the importance of wholeness, harmony, and continuity, and other of the more philosophical aspects of Froebel's pedagogy. He emphasized that the kindergarten was not intended to "supplant family education" but to "improve" it and "place it on a sound basis," and he was especially concerned that the kindergarten "not be a school." Warning of the dangers of schools where "precocity" was "encouraged at the expense of sound development" and "the unreasonable parent" was "gratified and the outsider dazzled by the wonderful attainments of the unconscious little sufferers," Hailmann took pains to counteract any tendency to turn the kindergarten into an academic institution.[10]

The most influential of these early German-American kindergarten manuals was Maria Kraus-Boelte and John Kraus's two-volume *Kindergarten Guide*, published by Ernst Steiger in 1877. Maria Boelte, niece of German writer Amely Boelte, had studied kindergarten methods in Hamburg with Froebel's widow for two years before going to England, where her aunt had connections in the German community. There, she taught in urban kindergartens with the Ronges and set up a charity kindergarten and exhibit of kindergarten work at the London International Exhibition in 1862. Boelte was struck by the differences she saw between the aristocrats' children whom she had taught in Germany and the poor children in the London kindergartens. When she returned to Germany in 1867, however, she was discouraged by the conservative resistance and class divisions that slowed the progress of the kindergarten movement in that country. Her aunt then arranged for her to meet in London with Elizabeth Peabody, who had been trying to convince Boelte to come to the United States. Boelte's correspondence with John Kraus, a German educator working in Washington, D.C., helped persuade her to accept Peabody's offer.[11]

Peabody got Boelte a job teaching kindergarten at Henrietta Haines's private finishing school in New York. Boelte soon married John Kraus, and in 1873 they opened the New York Normal Training School for Kindergarten Teachers, Kindergarten and Adjoining Classes, where they began offering a full two-year course of Froebelian training. Like their course, their *Kindergarten Guide* was the longest, most complete, and most detailed of any of the manuals.

Bertha Meyer Ronge's *Aids to Family Government* (1879) was the most politically radical of the German kindergarten texts available to American parents and teachers. An avowed feminist, Ronge began her book with a plea for increasing women's rights, particularly that of choosing an occupation and avoiding "a repulsive marriage for the sake of a home." More of a social theorist than her sister Margarethe Meyer Schurz, Ronge emphasized the importance of Froebelian education as a means of advancing universal human culture. The most important effect of the Froebelian kindergarten, according to Ronge, was its larger influence on the home and society. The child returned from kindergarten happy because it had been given work that had engaged its mind, thus making it content. At home the child listened "without compulsion" and willingly gave up its own wishes if required to do so. The "joy, love, and peacefulness" that the child brought home from kindergarten then "spread among the other members of the household, and the first step in morality, culture and happiness proceeding from the child is taken." Ronge concluded by recommending universal public kindergartens and Froebelian training for all girls and women.[12]

Elizabeth Peabody and the Beginnings of the American Kindergarten Movement

In the hands of German-Americans the kindergarten was perceived as a foreign importation; it took the involvement of American educators like Elizabeth Peabody and Susan Blow to Americanize the kindergarten and pave the way for its universal acceptance. Though already in her fifties when she discovered the kindergarten, Elizabeth Peabody became the best known of American kindergarten advocates. She first heard about the kindergarten from Henry Barnard, who had reported on the 1854 International Exhibit of Educational Systems and Materials in London in his *American Journal of Education*. Peabody learned more from an 1859 article in Boston's *Christian Examiner* by Edna D. Cheney and Anna Q. T. Parsons, which included a summary of Froebel's ideas by Baroness Marenholtz. The same year Peabody met Margarethe Meyer Schurz at an abolition meeting in Boston. Impressed by the intelligence and independence of Schurz's daughter, which Schurz attributed to kindergarten education, Peabody asked for more information. Schurz told her about Froebel's ideas and sent her a copy of the introduction to Froebel's *The Education of Man*.[13]

It is easy to see why Froebel's romantic educational philosophy would appeal to a female American transcendentalist like Peabody, who was already experienced in education. Transcendentalism, like other forms of romanticism, idealized women but did not give them any realistic role in society. The kindergarten offered women like Peabody a respectable, meaningful cause and the possibility of self-respecting, autonomous work. Single and perennially seeking more interesting, remunerative employment, Peabody immediately took up Froebelianism and opened the first English-speaking kindergarten in America in Boston in 1860.

Peabody's first task was to overcome resistance to the idea of schooling for young children. Her *Kindergarten Guide*, published in 1863 in a volume with *Moral Culture of Infancy* by her sister Mary Peabody Mann, stressed the differences between a kindergarten and a school. A kindergarten, she wrote, was "not the old-fashioned infant-school," nor a "primary public school," but a very different kind of natural community for young children, "a commonwealth or republic of children," as "contrasted, in every particular, with the old-fashioned school, which is an absolute monarchy." The mission of kindergartners was gently and lovingly to lead children through the Froebelian play activities, rather than forcing them. Indeed, Peabody's directions for playing Froebelian games emphasized that the kindergarten teacher "should always play with the children." The child's "own cooperation—or at least willingness"—was "to be conciliated and made instrumental to the end in view." Loudness and physical movement were permitted and even encouraged, albeit in a controlled fashion, a radical departure from the strictly enforced quiet of most primary school classrooms.[14]

The physical environment of a kindergarten was also different from a school's. Two well-lighted and well-ventilated rooms were "indispensable," one for "quiet employments" and one for music, singing, movement, and play activities. Instead of desks bolted to the floor, movable tables and chairs were to be set up to suit different activities. In addition to paper, pencils, chalk and slates, and a profusion of other materials, there was to be a piano or at least a hand organ or guitar for use in songs and games. Peabody even suggested that, if possible, special glass-walled kindergartens should be constructed "on the plan of the crystal palace," with storage areas, bathrooms, and wraparound chalkboards, all at child scale.[15]

The outdoor environment of a kindergarten was to be different from a school's as well. Kindergarten children were to have a special play area, preferably a grassy one rather than cement, and a real garden. The teacher was to organize and participate in outdoor games with the children. The teacher and children were to garden together, or, if a real garden was not possible, the teacher was supposed to bring nature indoors by giving each child a pot in which to plant flowers and by setting out communal window boxes. These activities were such a departure from traditional schoolwork that Peabody felt it necessary to explain that, despite its name, the kindergarten was not entirely an open-air program.

Though Peabody's initial kindergarten efforts were well received, she herself was afraid that her limited knowledge of Froebelianism might lead her inadvertently to foster precocious intellectual development. As she later wrote, "The quiet, certain, unexcited growth of self-activity into artistic self-relying ability which Froebel promised, did not come of our efforts; but there was on the contrary, precocious knowledge, and the consequent morbid intellectual excitement quite out of harmonious relation with moral and aesthetic growth." Peabody's solution was to seek deeper knowledge. In 1867 she visited model kindergartens in Hamburg and other cities and met with German Froebelians such as Maria Boelte, whom she invited to come to the United States. On her return fifteen months later, Peabody repudiated the first edition of her *Kindergarten Guide* and brought out a revised version incorporating her new knowledge of Froebel's true philosophy and methods. Her first efforts, she later confessed, had been "presumptuous attempts at practical kindergartens[,] . . . unconsidered experiments" that were "generally disappointing; for, in fact, they were only the old primary school, ameliorated by a mixture of infant school plays; and in the best cases, by object-teaching according to the plan of Pestalozzi."[16]

The main change in Peabody's second *Kindergarten Guide* was her new opposition to the teaching of academic subjects to young children. Her first guide had included sections on reading, geometry, geography, and other advanced academic subjects that were not part of the Froebelian curriculum. In the revised edition, she added footnotes and introductory sections explaining that she had been mistaken to combine academic subjects and methods with kindergarten activities. In a telling change of mind, she now argued that reading should "not come till children" were "hard upon seven years old," after "the kindergarten exercises on blocks, sticks, peas, &c." were "entirely exhausted." Kindergartning should be based on play, on accepting, not opposing, young children's "spontaneous" and "natural" activity (71) and "genially directing it to a more certainly beautiful effect than it can attain when left to itself" (35). Peabody now recognized that in the kindergarten it was "a serious purpose to organize *romping*" (15).

In the years following her return from Europe, by then in her mid-sixties, Peabody no longer engaged in classroom teaching but became one of the country's best-known kindergarten proponents, corresponding with leading educational and political figures, lecturing, and in 1873 founding the journal *Kindergarten Messenger*. Though more focused than her earlier educational journal, the first three volumes contained a wide variety of selections, including Wordsworth's "Ode on Intimations of Immortality in Childhood," and poems by William Blake, Matthew Arnold, and others. There was even an extract from John Ruskin's essay "Aratra Pentelica." But Peabody knew her audience wanted and needed practical information on kindergartning, and, for the most part, that was what she gave them.

The pages of the *Kindergarten Messenger* documented the expansion of the kindergarten movement in the 1870s. The section "Kindergarten Intelligence," which included descriptions of kindergarten classes and information about the spread of kindergartens nationally and internationally, grew so much that later issues were devoted almost entirely to reports on training schools, graduation exercises, and organizational business. Increasing numbers of exemplary kindergartens and training classes were cited, in places as far away as Japan, India, and Africa, and the number of advertisements for kindergarten books and materials increased as well.[7]

But Peabody soon realized that growth brought problems. Anyone could start a program, just as she had, based on oral descriptions and a little reading, and use the name "kindergarten" to attract students to what were really amalgams of academics and a small amount of Froebelian methods. Peabody used the *Kindergarten Messenger* to try to stop such unauthorized kindergartens from springing up. She published articles criticizing "false" kindergartens and unmasking and naming supposed kindergarten "impostors." "False" kindergartens catered to adults who wanted to see young children learn to read and write and study school subjects at an early age, rather than doing what was good for them— playing. A "genuine" kindergarten, according to Peabody, was characterized as much by what the children did not do as by what they did. It was "a company of children under seven years old, who do *not* learn to read, write, and cipher; nor to study objects unconnected with their own conscious life."[18]

Fear of the dangers of unchecked expansion also led Peabody to form a kindergarten organization. Modeled on the Froebel Society of London founded by Bertha Meyer Ronge, the American Froebel Society (later the American Froebel Union or AFU), was started in 1877 to prevent "misrepresentations of the principle, and consequent deterioration" of Froebelianism. Among other efforts, the AFU proposed granting degrees, an "M.K." or "Mistress of Kindergarten Art," and an "M.K.T." or "Mistress of Kindergarten Training," though nothing seems to have come of this proposal.[19]

If credentialing failed as an occupational control strategy for kindergartners, other methods succeeded. Peabody used the early nineteenth-century ideology of domesticity and "woman's sphere" to promote kindergartning as an occupation for American women. Borrowing from the earlier prescriptive literature on the importance of the mother's role in education, she proclaimed kindergartning to be the ideal solution to the problem of what educated American women should do with their lives. It was Froebel's genius, she stated, to have discovered a means whereby women might again assume a useful, natural role in society. Becoming a kindergartner, Peabody argued, was the noblest vocation to which a woman could aspire, "the perfect development of womanliness—a working with God at the very fountain of artistic and moral character."[20]

Peabody's efforts to promote kindergartning as a vocation for American women created a female alternative to the masculine models of professionalism evolving at the same time. Kindergarten ideology was characterized by a gender-linked definition of qualifications and expertise and by voluntaristic, antimaterialistic vocational ideals. Unlike most male professionals or tradesmen, who based their qualifications and expertise on training and mastery of specialized professional knowledge or technical skills supposedly un-related to their masculinity, kindergartners based their qualifications on their emotional capacity to love young children and on training in educational techniques thought to be linked to explicitly feminine types of behavior. And unlike male professionals, who were supposed to devote themselves to their clients' interests and be removed from personal financial concerns but who were also discreetly well paid for their services, kindergartners' occupational norms were explicitly voluntaristic, and they were extremely ill paid for their work.[21]

Peabody defined kindergartning maternalistically and equated it with mothering. But a biologically essentialist definition that linked kindergartning to mothering was problematic because Peabody, like almost all other early female teachers, was single. How could women who had not experienced motherhood and child rearing themselves have the authority to act like moth-ers to other women's children and tell mothers what to do? Peabody's answer was that motherliness was a quality of the soul, not the body. Being a wife and mother were "the highest of earthly relations . . . the complete initi-ation into 'the communion of the just made perfect,'" she said, but "MOTH-ERLINESS" was a quality "not confined to mothers of the body, and in some sad cases in this wicked world" was "really lacking in them." All "true" kindergarten teachers, however, were motherly, Peabody declared.[22]

Peabody extended this definition of mothering by comparing kindergartn-ing to another spiritual profession, the ministry. Like ministers, true kinder-garten teachers were responding to a calling, a conversion to childhood. Peabody had experienced such a conversion herself, and in her many talks to kindergartners in training, published in 1886 as *Lectures in the Training Schools for Kindergartners,* she described seeing others accept the "redeeming vocation of childhood." They began to "feel it even in the training school," she observed. "'It is simply unutterable!' was the exclamation of one." This conversion experience was what set the true kindergartner on her path and gave her the right to act like a mother to other people's children. Mother-hood was the most primal of human experiences for a woman, but kinder-gartning was a close second. "The kindergartner," according to Peabody, was "the first minister of the gospel of life, after the mother." Kindergartning was "a vocation from on High."[23]

Peabody's depiction of kindergartning as a spiritual vocation was also grounded in antipathy to materialism, a central tenet of the ideology of "woman's sphere." Women's supposedly superior morality and selflessness compared to men were posited as a counterbalance to the encroachment of the masculine world of commerce and industry on society and family life. The "struggle for material good," Peabody warned kindergartners, was a "not unworthy" but "too predominant characteristic of American life." The antidote to increasing materialism was to rediscover childhood and be in close contact with the innocence, purity, and spirituality children embodied. Those lucky enough to minister to children "can have only this gospel to administer, if they are single-eyed and pure in heart from self-ends, 'Ye cannot serve God and Mammon.'" Kindergartning, Peabody exhorted, should not "be regarded as a *business, but as a religion.*" Of course, kindergarten teachers should be paid for their work, "like any other *minister of truth and light,*" but they must have a "higher aim than money." And since women should not wear themselves out and "half starve, for the sake of keeping a kindergarten," Peabody felt that only those who were "sufficiently free from other obligations" should be permitted "the privilege and luxury of working with God, on the paradisiacal ground of childhood."[24]

Peabody's insistence that kindergarten teaching was a religion rather than a business also served more secular ends. It preserved kindergartning as an occupation for middle- and upper-class women and protected it from schoolmen. Peabody's worry that "the sacred vocation of educator" was becoming "a trade" reflected the reality of a transition in the teaching force. As public schools expanded to accommodate growing immigrant and indigent urban populations, more men and women from lower social-class backgrounds, who were more dependent on their salaries, were being hired to meet the demand for teachers. At the same time, the organizational structure of urban schools was changing in ways that took responsibility away from teachers and placed it in the hands of primarily male principals and superintendents, who began applying industrial approaches to the management of education.[25]

Elizabeth Peabody had initially supported the idea of public kindergartens but soon changed her mind. At debates on the topic of charity versus public kindergartens at AFU meetings in the late 1870s and early 1880s she expressed her "great dislike of institutional life." "Natural relations," she stated, "were better for moral culture than artificial ones, even if parents were vicious," because of the difficulty of "keeping the heart" in an institution. Rather than taking control away from families and giving it to the state, Peabody hoped that privately sponsored charity programs might be sufficient to meet the needs of the poor and immigrant children who were filling America's cities in the late nineteenth century.[26]

Peabody thought the increasingly bureaucratic nature of public schools was inimical to the idea of kindergartning and to the interests of young children. She distrusted public school officials because she felt the "business character of superintendents had fallen below the philanthropic spirit which should always preside over education" and expressed concern that public schools had "deteriorated in spirit while apparently improving in form." Common school advocate Henry Barnard, who participated in the AFU debates, also emphasized the importance of keeping the kindergarten in private hands "to save it from the influence of *partisan politics* in the appointments of teachers and superintendents" and argued forcefully that the kindergarten should be left in "hands that loved it." School committeemen, according to Barnard, would not "be able to do what women who understood the needs of young children, could do."[27]

Peabody's voluntaristic ideology functioned as a means of both regulating access to kindergartning and increasing its status. High-minded ideals enhanced the identification of kindergartning with upper-class models of female beneficence and patrician civic responsibility. Records of some of the early kindergarten training schools confirm that most teachers came from middle- and upper-class backgrounds. The AFU was made up of women who were wives or daughters of wealthy and influential men. Among others, the membership included Pauline Agassiz Shaw and Ida Agassiz Higginson, daughters of Harvard's famed naturalist Louis Agassiz, both of whom married into affluent Boston families. Their social status and that of other AFU members and sponsors lent prestige to kindergartning and maintained a distinction between kindergarten teaching and elementary school teaching, which was rapidly being taken over by women from lower-class backgrounds who became the "hands" in the new urban education factories.[28]

Susan Blow, William Torrey Harris, and the Kindergarten Experiment in the St. Louis Public Schools

St. Louis educator Susan Blow was another formidable force behind the Americanization of the kindergarten. Born into a wealthy, cultured, intensely religious Presbyterian family in 1843, Blow was educated at home by private tutors and attended Henrietta Haines's private girls' school in New York

City. Visiting German kindergartens while traveling abroad with her parents convinced her that kindergartning was what she wanted to do with her life. She returned to St. Louis in 1871 and met superintendent of schools William Torrey Harris, who encouraged her to continue her interest in Froebelianism.[29]

Harris, who later became United States Commissioner of Education, was the best-known and most outspoken and intellectually inclined of a new breed of urban school administrators. Harris was born in Connecticut in 1835 and went to school there and in Providence, Rhode Island. In 1856, while studying at Yale, he had been impressed by a lecture given by Bronson Alcott, and after the Civil War he invited Alcott to address the St. Louis Philosophical Society, a group of German immigrants and schoolteachers who met regularly to discuss idealism. But Harris now found Alcott's ideas impractical, unsuited to the new realities of American urban and industrial life. Neither, apparently, was he much impressed by Elizabeth Peabody, who had begun a letter-writing campaign to convince him to begin a public kindergarten in St. Louis.[30]

Harris was impressed by Susan Blow, however, who had begun experimenting with Froebel's pedagogy while substitute teaching in the St. Louis schools, and their discussions of Froebelianism led to a long professional collaboration. As his annual reports make clear, Harris supported the kindergarten as an alternative to having young children out on the streets but disliked Froebel's blurring of the lines between schoolwork and play. Susan Blow seemed like someone who could maintain that important distinction; Blow, meanwhile, was eager to get kindergartens into the public school system. At Harris's suggestion, Blow went to New York in 1872 to study kindergarten methods under Maria Kraus-Boelte. After immersing herself in the minutiae of Froebelianism for a year, Blow returned to St. Louis and convinced Harris to provide her with a salaried teacher and space to start a kindergarten in the Des Peres School for the 1872–73 school year.[31]

St. Louis provided a hospitable climate for public kindergarten programs, which grew rapidly to include kindergartens in other schools throughout the city. Tensions between the city's large German population and other ethnic groups, however, led to some complaints about the appropriateness of German educational methods in American schools. Cost was also an issue. Harris himself was worried about the expense. By his calculations, kindergartens cost sixteen dollars per child per year, as opposed to twelve dollars for other grades, and this figure did not include salaries for the assistant teachers who worked as volunteers to receive kindergarten training. Since kindergarten sessions were only three-and-a-half hours long, Harris hit on the idea of double sessions, which most public kindergartens would eventually adopt. The drawback was that this schedule would prevent kindergartners from conducting the home visits and mothers' classes that gave kindergartning its unique, direct connection to private family life. But, as Blow noted in her report to Harris, in the five out of seven St. Louis schools with two sessions of kindergarten, the classes were taught by different teachers, presumably allowing teachers to continue fulfilling these additional duties but offsetting the savings of doubling sessions.[32]

Blow and Harris began their kindergartens by admitting young children between the ages of three and five, the "symbolic" stage of development on which, as Hegelians, they wanted to concentrate. Harris also wanted to reach younger children because he saw the kindergarten as the "transition between the life of the Family and the severe discipline of the School." For him, the sooner children adjusted to school and became rational, ordered beings, the better. He noted with pleasure in his *Twenty-First Annual Report* that primary teachers confirmed that "Kindergarten children submit more readily to school discipline than do children received directly into the primary room." This, Harris said, disposed of the argument that "the comparative freedom of the Kindergarten" would "unfit pupils for the regular school," one of the problems encountered by infant schools.[33]

This finding was not surprising given that Blow and Harris's "symbolic education," a somewhat abstruse, idiosyncratic mix of German idealism and other philosophical and psychological theories, fit well with the traditional public school functions of academic preparation and promotion of citizenship and civil order. Kindergartens in St. Louis were not intended to be a "paradise of childhood," Harris asserted, but a means of controlling the "gushing hilarity" of young children and enhancing their future intellectual development. In Harris and Blow's vision of child gardening, the kindergarten teacher was as much a philosopher as a nurturer, and the kindergarten more a mental refuge and academic and civic training ground than a playground or garden.[34]

Meeting the educational needs of differing social classes was a central factor in Harris's support for public kindergartens. In an 1880 report to the Department of Education of the American Social Science Association, which

Harris chaired, a subcommittee made up of Harris, Henry Barnard, and women's education advocate and social scientist Emily Talbot listed reaching "the proletariat" and neutralizing "the seeds of perverseness and crime in their earliest growths" as one of nine pedagogical and social objectives for kindergartens. Providing kindergartens for upper-class children was equally important to the public good, Harris argued, because wealthy children, who were "often left to the home training of ignorant or weak servants," inherited "great power of will," with the consequence that these socially advantaged children developed "caprice, waste[ed] their patrimony, and cost the State large sums to repair their excesses."[35]

Training was important because of the newness and uniqueness of Blow's and Harris's pedagogical views. To facilitate this training, Blow visited Germany in 1876, where she met with German kindergartners in Berlin and elsewhere. On her return, she began a series of lectures and classes for mothers and other women interested in kindergartens. A powerful public speaker, Blow's classes were very popular. She expanded them to include lectures on other educational topics, such as art and philosophy, and by 1877 was attracting more than two hundred participants.[36]

Despite this success, Blow and Harris had trouble convincing the Missouri court system of the legality of kindergartens. School entrance age had been an issue in St. Louis all along, as it would be in many other cities and states in the campaign to establish public kindergartens. Harris had finally received school board approval to extend kindergartning to children as young as three throughout the city. Beginning in 1878, however, legal actions began challenging the school board's right to use public monies to operate kindergarten programs for children under the age of six. In 1883, the Missouri Supreme Court upheld these complaints, and St. Louis schools were forced to change the entrance age to five and charge five-year-olds a quarterly fee of one dollar. Exhausted and depressed, Susan Blow withdrew from active kindergarten work in 1884. Harris left St. Louis in 1880, but as late as 1895, when he was the U.S. commissioner of education in Washington, D.C., he was still trying to get the Missouri state constitution changed to lower the entrance age to four.[37]

Popularization of the Kindergarten

St. Louis was more an early special case than part of a widespread trend, but private kindergartens continued to proliferate, spurred by a series of national and regional fairs and expositions and by the growth of the commercial kindergarten supply industry. Kindergartners used the 1876 Centennial Exposition in Philadelphia, which was attended by more than ten million Americans, to promote awareness and acceptance of Froebelianism. The exposition included a Woman's Pavilion with various exhibits devoted to aspects of the "woman movement." Prominent among these exhibits was a "Centennial Kindergarten" demonstration with a teacher and children in daily attendance.[38]

The Centennial Kindergarten sponsored by Elizabeth Peabody's Boston Froebel Society was one of the biggest draws of the exposition. The teacher, Ruth Burritt, had trained with Maria Kraus-Boelte in New York and Mary Garland in Boston. The children in attendance were eighteen orphans from a nearby charity home, and to make sure they arrived each day looking well dressed and acting well behaved, Burritt moved into the home with them.[39]

Not all coverage of kindergarten exhibits at the Philadelphia exposition was uniformly positive. Elizabeth Peabody's reports printed in the *New England Journal of Education* included some pointed criticism. She faulted Susan Blow's St. Louis exhibit, for instance, because of the perfection of the examples of children's handwork on display. Peabody had made sure the Massachusetts exhibit contained no such forced, "false" work, and she explained in one of her reports that kindergartning was more than "the mere *knack* of making children do pretty fancy-work."[40]

Peabody was especially critical of an exhibit by Anna Coe called the "American Kindergarten" that claimed to be an improvement on Froebelian methods designed especially for American audiences. According to Maria Kraus-Boelte's husband, John Kraus, Coe had even changed Froebel's famous motto, "Come, let us live with our children," to "Come let us live with our parents, instead of servants," an indication of her targeted market. In addition to Coe's arrogant and conscious deviation from Froebel and her inclusion of Bible lessons, Peabody criticized Coe's incorporation of academic subjects like geometry in the kindergarten curriculum. Coe responded that parents preferred her "American Kindergarten" curriculum to a pure Froebelian kindergarten and that her work seemed to be attracting favorable attention. In the end, Peabody resigned from the *New England Journal of Education* in a huff when the editors refused to stop carrying prominent advertisements for Coe's training school.[41]

The exposition featured commercial as well as non-profit kindergarten exhibits, marking the beginning of another important trend: the marketing of the kindergarten and kindergarten materials. The main commercial exhibits were those of the two competing kindergarten supply firms, Milton Bradley and Ernst Steiger, both of which sold numerous publications and materials through mail-order catalogs and stores. Steiger was, if anything, an even more avid kindergarten supporter than Bradley was. A German emigrant, he had written a book in German exhorting German-Americans to start home kindergartens and, with Peabody's support, broadened his market to include kindergarten materials and publications in English.[42]

These commercial exhibits did much to make kindergarten information and materials accessible to the home market. Mrs. Anna Wright, for instance, mother of Frank Lloyd Wright, recounted her excitement at seeing the kindergarten exhibits at the Centennial. When she got home to Boston, she rushed to Milton Bradley's to purchase kindergarten materials for her children and enrolled in Matilda Kriege's training class. While it is impossible to know how many other American mothers tried out Froebelian methods, records of kindergarten training schools suggest that many graduates started home kindergartens. Given the growing popularity of the kindergarten, it is likely that many less well trained American women also used kindergarten methods informally both with their own and with neighborhood children.[43]

The 1870s saw the growth of a new commercial market populated by new consumers: mothers and young children. Most early American toys had been simple handcrafted objects; fancier toys came from abroad, especially from Germany. But toys and home educational materials became a profitable business, and American manufacturers began specializing in producing toys made of different materials. When the mail-order house of Montgomery Ward began selling toys in the late 1870s, the market and availability expanded greatly. By 1900 Ward's catalog included kindergarten materials, among numerous other types of toys. In 1907 toy manufacturer Luis Reinecke predicted a bright future for educational toys and compared a "well conducted toy shop" to a "fine kindergarten."[44]

Commercialism brought potential problems as well as benefits. Toy manufacturers were usually more interested in selling their wares than in observing the finer points of pedagogical correctness. Merchandisers claimed to have the approval of kindergarten trainers but sometimes changed Froebel's materials as they saw fit. Bradley added alphabet letters to Froebel's blocks, for instance, calling them "The Original Kindergarten Alphabet and Building Blocks." What probably seemed like an insignificant alteration to Bradley radically changed the purpose of the blocks, turning them into a didactic teaching device rather than a symbolic play material.

Ever sensitive to signs of materialism in education, Elizabeth Peabody worried about the growth of the commercial kindergarten supply industry. As she wrote in 1879 to her friend and fellow kindergarten advocate Henry Barnard, "The interest of manufacturers and of merchants of the gifts and materials is a snare. It has already corrupted the simplicity of Froebel in Europe and America, for his idea was to use elementary forms exclusively, and simple materials,—as much as possible of these being prepared by the children, themselves."[45]

But popularization of the kindergarten continued. The 1880s and 1890s saw kindergarten exhibits at fairs and expositions all over the country. A model kindergarten conducted for the duration of the New Orleans Exposition in 1885 increased awareness of the institution in the South. And the ultimate exhibit took place in 1892 at the Columbian Exposition in Chicago, where private, charity, and public kindergartners from around the country put on displays and held conferences.[46]

As the private kindergarten movement grew, however, it began encountering criticism. Even some of Peabody's old transcendentalist friends began taking Froebelianism to task for its excessive rigidity. At a meeting of the AFU in 1877 in celebration of Froebel's birthday, the poet and essayist Francis Hedge said that he was suspicious of Froebelianism "because it was a system." Hedge believed "the best thing to be done for children was let them alone, but give them freedom and opportunity." Peabody smiled at Hedge, who had admitted to "ignorance of Froebel's system," and observed that though she approved of giving young children freedom and opportunity, simply letting them alone would only cause them to become "victims of their own ignorance and caprices."[47]

The criticism that must have stung Peabody the most was the publication in the *New England Journal of Education* of anonymous letters condemning Peabody's reverence for Froebel and her vision of kindergartning as a religion. "Let us prune off all this kindergarten cant and bigotry," one letter stated, "and not treat Froebel as if he were Christ, his system as if it were a religion, and therefore incapable of improvement, and his pupils as if they were his infallible saints." After all, this anonymous critic from St. Louis wrote, education was a "progressive science and *not* merely . . . a religion and a philosophy."[48]

In poor health, her energy flagging, Peabody continued to be involved with the kindergarten movement until her death in 1894 at the age of ninety. Blow came out of retirement in the 1890s to become the most vociferous defender of orthodox Froebelianism. But the crusade to preserve Froebelian purity was a lost cause. The control of the American kindergarten movement shifted to younger women working in charity kindergarten organizations who concentrated more on young children's mental and physical development than on their morality and spirituality. With the change of focus from immortality to reality, from the state of children's souls to the state of their bodies, minds, and daily lives, kindergartners came to recognize that American cities were not a paradise for young children and that private kindergartners had a public responsibility to do what they could to help "other peoples' children."

Chapter 5   Educating "Other Peoples' Children"

The Free Kindergarten

Movement in America

The rapid industrial growth and urbanization of the United
States after the Civil War were perceived as harmful to children.
Increased rates of immigration and high birth rates among immigrants were also a cause of concern as more and more young
children from different cultural backgrounds flooded city streets.
Some of the private wealth amassed during the Gilded Age of
economic expansion of the 1880s and 1890s was directed to helping these children through free kindergarten associations, some
115 of which were in existence by 1890.[1]

Froebelian pedagogy began to change as teachers in these free
kindergartens began ministering to young children's physical as
well as educational needs and educating mothers from different
cultural and social-class backgrounds. Academicians and educators began looking to science to create rationally structured educational organizations and scientific pedagogy designed to deal
with the problems created by industrialization and urbanization.
These new psychological views of education produced the first
scientific critique of Froebelian kindergarten pedagogy. Psychologist and child study advocate G. Stanley Hall in particular
voiced concerns about whether the kindergarten was harmful to
young children physiologically and psychologically. Unlike
Amariah Brigham's earlier warnings on precocity that had ad-
versely affected the infant school campaign, however, Hall's
challenge did not sound a death knell for kindergartens. Instead,
a new generation of American kindergartners began modifying
Froebelian pedagogy along scientific lines. But some kindergartners continued to adhere to orthodox Froebelianism, and

deep divisions opened up in the American kindergarten movement. In Massachusetts, where Pauline Agassiz Shaw sponsored a network of free kindergartens and G. Stanley Hall promoted the study of children, kindergartners were torn between conservative Froebelianism and more modern methods. In the Chicago area, kindergartners Anna Bryan, Alice Putnam, and Elizabeth Harrison collaborated with progressive educators Francis Parker and John Dewey and advocated change or compromise. While in the slums of San Francisco, Kate Douglas Wiggin and her sister Nora Archibald Smith developed an ideology of children's rights that contributed to rationales for universal public kindergartens.

Most urban kindergartners were as intent on reaching mothers as children. They wrote books, made home visits, held mothers' classes, gave lectures, and started training programs and national organizations. Efforts initially focused on mothers from lower-class and poor backgrounds, but, as with earlier innovations in education for young children, the kindergarten mothers' education movement became very popular with women from the middle and upper classes. Though most charity kindergartens and mother's classes remained segregated along class lines, free kindergartners envisioned forging new bonds among women based on their shared commitment to improved child rearing and education and in so doing further popularized the kindergarten and expanded public responsibility for young children.

Charity Kindergartens and Child Study in the East

The extension of kindergartning to the children of the poor began in earnest in the late 1870s, with New York and Boston in the lead. Felix Adler, son of the founder of American Reform Judaism and himself the leader of the Ethical Culture Society, started a free kindergarten in New York in 1877 and spurred organization of charity kindergartens in other parts of the country through his frequent lecture tours. In the same year, Pauline Agassiz Shaw began a network of charity kindergartens in the Boston area. Other free kindergarten associations also were started in Eastern cities in the 1880s and 1890s.[2]

Pauline Agassiz Shaw was exemplary of a new generation of wealthy, socially conscious, socially active women who in the Gilded Age expanded their sphere of influence from the private home to the public arena by sponsoring projects related to children and education. Born in Neuchâtel, Switzerland, in 1841, Pauline Agassiz lived with relatives in Europe after her mother's death in 1848 and then joined her father, naturalist Louis Agassiz, and his second wife, Elizabeth Cary Agassiz, in Cambridge, Massachusetts. There she attended a special school for girls run in their home by her stepmother, who later became the first president of Radcliffe College. Reared in a heady intellectual environment that valued moral rather than material worth, Pauline Agassiz's life changed dramatically in 1860 when, at the age of nineteen, she married Quincy Adams Shaw, whose personal fortune included the Calumet and Hecla Mining Company. Pauline Agassiz Shaw was determined to put her new wealth to good use. With Elizabeth Peabody's encouragement, she became deeply involved in philanthropic support of kindergartens, financing kindergartens, sponsoring lectures, classes, and a training school, and even underwriting pathbreaking psychological research on young children and the effects of the kindergarten.[3]

Since Elizabeth Peabody's initial private kindergarten attempt in 1860, only a few kindergartens had opened in Boston. After kindergartners Matilda and Alma Kriege had returned to Germany, having had little success with their private Boston kindergarten, they were replaced by one of their pupils, Mary Garland, whose kindergarten and training school were a success. Another private kindergarten was started at the Chauncy Hall School, which had begun admitting girls as early as 1858. Then, in 1877, Pauline Agassiz Shaw opened two charity kindergartens, one in Brookline and one in Jamaica Plain. By 1883 Shaw's two kindergartens had expanded to thirty-one, some located in public school buildings. Shaw took care of all the expenses—the teachers' salaries, furniture, supplies, and heat; the school system provided the space.[4]

The best known of Shaw's kindergartens were the two in the Cushman School in Boston's crowded North End. There, in an area "filled with the poorest and most degraded classes," as described by Progressive educator-reformer Francis Wayland Parker who worked briefly as a primary school supervisor in Boston, "Poles, Russians, Italians, Bohemians" and working parents of many other nationalities were forced to "turn their children out into the streets in the morning to care for themselves." Shaw's teachers brought these "neglected waifs and strays" into "home-like Kindergartens" where their "faces were washed, and their clothes made clean and comfortable" and "lunches of bread and milk were served daily at ten o'clock." Teachers also made home visits, conducted mothers' meetings and classes, and did all they could to encourage parents to become more involved with their children. As Parker commented, the children at the Cushman School kindergarten were joyful, with hearts "full of true happiness, the joy of doing, of overcoming, of growing." But on seeing this happiness, Parker also immediately thought of the "terrible problems of anarchy, of socialism, of trade oppression, of trade-unionism" the kindergarten could prevent.[5]

Shaw's kindergartens were the site of some of the first child study experiments in America. Beginning in September of 1880 she paid for substitutes so that four of her most capable teachers could help G. Stanley Hall survey what young children knew when they entered primary school. Born in 1844 in Ashfield, Massachusetts, Hall was the first American psychologist to study young children systematically. After graduating from Williams College, he went to Germany, where, like so many other American intellectuals of the period, he was much taken with Hegel's ideas. On his return to the United States, Hall visited William Torrey Harris and participated for a time in Harris's philosophical circle in St. Louis, but he soon became disenchanted with Hegelianism. After teaching philosophy at Antioch College, he went to Harvard where he studied philosophy and psychology under William James. In 1878, he received the first doctorate in psychology awarded in the United States. Hall then returned to Germany where he studied in Carl Ludwig's and Wilhelm Wundt's psychology laboratories and became interested in the evolutionary philosophy of Ernest Haeckel. He also toured German schools and became knowledgeable about European pedagogical reforms.[6]

Hall came back to America in 1880 convinced that the key to understanding human development, or what was then called the history of the race, was studying young children from an evolutionary perspective. From Haeckel and others Hall had picked up the idea that ontogeny recapitulates phylogeny, that is, the development of an individual organism repeats stages in the development of its species. He also adopted the concept of "culture epochs" from German pedagogues Tuickson Ziller and Wilhelm Rein, who postulated that school curricula should repeat the stages of cultural history; as Hall and others came to believe, human embryos went through a fish stage, young children's play repeated the social organization of primitive tribes, and schoolchildren should study the Greeks, then the Romans, and so on, in evolutionary and historical order. Hall eventually developed these notions into an overall theory of "genetic psychology," in which he claimed to trace the biological origins of human mental development.[7]

Hall collected a huge amount of data in Shaw's Boston kindergartens. Under his direction, the four kindergarten teachers paid for by Shaw surveyed about two hundred children ranging in age from four to eight years old, most of whom were five or six at the time of the study. Each teacher would interview three children at a time, asking some 134 questions about objects in the environment, the weather, and other subjects in order to test their knowledge of the natural world. Sixty or so other teachers also participated in the study.[8]

The results of Hall's research provided strong support for kindergarten education for young children. Like German researchers whose work he reviewed, Hall found in a "striking way the advantage of the kindergarten children, without regard to nationality, over all others." This advantage was even more striking because, as Hall stated, most of the kindergarten children "were from the charity kindergartens, so that superior intelligence of home surroundings can hardly be assumed." All but four of the nearly thirty primary teachers Hall questioned also thought the kindergarten children did better in school, though at first they had found them "more restless and talkative."[9]

Despite this vote of support for the kindergarten, the overall findings of Hall's study were negative. Most young children entering school in Boston knew shockingly little about the natural environment. Eighty percent did not know what a beehive was; 77 percent did not recognize a crow; 72.5 percent did not know a bluebird; 65 percent did not know an ant; 63 percent did not know a squirrel; 54 percent did not know a sheep; 33.5 percent did not know a chicken; and 18.5 percent did not know a cow. Most of the children said they had never seen hail (73 percent) or a rainbow (73 percent) and had no conception of an island (87.5 percent). Almost all (90.5 percent) did not know where their ribs were, and 65.5 percent did not know where their ankles were, though most—78.5 percent—did know their right and left hands (18–20).

Modern standards would deem many of Hall's questions culturally biased; examiners did not ask the children about objects from their everyday urban environment, for instance. The fact that Boston children knew their numbers (only 28.5 percent did not know the number 5 and only 8 percent did not know the number 3) and colors (only 15 percent did not know green and only 9 percent did not know red) and said they had seen stars and the moon (only 14 percent and 7 percent, respectively, had not) suggests that they did much better on more familiar items (18–20).

Hall attributed the ignorance he found to city life, and he was not alone in drawing this conclusion. Hall thought that children who grew up in cities were being cheated because city life was "unnatural" and "inferior in pedagogic value to country experience." The solution was to send children to the country and to kindergarten. "The best preparation parents can give their children for good school training," Hall stated, was "to make them acquainted with natural objects, especially with the sights and sounds of the country, and to send them to good and hygienic, as distinct from the most fashionable, kindergartens." By "good and hygienic" Hall meant kindergartens where children had plenty of time to play outdoors and study nature rather than doing a lot of fancy paper cutting indoors (26–27).

It is easy to understand why Hall recommended kindergartens as the next best thing to country life. Descriptions of kindergartens in Boston in the 1880s are replete with rural realia. Lucy Wheelock, a novice kindergarten teacher at the Chauncy Hall School during this period, turned her classroom into a veritable bower of flowers and animals. There were "geraniums blooming in window boxes" and "small pots with growing bulbs." A "wet sponge placed in a deep dish was sown with grass seed, which soon sprouted and showed us a ball of green." Children brought in caterpillars and watched them turn into butterflies. A nature shelf featured "a twig of pine cones, a branch of an oak tree with a cluster of green acorns, sea shells, chestnuts and other nuts." There was even a "large wasp's nest fastened to a branch of an apple tree" hanging from a cabinet. With classrooms like this, no wonder the children who attended kindergarten were better at identifying natural objects than were the other children in Hall's study.[10]

Hall saw child study as a broad, interdisciplinary movement encompassing pedagogy, anthropology, pathology, and psychology, and when he became the first president of Clark University in Worcester in 1888, he tried to make that institution the center of a new kind of popular, populist psychology that linked academia and schools. In 1891 he founded a journal, *Pedagogical Seminary*, in which he began sending out questionnaires and publishing the results of child study research. His messianic vision was well received by teachers, especially kindergarten teachers, and in the 1890s child study developed into a national movement involving thousands of teachers and parents throughout the country.[11]

In 1892 Hall began a series of special summer sessions at Clark that attracted free kindergartners from around the country. Among the leaders of the charity kindergarten crusade who attended the 1894 session were Anna Bryan, Alice Putnam, Alice Temple, and Nora Archibald Smith. In addition to lectures on experimental psychology, pedagogy, anthropology, biology, and other topics, the Clark Summer School of Higher Pedagogy and Psychology included cultural and social events and outings. The teachers had access to all of Clark's facilities, including the psychological laboratories where, according to a report on a later session in the *Kindergarten Magazine*, daily sessions consisted of "practical experiments, physiological investigations and studies, and discussions of these studies in both lecture and classroom form." Hall even invited some of the kindergartners to be his house guests. In her autobiography, Lucy Wheelock recalled unforgettable "evenings spent on Dr. Hall's vine-covered porch after the day's lectures were ended."[12]

Hall asked kindergartners Anna Bryan and Alice Putnam from Chicago to design a special kindergarten "topical syllabus," as Hall's questionnaires on subjects such as children's appetites, fears, anger, and so on were called. Their syllabus included more than a hundred questions grouped under seven headings: "hygiene," "gifts and occupations," "games and plays," "music," "stories," "miscellaneous" (questions about the length of sessions, the age of the children, and so on), and "special points" (pedagogical questions, including queries about teacher training).[13]

The questions on Bryan and Putnam's syllabus reveal the extent to which some kindergartners in the 1890s were beginning to modify and critique Froebelian pedagogy. Bryan and Putnam asked teachers whether they thought "a fixed regime, as of gifts and occupations, allow us to find out or to develop the natural interests and aptitudes of children?" Teachers were also asked to critique the relative worth of different Froebelian and non-Froebelian activities, games, and toys and whether the abstract concepts underlying the order of the gifts and occupations had "any educational value, and if so what, and for whom?" It is unfortunate that the replies they received have been lost; they would have provided a rich source of documentation on changing kindergarten practices.

Two themes in particular ran through the questionnaire: the need to prevent fatigue and the need to modernize. Teachers were asked to comment on whether they thought Froebel's methods required too much "fine work," whether his materials were "too small," and if the work required "too many repetitions." They were also asked how Froebel's general principles should be "modified or restricted, to conform to more modern views of evolution, anthropology, child study, & c." Clearly Hall was beginning to see child study research less as support for the kindergarten than as an aid to understanding developmental problems the kindergarten might cause.

Hall's main worry was about muscular development. He theorized that "fundamental" and "accessory"—what today would be called large and small—muscles developed successively. Applying this law specifically to the kindergarten, he said that certain important changes needed to be made. "No one believes more heartily in the kindergarten than I do," he stated, "[but] I think when you take 4, 5 or 6 year old children and set them at this fine work of weaving delicate strips of paper and at other delicate processes it is putting the accessory before the fundamental." Such activities "revers[ed] nature's process." The solution, he said, was to change the size of kindergarten materials so that their manipulation would not require fine motor coordination. "Small writing, small figures, fine lines, and everything which puts undue strain on the delicate muscles that are not developed until a later period [should be] put away from the primary school." To modern ears, this sounds obvious and right, but at the time the idea represented a revolutionary modification of Froebel's methods, which involved much detailed handwork.[14]

With characteristic exaggeration, Hall expanded his ideas on the dangers of early fine motor exercise to include the possibility of permanent neurological damage, neurosis, and disease. In a speech on child study in summer schools, he reported direly that researchers had found chorealike symptoms in some children who had overtaxed their small muscles for even a short period of time. "Little children of six," Hall warned, "have very little power to use the hands at all." Their finger muscles were easily tired, and "choreic symptoms result if these muscles are put through any kind of exercise that involves fatigue, so that we found all the symptoms of chorea in something like 15 percent of the children who used these muscles for five minutes." These findings could lead to only one recommendation: "Do not admit kindergarten methods of manipulating little bits of paper and tooth picks. . . . They directly cultivate 'Americanitis' and tend to stamp a neurotic temper on children, because fatigue is the beginning of every disease of the nervous system."[15]

Like infant school pedagogy, kindergarten methods were now in danger of being seen as rigid, developmentally inappropriate, and physiologically damaging to young children. Some kindergartners had already begun modifying Froebelian methods and were interested in experimenting with child study and adapting Froebelianism accordingly. Lucy Wheelock, for example, had already recognized in the 1880s that some of Froebel's methods were not developmentally appropriate. "I soon discovered," she wrote in her autobiography, "that the six colored balls of the first gift and the wooden sphere, cube and cylinder were playthings for the child in the cradle and not for the four-year old, so I dropped them from my program." Later, she continued, "I also gave up the fine pricking and the drawing on paper marked off in small squares at the time when Dr. Stanley Hall was criticizing the fine work as a great strain on the eyes and smaller muscles."[16]

Her deviance from Froebelian orthodoxy, however, earned Wheelock the brand of "heretic." Traditional Froebelianism remained strong in Boston. Pauline Agassiz Shaw had invited two of Susan Blow's students, Laura Fisher and Clara Beeson Hubbard, to come to Boston in the fall of 1883. Fisher, in particular, shared Blow's intense dedication to Froebelianism and was to have a long-lasting influence on kindergartens in Boston through her appointment as supervisor when the Boston Public Schools adopted kindergartens. As late as 1914, orthodox Froebelian pedagogy was in use in Boston kindergartens, and State Commissioner of Education David Snedden even suggested in his annual report for that year that this resistance to scientifically based methods accounted for the relatively slow adoption of kindergartens in Massachusetts generally. In the Midwest and West, however, free kindergartners were experimenting more freely with Froebel's methods.[17]

Child Study and Teaching Mothers in the Midwest

In the late 1880s and 1890s the locus of the kindergarten movement and of educational reform generally shifted from New England to the Midwest. The early influence of Susan Blow and William Torrey Harris in St. Louis was felt throughout the region; William Hailmann and his wife Eudora brought new ideas to Milwaukee, Detroit, and elsewhere; and Chicago became the center for Progressive educational ideas and programs. Francis Parker had moved to Cook County Normal School, where he continued experimenting with curricular innovations. John Dewey did seminal research in psychology while at the University of Chicago and utilized kindergarten techniques at the Laboratory School he and his wife Alice Chipman Dewey directed there. And a kindergarten was one of the first programs Jane Addams organized at Hull House, her model social settlement. Kindergartens were also begun in other midwestern cities.[18]

Anna Bryan's work in free kindergartens in Louisville and later in Chicago was especially important in pointing the way to new conceptualizations and implementations of kindergarten policy and pedagogy. Born in Louisville in 1858, Bryan had heard about the kindergarten while visiting relatives in Chicago and enrolled in a training school run by Alice Putnam of the Chicago Free Kindergarten Association. After completing a short course in 1884, she taught at the Marie Chapel Charity Kindergarten and in 1887 returned to Louisville to direct a kindergarten being organized by women from the Union Gospel Missions. Bryan convinced the women's group to form a Free Kindergarten Association, which met for the first time on November 30, 1887.[19]

One of the association's early reports discusses the efficacy of kindergartens as a means of preventing urban crime, promoting "the public good, on the side of law, order and commercial prosperity," and combatting the "poisonous atmosphere" of some homes. Error, Bryan stated in an article on the kindergarten and philanthropy, was "as much the result of ignorance as natural depravity," and "with a careful arrangement of earliest impressions and experiences, it is possible to grow tissues and form molds for thought and feeling." But dire consequences could result if environmental amelioration was not instituted properly. It was better to let people starve than to leave their "undirected energies" without "wholesome occupations"; otherwise, with the strength they gained from being given free food but not education, the poor could "turn against us in anarchy and rebellion."[20]

Bryan, like other charity kindergarten supporters, did not believe that the kindergarten should be a replacement for the family or a way of relieving women's responsibility for mothering. "We cannot take the child from the home," Bryan stated, "nor would that be well for either child or parent." Nor could society "go into the homes daily and effect permanent reform there." But the kindergarten could bring about this needed reform indirectly, by changing families, particularly mothers, through their children. "The kindergarten does not relieve the mother of responsibility, but rather, through its subtle influence, its transforming power over the little ones through song and play, strengthening the family relations, and binding the child closer to the mother, it arouses her to a sense of duty."[21]

Bryan was one of the first American kindergartners to break with Froebelian orthodoxy. She began experimenting with new teaching methods on her own in Louisville in the late 1880s even before she was exposed to G. Stanley Hall's ideas at the Clark University summer school in 1894. Intellectually independent by nature, Bryan encouraged kindergartners to decide for themselves about what was best for young children rather than following Froebel slavishly. In an 1890 address to the Kindergarten Department of the National Educational Association, she criticized Froebel's followers for having turned his "ministry" into a "personal cult." Some Froebelians, Bryan stated, had become "servile imitators" who failed to "distinguish between the idiosyncrasies of the man and the universals he reflects." Because Froebel had developed a "complete and comprehensive . . . system," there was a "great danger and temptation," she asserted, to mistake his work as "a prescribed, formal line of teaching, instead of tools to be skillfully and discriminatingly used."[22]

Distinguishing between what she called "free play" and "dictation play," Bryan argued that the key to meaningful learning was for a child's consciousness to pass through "*not* a *passive, literal* sequence, but an *active, creative* one" (577). The kindergarten teacher's appropriate role was to help children with "thinking about and finding relationships for themselves" rather than forcing children's interests to be "subordinated to material" (575). Bryan's main pedagogical innovation was to begin incorporating themes from children's daily lives into the sequence of Froebelian gifts and occupations. Using the example of a play based on a trip to grandmother's house, she demonstrated how instead "of teachers furnishing moves to be copied, the child himself created the moves by the suggestiveness and relatedness of ideas, and is thus led to consciously work out the thought; to compare, measure, relate, judge, to determine the kind of form required by the necessities of the case, and thus to arrive at a conclusion" (576). Though seemingly a small shift, the introduction of child-initiated topics to teacher-controlled curricula and of imperfect reality to artificial naturalism was an enormous change that was to have a lasting effect on preschool pedagogy.

One visitor to the Louisville free kindergartens described activities designed by Bryan's teaching assistant, Patty Smith Hill, whose career would span the kindergarten and nursery school movements. During the occupations the children sewed designs of objects they themselves had talked about rather than Froebel's abstract or formal patterns. When it was time to play with the gifts, the children made beds, chairs, tables, stoves, and cupboards with the blocks instead of the prescribed stylized designs. And during the plays the children took the roles of real objects like clocks and "other *useful articles*" and played games in which they delivered mail and did other real things they had seen real people doing.[23]

Born near Louisville in 1868, Patty Smith Hill was the daughter of a Princeton-educated Presbyterian minister who was the president of a women's college; her mother had done college-level course work through private tutoring. After graduating from the Louisville Collegiate Institute in 1887, Hill attended Bryan's new kindergarten training program and then in 1889 became her assistant. And though Bryan did not make the connection between pedagogical innovation and political progressivism, her young assistant did. Hill, who had been interested in child study before she attended the Clark summer sessions with Bryan, saw that the universality of the scientific laws of psychological development cut across class barriers and thus must cut across political barriers as well. Whether rich people liked it or not, the "minds of the prince and the pauper unfold in obedience to the same divine laws, which, if violated, in either case must inevitably result in evil." Given that children develop through biologically equal processes, they should be treated equally by society. Though pedagogical methods might "differ somewhat, according to environment, the principle is the same for both classes," Hill stated. She even suggested that children from different class backgrounds should be enrolled in the same kindergartens. "It is wonderful to see the extremes of society meet under the guidance of a skillful teacher to unfold and blossom," Hill exclaimed, "not only by the same laws and principles, but even, in some cases, under the same methods."[24]

Bryan's and Hill's work in the Louisville free kindergartens influenced the kindergarten movement in the rest of the Midwest and elsewhere. Their presentation at the 1890 NEA meeting attracted attention, and more than three thousand visitors came to observe the Louisville free kindergarten programs. In 1894 Bryan returned to Chicago and left Hill in charge of the kindergartens in Louisville. Bryan's pedagogically liberating influence was felt in Chicago, where she became director of kindergarten training at the Armour Institute and worked closely with Francis Parker, John Dewey, and others in the center of the Progressive education movement.[25]

The charity kindergarten movement in Chicago was initiated by a married mother, not by a single female kindergartner, and programs in Chicago bore the stamp of this orientation. Kindergarten organizing in Chicago began in 1874, when Alice H. Putnam started a mothers' class to study Froebel. Putnam had become interested in the kindergarten as a means of improving the education of the two elder of her own four children. Putnam, born in Chicago in 1841, the daughter of a prosperous merchant who was founder of the Chicago Board of Trade, also saw the kindergarten as a way of contributing to the improvement of her natal city, for which she cared deeply. Elizabeth Peabody's exhortation to mothers to become more informed about education spurred her to form a study group made up of ten or twelve of her friends, including three men, who began reading Froebel's *Mother Play*.[26]

Putnam was a model of maternalistic politics, of how women in the Progressive Era extended private caring to public commitment and connected the domestic sphere of their own homes and families to that of other women's homes and families and then to the public domain of urban reform. Putnam found ways of combining her own mothering with working to help others to become better mothers. Realizing that she needed kindergarten training, Putnam took her oldest daughter with her to Columbus, Ohio, where she studied in a training school run by Anna J. Ogden. In 1880 Putnam took over a training class Ogden had started in Chicago and directed it until 1910 under the auspices of the Chicago Froebel Association (which Putnam's original study group became in 1880). Putnam was also directly involved in the founding and operation of the Chicago Free Kindergarten Association and the Chicago Kindergarten Club, both of which sponsored various programs throughout the city.[27]

Though she had studied under Susan Blow in St. Louis and with Maria Kraus-Boelte in New York, Putnam was child- rather than method-centered in her pedagogy and put children's interests before that of maintaining Froebelianism as an educational doctrine. "Let the children lead you, and you will not go far astray," Putnam told her students. "Study them, and let their actions serve as your guide." She was much influenced by Francis Parker, one of the leaders of the Progressive education movement, whom she helped bring to the Chicago area in 1883.[28]

When in Germany, Parker had learned of new educational methods, including Froebel's kindergarten (which he termed the "most far-reaching educational reform of the nineteenth century"), and had begun reconceptualizing the school curriculum as an integrated whole. In Quincy, Massachusetts, he had started reading and language arts programs based on what today would be called a combined whole-language, phonetic approach. After reading about the Quincy Method, Putnam had attended a summer school Parker ran on Martha's Vineyard. The experience so impressed her that she helped Parker gain appointment as principal of Cook County Normal School in Chicago. Wanting as ever to combine her private and public life, Putnam moved her family to a house in nearby Englewood so that her three daughters could attend the school attached to the normal school. Putnam herself taught kindergarten and was the kindergarten trainer at Cook County Normal School for some years and joined the group of Progressive teachers working with Parker.[29]

Putnam was also involved in kindergarten efforts at Hull House, the settlement house Jane Addams started in 1889 in Chicago's crowded Nineteenth Ward, and at the University of Chicago, two other centers of social and educational reform in Chicago. Addams supported the kindergarten both as means of providing child care for indigent mothers and as an educational program for young children. Particularly interested in the opportunities for association and social development the kindergarten offered to children, she raised money to expand Hull House's facilities to include a children's building. As the projected costs of the new building mounted, Addams asked Alice Putnam whether she would move her training school to the site and support the project. Putnam enthusiastically agreed and for seven years made the long commute from her suburban home to the West Side to supervise the kindergarten training school at Hull House.[30]

Even more impressive than Elizabeth Peabody's fantasized "crystal palace" for children, the four-story red brick children's building that opened at Hull House in 1896 was a prototype for the kind of comprehensive services to children and families that Progressives like Addams and Putnam hoped would reform society. Designed by the Chicago architectural firm of Pond and Pond, the building included space for children's clubs, a nursery school–like "baby department," a day nursery that ran from seven in the morning until seven at night, children's art and music studios, a kindergarten, and a kindergarten training school. John Dewey himself opened this paradigmatic Progressive structure, saying: "The most significant thing about this building is that it stands for one's faith in childhood."[31]

But though Dewey supported the kindergarten at Hull House and was a guest lecturer at Alice Putnam's training school, he was ambivalent about the Froebelian kindergarten generally. The classes for four- and five-year-olds at the Laboratory School of the University of Chicago that he directed from 1896 to 1903 offered kindergartenlike activities and were taught by teachers trained by Anna Bryan, yet he refused to let them be called a kindergarten, terming them the "sub-primary department" instead. Dewey's main objection to the traditional kindergarten was the imitative copying of Froebelian activities that Bryan called "dictation play." As always, Dewey sought balance. "Nothing is more absurd," he wrote concerning Froebelian pedagogy, "than to suppose that there is no middle term between leaving a child to his own unguided fancies and likes or controlling his activities by a formal succession of dictated directions." The teacher's job was to suggest activities that would "*fit in* with the dominant mode of growth in the child," to serve as a "stimulus to bring forth more adequately what the child is already blindly struggling to do."[32]

The kindergarten children at Dewey's University of Chicago Laboratory School played games related to their homes and family members and made practical objects they could use. They played at washing clothes, wove rugs from quarter-inch-thick candlewick, and cooked their own lunches of semolina and other cereals, a suggestion the children came up with themselves. The guiding principle was that the activities and materials had to be "real." This was Dewey's other criticism of Froebel: that kindergarten children performed artificial, symbolic representations using objects made of "artificial" materials, such as planting grains of sand instead of real seeds or dusting an imaginary room with an imaginary broom. The materials young children used, Dewey stated, should be as "direct and straightforward, as opportunity permits."[33]

The lectures and writing of another Chicago kindergartner, Elizabeth Harrison—who herself was not a mother—probably reached into more homes and brought more mothers into the kindergarten movement than did anyone else's. Born in 1849 in Athens, Kentucky, Harrison attended public schools in Davenport, Iowa, and in 1879, at a friend's invitation, went to Chicago to see the kindergarten in which her friend's daughter was enrolled. Much impressed, Harrison stayed, attended Alice Putnam's training school, and became Putnam's assistant for a year. Then, like Putnam and so many other kindergartners, she went to St. Louis to study under Susan Blow and then to New York to train with Maria Kraus-Boelte before returning to Chicago to teach in a private kindergarten.[34]

Influenced in part by Froebel's emphasis on mothers in his *Mother Play*, Harrison began looking for ways to involve mothers more directly in kindergartning. In 1883 Harrison and Alice Putnam started the Chicago Kindergarten Club and invited mothers to join along with their children. Harrison also began explaining Froebelianism to the club's affluent female members. In 1885 she began a small training class with five students and two mothers on Froebel's *Mother Play*. In 1887 a wealthy member of the Chicago Kindergarten Club, Mrs. John N. Crouse, visited this class and was so impressed that she offered to back Harrison financially and set about organizing mothers' classes throughout Chicago.[35]

Two years later Harrison and Crouse became codirectors of the Chicago Kindergarten Training School, the first large-scale American institution to provide women with education for motherhood. They went to Germany to learn more about Froebelianism from Henriette Schrader-Breymann, Baroness Marenholtz-Bulow, and others in the German kindergarten movement and, on their return, extended the training course to three years and renamed it the Chicago Kindergarten College. This "unique school for motherhood," as Susan Blow described it, enrolled some five thousand women in its courses between 1886 and 1895 and eventually became the National College of Education, now National Louis University, in Evanston, Illinois.[36]

Drawing from both Froebel and scientific child study in her mothers' classes, Harrison sought to make conscious and stronger the unconscious "nurture element" she thought was immanent in all women. By "nurture element," she told the kindergarten department of the National Education Association in 1903, she did not mean "sentimental gush, nor do I refer to the morbid love of self-renunciation which is sometimes called unselfishness; but rather that deep spiritual element in woman which makes her intuitively feel the weakness or need or discouragement of another when her more outward-looking brother has not yet perceived it, and that makes her rejoice in serving, rejoice in growing, that she may serve the more and the better." Once "rationalized and made a conscious power," Harrison argued, this "spontaneous unconscious nurturing element" empowered mothers to go beyond "merely . . . an individual work of love that concerns their own children" to do "great world-work whose influence will go on for generation after generation."[37]

Though maternalist ideology did not require motherhood for its leaders and many leading maternalists were unmarried, Harrison encountered some resistance because she was not a "real" mother herself. Nonmothers had written child-rearing guides in the early nineteenth century, and *only* unmarried women were permitted by tradition or law to be public school teachers in many parts of the country in the nineteenth and early twentieth centuries, but the tradition of teaching young children was somewhat different. Dame school teachers, for example, had usually been married women with children of their own. "How can a woman who has never given birth to a child teach mothers?" Mrs. Crouse was frequently asked when helping to organize Harrison's classes. This concern may have stemmed from notions of what was appropriate for younger children, but it was also a sign of the increasing awareness of the complexity of child rearing as well as of the increasingly biologically deterministic mind-set of science and society in the Progressive Era.[38]

To dispel this distrust Harrison tried to make mothers as comfortable as possible in her classes and to involve them in the kindergarten movement generally. She recommended that kindergarten teachers visit the children's homes and invite mothers to birthday, Valentine, Christmas, and Easter parties in the kindergarten. Soon the mothers' class would become a "social club" in which women could make new friends while learning how to be better mothers. Harrison suggested that in immigrant neighborhoods kindergartners show pictures of "famous places in the 'old country'" and have one of the mothers who spoke English reminisce about "their own early days or their trip across the Atlantic." This of course should be followed by showing pictures of "famous and beautiful places and buildings in America" so that the mothers would be proud of their new land.[39]

While these activities may not have made poor immigrant women feel very comfortable, Harrison's belief in the possibility of interclass communication among women was genuine. Harrison thought kindergartners had much to learn from mothers. "The mothers themselves will teach [the kindergartner] many things and give her flashes of insight far deeper than they realize," she declared. Such mutual dependency was the foundation of democratic society, Harrison argued, and its lack the source of class conflict, though people from different class backgrounds and occupations did not seem to know this. But, as she observed in "Hints for Mothers' Clubs," one could not expect the anarchist, whose hungry children were crying, nor the "comfortable, satisfied millionaire" to understand or solve this social problem. The solution lay in socializing young children differently in the kindergarten, where the rich man's child could play at being a worker and where all children, poor and rich, could "grasp the true sense of dependence." The potential of the kindergarten to prevent class conflict and to promote cross-class communication was the great hidden agenda of the kindergarten, and Harrison wanted people to know it.[40]

Harrison's talks to mothers were published in 1890 as *A Study of Child Nature from the Kindergarten Standpoint,* a work that became the most popular and widely read of all kindergarten books for mothers. Though Harrison thought the way to understand little children was through Froebel's "science of motherhood," her ideas had much in common with earlier nineteenth-century child-rearing manuals. Mothering, she stated, was based on three "facts": children had instincts that could be trained "upward or downward," these instincts manifested themselves early, and mothers' "loving guidance" could be "changed from uncertain instinct into unhesitating insight." But Harrison was really more interested in teaching children self-control than in scientific explanations of child development.[41]

Like many Progressives, Harrison was relentlessly optimistic and future-oriented, and sometimes somewhat smarmy. She criticized George Eliot and *Middlemarch,* for instance, for emphasizing "the discordant side of life, rather than the harmonious one," saying that "the great Englishwoman" was not as "helpful or as wholesome as many a writer who has less brain power and artistic skill than she, but who leaves us with a strong feeling that right rules in God's universe." What was most important for mothers, Harrison asserted, was to emphasize the positive in child rearing (24-25).

In chapters on training the senses, mind, and emotions, Harrison elaborated on the importance of wholesomeness. She was greatly disturbed by sensuality in general and inveighed against high living, degeneracy, gluttony, and, of course, intemperance, stating that the "perfect character" was "the character with the perfectly controlled will" (43). She condemned the "fashionable parties for children" in vogue among the upper classes and warned mothers about children's fancy dress and other activities that might turn children into epicures (54). Not surprisingly, a comparison of toys from different countries based on cultural stereotypes ended with a recommendation of homey, healthy German toys rather than fancy French dolls (58). In all matters of taste, simplicity was best for children.

Harrison's other main message was the importance of teaching children "the joy of unselfishness" so that they could "enter upon *True Living*" (81).

Training children *"through love"* to give up their own will to others was, in Harrison's maternalistic view, the key role mothers played in society (87). She told mothers how to cultivate "the 'love-force'" that was "woman's greatest instrument of power" (89). During punishment, for example, mothers should always reassure their children that it was the wrongdoing, not the child, that was the problem and that they could still count on "the everlasting arms of love" (140). In other modern-sounding advice, Harrison recommended what today would be called structured choices, letting children choose between two acceptable options such as being quiet or leaving the room. But these were mere devices to help mothers out of sticky situations. The really important thing was to develop children's character and self-control. Reading about and celebrating heroes could be helpful, as could the force of public opinion. Ultimately, however, parents had to teach their children that free will was not the ability to do what one wanted "but the power to compel one's self to obey the law of right, to do what ought to be done in the very face of otherwise overwhelming impulse" (163). If a woman could raise a secure and self-controlled child, Harrison concluded in her final chapter on faith, she had done everything a "mother-heart" could crave (207).

The enormous popularity of Harrison's book—it went through some fifty printings and was translated into at least eight foreign languages—may have been due to her emphasis on morality, character training, faith, and other spiritual themes that have always been compelling to the mainstream of American parents. Above all, she was a pragmatist and a moderate. Though she paid lip service to science, she told mothers what they wanted to hear and answered many commonly asked questions. Her digressions on children's food and toys and especially her discussions of how to teach children self-control outlined a new Progressive approach to discipline that would become the hallmark of modern American child rearing.

Harrison's mission to mothers culminated in the Chicago Conference of Mothers in 1894, the forerunner of the National Congress of Mothers and Parent-Teacher Associations. Special railroad rates were arranged so that women could come to the weeklong conference from all parts of the country. Pediatricians, kindergarten teachers, and trained kindergarten mothers addressed the assembled group on topics such as prenatal influences, the nursery, clothing, food, and various other kindergarten-related subjects. Harrison participated in an unplanned but very popular discussion session on why "children of *all* classes" should be in kindergarten for "part of each day," talked about storytelling for young children, and answered mothers' questions. Alice Putnam spoke on the subject of "Constructive and Destructive Games," using examples of her own son's behavior to discuss how to channel boys' aggressive play. And Alice Merry, a Progressive Era superwoman described as "a living example of the modern emancipated mother, who not only practices dress reform, common sense, and kindergarten, but has time to tell other women how to go and do likewise," gave a popular session on how to conduct a kindergarten, organize mothers' and fathers' meetings, and at the same time manage "her own household and little ones." Appropriately, John Dewey, introduced as the "'latest utterance' in the psychological world," closed the conference with a speech on how parents were actually psychologists with the very important mission of rescuing civilization from disintegration. *"To be a psychologist is simply to be interested in people,"* Dewey declared, defining the populist Progressive vision of psychology. Civilization was in danger, he concluded, because of "want of discipline and authority"; the solution was to "go deeper into the nature of the child and find there the true basis for discipline and authority . . . the moral center of gravity"—self-control.[42]

Dewey also addressed kindergartners who attended another popular conference Elizabeth Harrison helped organize, the School of Psychology, held under the auspices of the Chicago Kindergarten College in April 1889. All the leading psychologists of the day spoke at the conference, but it was William Torrey Harris who pointed to the future of kindergarten and psychological debates in his comments and closing remarks. "There are two dangers I would point out," Harris stated prophetically, "1st, That of turning the kindergarten into a sub-primary school; a sort of puny, insignificant primary. 2nd, There is an infinite amount of soft sentimentality about the kindergarten."[43]

Harris's final address, "Two Kinds of Psychology," foreshadowed the upcoming conflict between cognitive-developmental or what he called "rational psychology" and behavioristic-experimental or what he called "empirical psychology." Harris also spoke of the newly defined problem of arrested development. Arrested development could occur, Harris explained, when a child had been drilled to such an extent on some academic topic that he or she became fixated on it alone, as when a teacher's focus on counting over understanding mathematical relationships led children to love "to count better than to think of causal relations." Harris was afraid that kindergarten children might become "haunted with symmetry" and thus fixated "on a lower stage of art," for instance. And spending so much time on Froebel's complex geometrical forms might focus the child's mind on "analyzing all physical forms and their parts to such a degree that the analysis gets in the way of his thinking about the causal relations." To prevent such arrested development, Harris concluded, teachers needed the services of both kinds of psychology. The "rational" aspect of child study could provide the observational skills and information necessary for teachers to understand children's development better, and the "empirical" side could "formulate a great many useful rules which will be of practical aid to the teacher in curing her pupil of one-sided development." In general, however, Harris saw the kindergarten as a positive, healthy influence on children's development, and for the time being at least, this optimistic view carried the day. The kindergarten was conceived as part of the solution, not the problem.[44]

Free kindergartners in the Midwest melded the universalism of psychological concepts of development and of mothers' concerns for young children into a new ideology that would transform the kindergarten from a class-segregated private program for the affluent or a charity for the urban poor into universal public early education. This policy transformation was enhanced and consolidated by the work of women working in free kindergartens in the West.

From "Conscious Motherhood" to "Children's Rights" in the Far West

Fittingly, it was in the more open, less class-structured society of the American West that the ideological framework for universalizing education for young children evolved most fully. The book that laid the groundwork for this new ideology was written by a German kindergartner who had emigrated to America in the late 1860s. Born in Munden, Germany, in 1818, Emma Marwedel was probably trained by Froebel's second wife, Luise Froebel, and was very active in the German kindergarten movement. In 1867, when Marwedel was director of a new Girls' Industrial School and kindergarten in Hamburg, she spent time explaining Froebel's methods in detail to Elizabeth Peabody. (In fact, Peabody attributed to Marwedel the deeper understanding of Froebelianism that caused her to change her views about academics for young children.) Encouraged by Peabody, Marwedel emigrated to the United States and began a private school and kindergarten training program in Washington, D.C., in 1871. In 1876 she moved to Los Angeles, where, with the support of Caroline B. Severance, a social reformer and leader of the women's club movement, she started the California Model Kindergarten and the Pacific Model Training School. She then moved to the San Francisco area, where in 1878, at the instigation of Felix Adler and with the financial support of Phoebe Apperson Hearst, wife of railroad and mining magnate George Randolph Hearst, she helped found the San Francisco Public Kindergarten Society and the Silver Street charity kindergarten and in 1880 opened another training school. Though Marwedel died destitute in Oakland, California, in 1893, her training schools and ideas had great impact on the kindergarten movement in the West.[45]

Published in 1887, Marwedel's book *Conscious Motherhood*, which was dedicated to Elizabeth Peabody, G. Stanley Hall, and Mary Peabody Mann, was the quintessential expression of maternalist ideology. Marwedel's main theme was that for children to develop to their full potential, as was their individual right, women needed to be trained for motherhood and in kindergarten philosophy and techniques. The idea of conscious motherhood had not developed earlier, Marwedel argued, because of the "error of accepting this instinctive power of motherhood as *complete* and sufficient" and "the error of limiting women's power to their own families" and condemning women to "dependence and ignorance" of themselves and of their "duties."[46]

The United States, Marwedel proclaimed, needed *"to revise those laws"* that concerned *"the home!"* Why should women have *"to beg through a whole generation"* for their *"equal rights?"* They should be "set free" to use their judgment in child rearing and *"made responsible"* in their duties as mothers (73). The principal right Marwedel thought should be granted to mothers was child custody, which was generally awarded to fathers. Though for more than two thousand years, women had been entrusted by society with the development of children's spirituality and selfhood, they remained "unfree" because they were not *"legally* recognized as independent and responsible for *their* OWN children" (223).

Marwedel lamented that the world was not yet ready to ensure the child "that sacredest of birthrights, the right to be well born," by regulating marriage (40). Short of this, she stated that children's rights, and mother's responsibilities, should begin at conception, or before. Mothers had a duty to "preconceive" their children with love. Good child rearing and early childhood education should then commence in the womb. From "the instant that a mother knows herself pregnant," Marwedel insisted, "she should begin the education of her unborn infant" (41). The "breeding mother" should think "exalted" thoughts, get proper exercise, and, above all, practice self-control (42).

Since every child should also have the right to a protected and "inviolate childhood" (85) and the right to achieve his or her highest individual potential, mothers must be "tacitly pledged to assist every child to reach the highest that is possible to him, that is, the complete development of his individual organization" (88). Marwedel then described in detail the environment and experiences to which she felt children were entitled. The ideal nursery, for example, should be filled with objects from nature, simple toys, and appropriate children's literature. She favored an "unpretentious" Christmas with a tree but without Santa Claus, the appearance of whom she found "loud, noisy, and meaningless" (241). She also recommended that every home have a sand table placed where children could play undisturbed and that both little girls and little boys play with dolls so that they would learn to be nurturing. She ended with a plug for her own specially designed kindergarten program and materials.

Emma Marwedel's student Kate Douglas Wiggin expanded the idea of mothers' responsibilities to their children into a concept of society's responsibilities to children and children's rights. Born Kate Douglas Smith in Philadelphia in 1865, to a distinguished New England family, Wiggin moved to a small village in Maine when her father died. She enjoyed what she later recalled as an idyllic childhood, attended dame schools, a female seminary, and, briefly, Abbott Academy in Andover, Massachusetts. In 1873 the family moved to Santa Barbara, California. When her stepfather died, Wiggin turned to writing and teaching to earn money. She was introduced to the kindergarten by Caroline Severance, at whose Los Angeles home she boarded while attending Emma Marwedel's training class. Wiggin returned to Santa Barbara to teach kindergarten and then moved to San Francisco in 1878 when Emma Marwedel asked her to become the first teacher of the Silver Street kindergarten.[47]

Situated in the Tar Flat slum area, Silver Street fulfilled Wiggin's desire to "plant a child-garden in some dreary, poverty-stricken place in a large city, a place swarming with unmothered, undefended, under-nourished child-life." Silver Street enrolled children from Irish, American, German, English, Scottish, Scandinavian, French, and Portuguese backgrounds and included at least one African-American, one Japanese, and several Mexican-American children. Their parents were of three types, according to Wiggin: "petty tradespeople, such as old-clothes men, small saloon-keepers, rag-dealers, tailors"; workers such as a "peddler, tin-mender" or "day-laborer"; and "absolute criminals." The biggest problem Wiggin saw was alcoholism and its effects on family life.[48]

The parents and some of the children were initially suspicious of the kindergarten. On being given a drum to play in a kindergarten parade, one five-year-old boy "went into fits of laughter, and between the paroxysms ejaculated—'A drum? Well I should smile. What'll yer hev next? This *is* a h—l of a school!'" But Wiggin prided herself on her ability to work with children from diverse backgrounds and to reach out to their mothers, whom she spent hours visiting. Eventually, children and parents alike were won over by her high spirits and hard work and came to greet her warmly as the teacher of "The Kids' Guards," as they called the kindergarten.[49]

The reports of the Public Kindergarten Society of San Francisco, which supported Silver Street, documented the cost-effectiveness of kindergartning as an antidote to urban problems, and Wiggin's kindergarten became known for transforming the lives of urban families. Stories such as that of "Jack," whose errant father returned to the family after receiving a sample of his kindergarten work, became the stock-in-trade of charity kindergarten lore. Wiggin perfected the genre in *The Story of Patsy,* written in 1882 to raise money for Silver Street. In this sentimental classic, which set the tone for Wiggin's enormously successful career as the writer of works such as *The Bird's Christmas Carol* (1887) and *Rebecca of Sunnybrook Farm* (1904), "Kate," an exhausted kindergartner resting from a hard day's work at Silver Street, is awakened from a nap by "Patsy," a small nine-year-old boy who says he should actually be considered three years younger because of the time he lost recuperating from a broken back after his drunken father threw him down a flight of stairs. Though the charity kindergarten is overcrowded, Kate accepts the child and helps his stepfamily move into a larger apartment. Patsy gradually stops speaking in slang, but his health continues to deteriorate, and he dies in his teacher's arms. His last words are "I guess—Heaven—is kind o' like—our Kindergarten . . . only bigger, 'nd more children."[50]

Wiggin's articles on the kindergarten were collected in *Children's Rights* (1894), one of the clearest statements of emerging Progressive maternalist ideology on society's responsibilities to children. Subtitled *A Book of Nursery Logic*, *Children's Rights* began by denouncing the founding of the Society for the Prevention of Cruelty to Animals before the Society for the Prevention of Cruelty to Children and calling Rousseau's *Emile* "a gospel for children's rights." Wiggin then laid out five basic rights to which she thought children should be entitled and provided detailed descriptions of what these rights should consist of in everyday life and what mothers should do to meet them.[51]

First, like Marwedel, Wiggin thought children should have the right to be "well born," though she did not elaborate on how this could be ensured (10). Second, she thought children should have the right to a lengthy and protected childhood. In what would become one of the clarion calls of the early education movement, she criticized the "hurry" and "worry" in American homes that took away time from children (13). Childhood, she asserted sadly, was "an eternal promise which no man ever keeps." Third, every child should have the right to "a place of his own, to things of his own, to surroundings which have some relation to his size, his desire, and his capabilities." Parents should be required to provide their children with their own rooms, child-sized furniture, and an interesting, educational home environment filled with good books, music, artwork, and playthings (15). Fourth, children should have the right to fair discipline. They should be taught and governed by the same laws under which they would eventually live. This was something Wiggin thought parents were not "generally wise and patient enough" to do; instead, they confused causes and effects in children's lives so that children could not see the logic of things (18). Particularly worried about mothers afflicted with "the lust of dominion" who would "*en*velop instead of *de*velop" their children's minds and "weaken [their] power of choice" (84), she argued that children should be given more freedom as they got older (19–20). Last, children should have the right to expect examples of good behavior from their parents. Thus, Wiggin thought, in addition to providing good genes, time, space, things, and treatment, mothers should talk and act appropriately. And to fulfill all these rights for their children, of course mothers needed kindergarten training.

The rest of the book, which included some chapters written by Wiggin's sister, Nora Archibald Smith, dealt with the kindergarten and social reform and the public schools. Pleading for support for public kindergartens, Wiggin listed the commonly stated rationales of preparation for school and socialization of immigrant children. She observed, however, that the familiar argument that the kindergarten prevented crime "on calm reflection . . . appears an exaggerated statement" (110). More important, she emphasized, was the value of kindergartens as a unique educational experience to which young children should have a right. The state should assume responsibility, she concluded, when a child "*needs* education," not at an arbitrary age. And this right to education, Wiggin argued, should extend to all young children, rich and poor, to what she called "other people's children," not just to those who could afford it (182).[52]

Kate Douglas Wiggin's younger sister, Nora Archibald Smith, was even more radical in her views of society's responsibilities to children. Born in Philadelphia in 1859, she, too, spent her girlhood in rural Maine and then moved to California, where she graduated from Santa Barbara College in 1877. Following college, Smith, who spoke excellent Spanish, ran a private school in the town of Magdalena, in Sonora, Mexico, and then became the head of the girls' department of the public schools in Tucson, Arizona. In 1880 she moved to San Francisco where she became one of the first pupils at Wiggin's California Kindergarten Training School associated with the Silver Street kindergarten; from then on, she was an enthusiastic and active kindergartner like her sister, taking over the training school when Kate married Samuel Bradley Wiggin in 1881.[53]

Nora Archibald Smith's book for mothers, *The Children of the Future* (1898), resembled her sister's but focused more on mothers' classes and on how to deal with different types of "difficult" children, a topic in which mothers expressed much interest. Smith emphasized that mothers from all social-class backgrounds needed kindergarten training. There were "as many shallow, weak, careless, stupid, morally obtuse mothers among the rich as among the poor," she asserted, and the ignorance, carelessness, prejudice, and even the "not infrequent brutality" of poor women toward their children was more forgivable because these mothers "knew not what they did." Citing examples of women's clubs and study groups on other topics, Smith argued that young children should be just as "legitimate an object of respectful study as a starfish, or a microbe, or a plant." If women were reading pamphlets on "The Internal Relations and Taxonomy of the Archaean Terranes of Turkestan, with Notes on the Pre-Paleozoic Surface of the Island of

Nova Zembla," then they should also be training for the "priestly office" of motherhood by reading Froebel's works and learning about storytelling, children's literature, and scientific child study.[54]

Smith suggested holding informal meetings during which mothers could bring up problems and have group discussions. Though she thought classes for poor mothers should be identical to those for rich mothers, she recommended that they be simpler and cover more "restricted" topics (52). The kindergartner in charge, Smith wrote, should put on her best dress and try to bring "a little innocent gayety to these dull, imprisoned lives." There should be refreshments, and a daintily set table; in "bounteous California, where blossoms may be had for the asking," the room could even be turned into a bower of flowers that the mothers could take home (53). Making the classes nice was especially important for poor mothers because these women with "tired backs" and "sad hard mouths" never had the chance to read, see fine pictures, or hear sweet music (56). Some of the mothers might understand only one or two of the ideas, but this could happen with any audience, regardless of class background.

Smith discussed the kinds of problems mothers brought up during the classes and the difficulties they were having with their children. Chapters addressed how to deal with sullenness, temper tantrums, selfishness, lying, and other problem behaviors, usually ending with a recommendation that the child attend kindergarten. The rest of the book concentrated on kindergartens and social reform and revealed Smith's egalitarianism. On the topic of manual training, for instance, which conservatives saw as the main benefit of the kindergarten for poor children, Smith stressed the importance of handwork as an expression of and means to connect inner and outer states, rather than as insurance for future jobs. A believer in both upward and downward social mobility, Smith argued that the "poor of this year may be the rich of fifteen years to come, and the rich of to-day may be, by and by, among the poorest" (135). And not only were wealth and poverty mutable; so was temperament. One had to believe, Smith declared passionately, that "the leopard could change his spots, or the whole scheme of the universe was wrong, and we were the blackest detail in the plan" (156).

The Silver Street kindergarten and training school flourished until its destruction in the earthquake and fire of 1906. Other charity kindergartens also were begun in the San Francisco area, under the direction of Sarah B. Cooper of the Golden Gate Kindergarten Association. Impressed by what she had seen during a visit to Silver Street in 1879, Cooper began doing kindergarten work with her Bible class. Probably because her cousin Robert G. Ingersoll was a well-known atheist, Cooper's work came under scrutiny; she was tried for heresy but eventually exonerated by the San Francisco Presbyterian Church. She then went on to gain the patronage of Phoebe Apperson Hearst, who supported her until her tragic death at the hands of her suicidally depressed daughter, who asphyxiated Cooper and herself in 1896.[55]

From these beginnings in Los Angeles and San Francisco, the charity kindergarten movement spread to other parts of the West. Presbyterian missionary kindergartners like Mariette Ward, Isa E. Dwire, Anna C. Krohn, Bertha Little, and Alice Blackford working in "plaza" kindergartens in New Mexico around the turn of the century developed bilingual kindergarten methods and other means of bridging the gap between Anglo and Hispanic culture. Research on women teachers in Texas has uncovered the records of Leonor de Magnon in Laredo and Jovita Idar in San Antonio, politically radical Latina free kindergartners who openly opposed the treatment of Mexican-Americans by the United States government.[56]

Possibly because kindergartens for Native American children isolated them in the more controlled environments of government-run Indian schools, reports of "successful" cultural transformation were more common. German-American kindergarten pioneer William N. Hailmann, who was appointed director of government schools for the Bureau of Indian Affairs in 1894, started more than forty Indian school kindergartens. Thomas Charles, after visiting two of these kindergartens in Albuquerque and Santa Fe, New Mexico, in 1895, declared the kindergarten to be the solution to the "great 'Indian problem.'" Native American children who attended kindergarten, he observed, learned to speak English, became "less self-conscious," and had "better manners and habits" than older Native American children who had not. And Lucie Calista Maley, a teacher in an Indian school kindergarten in the mid-1890s, described how she taught Native American children to become more Western in their attitudes toward self, property, and nature by giving each child individual responsibility for taking care of the plants in his or her own garden and by teaching them not to kill ants, for instance, and to appreciate the beauty of animals.[57]

In the 1880s, 1890s, and 1900s, the free kindergarten movement was transformed from a Gilded Age charity for the children of the urban poor and their families, who were thought to be individually at fault for their own degraded social position, to a Progressive social program that provided comprehensive educational services to children, mothers, and families entitled to these services as civic rights. Science affected policy rationales for kindergartens, as seen in the impact of G. Stanley Hall's ideas on the thinking of Anna Bryan, Alice Putnam, and Patty Smith Hill. But the culture and context of American urban life was probably the most powerful catalyst for these concomitant transformations in policy and pedagogy. Urban kindergartners working in free kindergartens in Boston's North End, on Chicago's Southside, and in the Tar Flat slum of San Francisco were surrounded with tangible evidence of what looked to them like the inability of families to socialize and educate their children. There was obviously a great need for kindergartens for "other peoples' children." Though many local obstacles impeded the provision of universal kindergartens, this glaring need and the ideology of children's rights legitimated the idea of public assumption of responsibility for the education of everybody's young children.

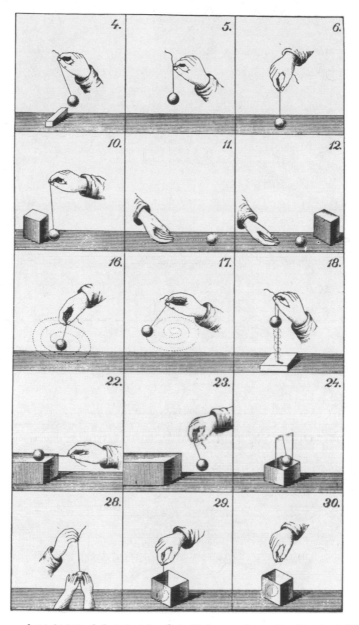

1. Plate 1 of *Friedrich Froebel's Pedagogics of the Kindergarten* (trans. Josephine Jarvis [New York: D. Appleton and Company, 1895], 338) shows directions for how to use Froebel's first gift, the ball.

Der kleine Gärtner.

Komm, wir wollen in den Garten,
All' die Pflänzchen dort zu warten:
Wollen sie gar schön begießen.
Das die Knöspchen sich entschließen.
    Die Knöspchen sich entfalten nun;
    Sie grüßen Dich mit süßem Duft,
    Womit sie durchwürzen die ganze
        Luft.
    Belohnend ist es, wohlzuthun!

2. "Der kleine Gärtner" (The little gardener), from *The Mottoes and Commentaries of Froebel's Mother Play* (trans. Henrietta R. Eliot and Susan E. Blow [New York: D. Appleton and Company, 1895], 228) includes a drawing of hands *(top)* showing how to do the fingerplay that accompanied the song.

3. In this etching captioned "Infant School—Kinder Garten Exercise," small groups of children, teachers, and assistants are doing different Froebelian handwork occupations, while other children sit in bleachers being read or lectured to, as was often the practice in infant schools early in the twentieth century. (The Bettmann Archive)

4. This sketch by E. R. Morse of a public kindergarten in Boston shows children modeling objects in clay. (The Bettmann Archive)

5. On the blackboard on the back wall in this 1876 photograph of a kindergarten are the exact Froebelian patterns the children are copying with rods. (The Bettmann Archive)

6. The packed gallery of adult observers and people waiting in lines outside the window in this illustration by Frank Leslie show the keen interest in the model kindergarten class conducted at the Centennial Exposition in Philadelphia. (*Frank Leslie's Illustrated Historical Register of the Centennial Exposition 1876* [New York: Frank Leslie's Publishing House, 1877])

7. The children's building at Hull House. Pond & Pond, Architects, Chicago. (*Kindergarten Magazine* 8 [February 1896])

8. At the Pratt Institute Model Kindergarten in New York City, each child had an individual plot in the garden, at the center of which was a communal plot, as prescribed by Froebel. (*Kindergarten Review* 17 [April 1907], 467)

9. Members of a mothers' club in Brooklyn, New York, making baskets as instructed by a kindergarten teacher standing at right. (*Kindergarten Review* 17 [April 1907], 475)

10. The George William Curtis Kindergarten, maintained by bankers and brokers, under auspices of New York Kindergarten Association, was one of many charity kindergartens sponsored by different organizations across the country. (*Kindergarten Magazine and Pedagogical Digest* 19 [May 1907])

11. The interior of school no. 1 of the Stanford Memorial Kindergarten in San Francisco shows a picture of Leland Stanford, Jr., the deceased son of Jane and Leland Stanford for whom this kindergarten and Stanford University were named. The children did Froebelian parquetry designs on special tables inscribed with inch-square grids. (The Bettmann Archive)

12. Children in the Hampton Institute Kindergarten play rhythm bands instruments. Hampton, Virginia, c. 1900. (Camera Club collection, Archives, Hampton University, reproduced by permission)

13. Children in the Hampton Institute Kindergarten sweep the floor and dust the classroom as part of a curriculum that focused on manual training and preparation for domestic service. Hampton, Virginia. (*The Southern Workman* (October 1907), Archives, Hampton University, reproduced by permission)

14. Children play with hardwood unit blocks designed by Patty Smith Hill and Harriet Johnson. The caption reads: "You can walk up my bridge on one side and down on the other." "Isn't mine pretty? Don't touch it. It might fall." (Julia Wade Abbot, *The Child and the Kindergarten*, U.S. Department of the Interior, Bureau of Education Kindergarten Circular No. 6 [Washington, D.C.: GPO, 1920], nn.)

15. The changing seasons were a perennial theme of kindergarten curricula, as seen in this photograph from Julia Wade Abbott, *The Child and the Kindergarten*. Abbott's caption reads: "Do you see all the things the farmer gets from his garden in the fall? and we found the leaves and the berries ourselves. We're singing a sing about it—'Sing a song of seasons, Something bright in all.'"

16. Many features of the modern kindergarten, such as indoor plants, nature study, and group peformance with percussion instruments were in place by the 1920s. (Julia Wade Abbott, *The Child and the Kindergarten*, 25)

17. The four-year-olds in this public kindergarten in New York City are wearing overalls for their dancing lesson, part of their everyday curriculum at P.S. 41. (The Bettmann Archive)

18. At Margaret McMillan's original nursery school in the Deptford section of London, the children spent time outdoors and the building was open to the air on one side. (Emma Stevinson, *The Open-Air Nursery School* [London and Toronto: J. M. Dent; New York: Dutton, 1923], follows 24)

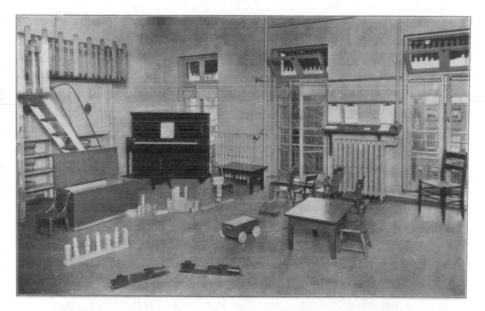

19. The specially designed indoor play equipment at Harriet Johnson's Bureau of Educational Experiments nursery school in New York City in the 1920s included climbing apparatus and a loft. The caption reads: "The play-room-adult furnishings are eliminated as far as possible." (Harriet M. Johnson, *A Nursery School Experiment* [New York: Bureau of Educational Experiments, 1922], 6)

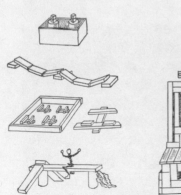

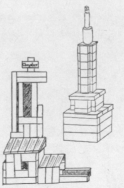

20. Children in nursery schools in the 1930s made block buildings based on real-life structures they had seen, such as the Chrysler Building in New York City, rather than Froebel's abstract models of towers and churches. Illustration from Harriet Johnson, *The Art of Block Building* (New York: John Day, 1933), 42–43.

21. Young children were sent home from nursery school if they failed the morning health inspection administered by nurses or teachers. (*Children's Centers*, ed. Rose H. Alschuler for the National Commission for Young Children [New York: William Morrow, 1942], 87)

22. During World War II volunteers provided preschool education and care for the children of working mothers. The caption for this WPA photograph of the Emerson Nursery School in Burbank, California, reads: "You could volunteer to help with war-worker's children in a nursery school." (Dorothy W. Baruch, *You, Your Children, and War* [New York: D. Appleton–Century, 1942], photograph by Jack Prescott), follows 174)

23. Dorothy W. Baruch's book, *You, Your Children, and War*, documented the effects of war on young children and suggested ways nursery school and kindergarten teachers could modify their classroom practices during wartime. The caption for this photograph of two boys in Mrs. Bell's Kindergarten in Los Angeles reads: "We're airplane men. We're shooting you dead." (Photograph by A. Pierce Artran, follows 32)

24. In the 1940s, fathers as well as mothers were encouraged to become more involved in their young children's emotional and social development. The caption reads: "Children need a lot of affection to live with stamina in a world at war." (Dorothy W. Baruch, *You, Your Children, and War*, frontispiece, photograph by A. Pierce Artran)

Chapter 6 "The Land of Childhood"

The Establishment of Public

Kindergartens in America

In the late 1880s the movement to establish public kindergartens that had begun in German-American St. Louis in the 1870s spread to Boston, Chicago, San Francisco, New York, and other cities and towns in the northeastern, midwestern, western, and mid-Atlantic states. Only the South and Southwest were slow to join the campaign, and rural areas everywhere lagged behind the rest of the country. A United States Bureau of Education survey documented an increase from forty-two public and private kindergartens in 1873 to almost three thousand in 1898, with enrollments of some 200,000 children. By 1910 the United States Census counted 396,431 children under the age of six attending school. But even with this near doubling within a decade, only 3.1 percent of American children under six were receiving education.[1]

As charity and other private kindergarten associations were subsumed into urban school systems, frequently intact, a battle for control began between female kindergarten directors and male principals and administrators. Under whose jurisdiction did the kindergarten lie? Who would make decisions about budgets, hours, and class sizes? Even though kindergartners fought to maintain some of the hallmarks of their distinctive approach to child gardening, the answers to these questions worked out in individual and local skirmishes gradually caused kindergartens to become more like the school systems into which they had been incorporated.

Internecine war heated up as kindergartners struggled to define what kind of pedagogy would prevail in public kindergarten education. Would orthodox Froebelianism remain the guide, or would child study and other new psychological ideas be the knowledge base for public kindergarten practice? What should be the relationship between the kindergarten and elementary education? Kindergartners debated these issues at the many conferences held during the 1890s and first decades of the twentieth century, especially at meetings of the International Kindergarten Union.

A Tale of Three Cities

In May 1887 Pauline Agassiz Shaw asked the Boston School Committee to consider adopting her free kindergartens into the public school system. Shaw's request was referred to the Committee on Examinations headed by Dr. Samuel Eliot. Eliot then asked Superintendent Edwin P. Seaver to circulate a questionnaire to the city's primary school teachers. Their responses favoring the kindergarten by a margin of seven to one, Eliot's committee reported back positively, and despite being in somewhat tight financial straits, in 1888 the Boston School Committee readily appropriated twenty thousand dollars for public kindergartens.[2]

According to Superintendent Seaver, the key to establishing public kindergartens was to prove their cost-effectiveness. "There is just one way in which the financial difficulties can be removed, and that is by means of an object lesson long enough continued to convince the people that every dollar that goes into the payment for kindergarten instruction is a dollar better expended than any other dollar in the whole school expense," Seaver told the National Education Association in 1890. If kindergartens made sense financially, as Shaw had proved to Seaver and Boston's notoriously fiscally conservative Yankee merchants, then they would be adopted. Because of the success of Shaw's privately financed experiment, the twenty thousand dollars needed to finance public kindergartens in Boston "came as easily as a five-dollar bill would come out of Judge Draper's pocket if I were short of money and wanted to get home," Seaver boasted to the NEA. And, "There has been no trouble in getting the money since—no difficulty at all."[3]

William Torrey Harris agreed with Seaver that money was the main issue but felt Boston was a somewhat special case. The "noblest and wealthiest people there have pleaded for the kindergarten," Harris stated at the same NEA meeting, and since Boston was "the second city in the United States in point of wealth . . . the question of expense is a very small matter to the Boston taxpayer." In poorer cities, Harris argued, the relative expense of kindergartens compared to other grade levels was a very important matter indeed. If "the expense per year for the education of the child in the kindergarten is as much as it is in the high school," Harris asserted, "it is a very valid objection to the development of the kindergarten." According to Harris, the way to "get it [the kindergarten] in a cheap way" was to have relatively large classes and employ aides and assistants. Harris said a system with only one trained kindergartner per class had cut kindergarten costs in St. Louis to $5.40 per pupil annually, much lower than in Boston and inexpensive enough for any school system.[4]

Cutting corners on kindergarten expenses, particularly on teachers' salaries, created other problems, however, as evidenced by the history of public kindergartens in Chicago. In 1892, the year of the World's Columbian Exposition in Chicago, the board of education adopted a few free kindergartens that had been sponsored by Alice Putnam's Chicago Froebel Association and Elizabeth Harrison's Chicago Kindergarten College. As in Boston, Putnam's free kindergartens had been successful, and money was no longer perceived as a major issue. In 1895 a local option law was passed allowing cities and towns to start public kindergartens, and the number of kindergartens in Illinois increased rapidly. Much of this growth, however, was subsidized by kindergarten teachers themselves, who were paid considerably less than other public primary school teachers. The maximum salary for a kindergarten teacher in the Chicago Public Schools in 1896–97, reported by Nina Vandewalker, was five hundred dollars, the same as the minimum salary for a primary school teacher, and kindergarten assistants were paid half that amount. To make matters worse, Chicago kindergarten teachers did not receive annual pay increases as primary teachers did; they were paid fifty dollars a month whether they were in their first or their fifth year of teaching.[5]

In January 1898 kindergarten teachers in the Chicago public schools formed a club to "uphold the 'honor and dignity' of kindergartners as progressive women, . . . demanding that we be given privileges that are ours by right of right." The Chicago Public School Kindergarten Association presented a petition to the school board signed by "128 kindergartners, and endorsed by more than 1,100 principals, grade teachers, and citizens" requesting that kindergartners receive annual salary increases based on experience. The kindergarten organization was also admitted to the Federation of Chicago Teachers, the radical labor group led by Margaret Haley. Chicago public school kindergartners felt this was "a great step . . . taken in the direction of making the kindergarten a necessary part of the public school system, instead of an accidental adjunct." Other urban teachers were beginning to affiliate with working-class labor unions rather than middle-class professional associations. In Chicago and elsewhere, the stereotype of the dedicated schoolteacher who worked for love of little children, not money, was beginning to crack, in part because the urban teaching force increasingly comprised women and men from lower-class and immigrant backgrounds who needed higher salaries to support themselves and their families. But salary alone was not the issue. Women teachers, even kindergartners subscribing to the vocational ethic that Elizabeth Peabody and others had so passionately preached, were beginning to connect self-esteem with money, as men had for centuries.[6]

The best recorded historic case of tensions between economic issues and dedication to the cause of young children arose in the establishment of public kindergartens in New York City. The impetus for the adoption of kindergartens into the New York public schools came from a private charity organization, the New York Free Kindergarten Association, founded in 1889 by a group of citizens concerned about the large numbers of younger children being turned away from the public schools because of lack of space. An article on these children appeared in the *Commercial Advertiser* in the fall of 1888. Wealthy businessman Daniel S. Remsen and his wife read the article, discussed the problem, and decided to do something about it. They contacted Progressive social reformer and board of education member Grace Hoadley Dodge, who put them in touch with kindergartner Angeline Brooks. The Remsens and a group of their friends then met with the crusading editor of *The Century*, Richard Watson Gilder, who began publicizing the kindergarten cause and served as the president of the New York Free Kindergarten Association for three years. Hamilton Wright Mabie, the reformist editor of *The Christian Union*, took over after Gilder, and together this group of journalists, educators, philanthropists, and social reformers, which also included Nicholas Murray Butler, president of newly founded Teachers College at Columbia University, started a network of free kindergartens and in 1892 convinced the city to appropriate five thousand dollars for public kindergartens.[7]

Once kindergartens got into the New York public schools, efficiency and existing bureaucratic structures determined their governance more than the reformist ideology that governed charity kindergartens. The New York Kindergarten Association's free kindergartens had served mostly Italian and Jewish children from the crowded, impoverished neighborhoods of the Lower East Side. Yet public kindergartens were opened in the schools that had the space, which often were not in the most populous or needy areas, because establishing kindergartens where they were most needed would have cost more money and cut into the budget for existing programs for older children. The needs of younger children, it seems, were at the bottom of the list. This financial decision also documents the difference between the needs-based ideology of charity kindergartens and the universal entitlement rationale of public kindergartens, which decreed that all children, rich or poor, deserved the best education public finances could provide.[8]

Kindergartens, Americanization, and the National Kindergarten Association

The problem of how to Americanize the large numbers of immigrants who flocked to this country in the years just before and after the turn of the century was one of the paramount social issues of the day. As New York kindergarten advocate James Bruce emphasized, kindergartens were a particularly effective method of Americanization because they reached children when they were very young and their natures were "still plastic." Young children could be "so swayed and molded as to grow up Americans, to absorb by natural processes, by normal unconscious assimilation, the tone and tendencies of our social and political structure." "They can breathe in the American spirit," Bruce argued persuasively, through the kindergarten's "songs and flag drills, by its elementary patriotic exercises."[9]

The adoption of kindergartens by public schools nationally was greatly propelled by concerns about Americanization. During World War I, in particular, the important socializing function of schools was emphasized for kindergartners, who were in direct contact with foreign-born families. A 1918 U.S. Bureau of Education pamphlet told kindergartners to "visit the immigrant mother oftener than American mothers," to teach English and civics in mothers' meetings because of the "danger" of the "new electoral power" these women's husbands wielded, and to help immigrant women find substitutes for their native foods. (A pamphlet that came out a year later, however, questioned whether it was in the American spirit to "rob the immigrants of . . . language, customs, racial traditions, religious beliefs" and suggested using mothers' meetings for "reviving . . . foreign customs of dress, food, music," so that they could be an "exchange of ideas . . . as well as the opening wedge for the tactful introduction of approved American customs.")[10]

Promoting the kindergarten as an agent of Americanization was apparent in the rationales behind the formation of the National Kindergarten Association, a political action group started by members of the New York Free Kindergarten Association and others in 1909. Based in New York City with a membership that included Richard Watson Gilder, Kate Douglas Wiggin, and Maria Kraus-Boelte, the NKA coordinated kindergarten campaigns nationwide and established links with other groups such as the National Education Association, the International Kindergarten Union, the General Federation of Women's Clubs, the National Congress of Mothers, and the National Council of Women. The NKA's first annual report began with a statement by Kate Douglas Wiggin that public kindergartens were needed as "the vestibule to our school work," as "a philanthropic agent, leading the child gently into right habits of thought, speech, and action from the beginning," to "help in the absorption and amalgamation of our foreign element," and for "social training" and the "development of the citizen-virtues, as well as those of the individual."[11]

The NKA's promotional efforts emphasized the fact that the United States was falling behind other countries in its provision of kindergarten education, citing statistics for Western European countries that had universalized the kindergarten or supported many more preschool programs per capita than the United States. In Italy, for instance, in 1907–08 3,576 kindergartens enrolled 343,563 children, and in Belgium in 1905 *"more than one-half"* of the 446,134 children between the ages of three and six attended kindergarten compared to the statistic of *"688 cities in the United States of more than 4,000 inhabitants, having no public kindergartens"* in 1907–08. Even Russia and Japan had kindergartens, the report noted (23–24).

Among the NKA's other activities was the distribution of a promotional film called *At the Threshold of Life* that, interestingly, focused more on the power of the kindergarten to change the life of an upper-class, native-born adult male than on its effect on a hapless immigrant child. The sentimentalized plot involved a crippled child, a kindergarten teacher who chooses her work over her lover, and a wealthy young man who converts to the kindergarten cause and in the process comes to understand and support his idealistic girlfriend's desire to work as a teacher. In the final scene, Roger, the boyfriend, writes the NKA a check for five thousand dollars and tells his girlfriend, Miss Gray, that he "will never again oppose her teaching." Whether persuasive or not, the message was loud and clear: if men wanted to marry intelligent, cultured, well-educated young women, they had better support the linked crusades for children's and women's rights of which the kindergarten was a prime example.[12]

The NKA also funded legal efforts to change state statutes or school board regulations to permit the expenditure of public funds to educate children under six. The annual report included a model kindergarten statute to be put before state legislatures that would permit towns and school districts to "establish and maintain" kindergartens for children from four to six years of age. The statute also addressed the problem of standards and quality control—a great concern of the NKA—by mandating that only kindergarten staff who had completed "a special course of two years' training in kindergarten work in a recognized training school" be employed (28).

In part because of the NKA, public kindergartens were established in many American cities in the years just before and after the turn of the century. In Washington, D.C., Louisa Mann, daughter-in-law of Horace and Mary Peabody Mann and founder of the Columbian Kindergarten Association, and Anna Murray of the National Association of Colored Women convinced Congress to appropriate eight thousand dollars for white kindergartens and four thousand for black kindergartens in the public schools in 1898. Free kindergartners in Philadelphia and elsewhere mounted similarly successful campaigns to incorporate child gardening into the public schools. In San Francisco the Golden Gate Kindergarten Society, the successor to the Public Kindergarten Society, finally managed to convince the school board to adopt public kindergartens in 1913. Though costs and restrictive state laws continued to pose stumbling blocks, by the beginning of World War I kindergartens had been adopted by most large public school systems and in smaller cities and suburbs nationwide.[13]

Kindergartens for African-American Children

The South and some states in the West were very slow to establish public kindergartens, especially for black children. According to National Kindergarten Association statistics, in 1916–17 only 2 percent of children between the ages of four and six were enrolled in kindergarten in Alabama, Arkansas, Georgia, and Mississippi, and only 1 percent were enrolled in North Carolina, Tennessee, and West Virginia; in Texas, Idaho, and Nevada only 1 or 2 percent of children were enrolled. Meanwhile, 26 percent of four- to six-year-olds were enrolled in Michigan, Wisconsin, and the District of Columbia, 28 percent in New Jersey, and 29 percent in New York state were in kindergarten.[14]

African-American children, according to a study done by Josephine Silone Yates, president of the National Association of Colored Women and author of a widely read column on education in the *Colored American Magazine,* were most likely to attend kindergarten in public systems that did not operate separate institutions for whites and blacks. But African-American children were sometimes denied admission to kindergarten even when they were permitted to attend upper grades. Southern school systems, particularly those in rural areas, were the least likely to provide kindergartens for African-American children. In fact, when Yates conducted a survey in 1901, she was unable to locate any public kindergartens for African-American children in the South. Howard University, Atlanta University, and African-American clubs, churches, and institutes, such as Hampton and Tuskegee, sponsored free kindergartens, however, and in the North, white charity groups and churches provided kindergartens for African-American children. Lucy Wheelock, for instance, was instrumental in organizing a free kindergarten in 1895 in Hope Chapel of Old South Church in what was then an African-American section of Boston, and similar programs were started in other major cities.[15]

Some whites argued that African-American children needed the kindergarten more than did white children, because of the manual training it provided, and some African-Americans concurred. An account of a weeklong visit to a kindergarten at the Hampton Institute in 1907 illustrates that vocational education seems to have won out over Froebelianism in most kindergartens for African-American children. The curriculum at the Hampton Institute kindergarten was based on the kitchen garden, an adaptation to domestic training developed in New York by Emily Huntingdon. Children began on Monday morning by dusting the room of "invisible dirt"; some then washed clothes with hot water and real soap, while others played with Froebelian gifts. In the afternoon, the children worked in the garden. On Tuesday morning the girls ironed, did some paper cutting and folding, and took care of their baby dolls while the boys did janitorial work; on Wednesday the children made furniture for a new doll they had been given. On Thursday the class visited an orchard to watch a farmer planting and then made farm tools out of clay. On Friday they did house cleaning and more janitorial work. Clearly, programs such as this were intended to train African-American children for domestic service and agricultural work as much as or more than they sought to educate in generic Froebelian fashion.[16]

Some African-Americans, however, like Anna J. Murray who organized kindergartens for African-American children in Washington, D.C., argued that African-American children, too, would benefit from the play experiences and "communion with nature" of the Froebelian kindergarten. Josephine Silone Yates actively promoted Froebelianism among African-American parents and advocated the universality of the kindergarten rather than its supposed specific advantages for African-American children. In a 1906 article in the *Colored American Magazine,* she stressed the importance of providing opportunities for play and an educational environment adjusted to harmonize with children's organic development. In another article, she described in detail the work of the Kindergarten Department of the National Association of Colored Women, headed by Haydee Campbell, and emphasized the importance of training more African-American kindergartners. Campbell, an Oberlin graduate, was chosen over white competitors to supervise kindergartens for African-American children in the St. Louis public schools, where she probably received training from Susan Blow and in turn trained a number of African-American kindergarten teachers. Louisville was another southern center for kindergarten training for African-Americans. In 1899 the Louisville Free Kindergarten Association opened a normal school class for African-American kindergartners; by 1905 seventeen African-American kindergarten teachers had trained there.[17]

The Training of Public Kindergartners

As Josephine Silone Yates, Haydee Campbell, and other kindergarten advocates realized, high-quality kindergarten training was the key to the success of the public kindergarten movement. The first generation of American kindergartners was educated in private training programs and in the very few public normal schools that offered courses in Froebelian philosophy and methods. After the turn of the century, public normal schools began replacing private training programs as a major source of education for kindergarten teachers. Private women's liberal arts colleges and private universities also became involved in kindergarten training.

Most private programs admitted young women who were high school graduates, but tuition and other admission requirements varied. At Lucy Wheelock's kindergarten training class in Boston, for instance, admission requirements were "an ability to sing, good health, a love of children, and a high-school education or its equivalent, and broad general culture." Applicants were to "furnish testimonials as to scholarship and moral character from the principal of the school last attended, or from some clergyman of their town and must be at least eighteen years of age." The tuition in 1894 was one hundred dollars for the first year and seventy-five dollars for the second, not including room and board or books and materials. The number of years required to receive a certificate or diploma also varied considerably, ranging from six weeks to two years, and this was source of much disagreement among kindergarten trainers. Though two years increasingly became the norm, kindergarten training was often somewhat shorter than the normal school course required for most elementary teachers.[18]

Unlike female seminaries, which emphasized the classics and religious education, or normal schools, which prepared teachers in school subjects, kindergartners studied Froebel intensively and did Froebelian activities as if they themselves were children. Special rituals, such as the celebration of Froebel's birthday, and other events reinforced students' senses of purpose and dedication to the Froebelian cause. Students at Lucy Wheelock's training school in the 1890s, for instance, took courses entitled "Survey of History of Pedagogy," "Applications of Pedagogic Principles," and "Psychology in Teaching" and studied science, music, and storytelling, along with courses on Froebelian philosophy, gifts and occupations, and games. In addition to works on Froebel and kindergarten guides, Wheelock's students read books such as J. P. Richter's *Levana* and Ruskin's *The Ethics of Dust* and *The Stones of Venice*. They also observed and student-taught in real kindergartens.[19]

Most early kindergarten training programs were one-woman operations whose success depended on the personality and energy of their directors, many of whom developed loyal followings among their students and supporters. From the few accounts available, many future kindergarten teachers seem to have enjoyed their training. But the enormous amount of handwork required—the laborious filling of notebook after notebook with intricate paper weavings, minute pinprickings, and so on—must have been tedious. Nor could the strictness with which some German-trained Froebelians treated their students have been appealing to many young women. In fact, some kindergarten trainees did protest the drudgery of their course work. Margaret Tillotson Edsall, who took kindergarten courses in Boston in 1887 and 1888, described "fearful" lectures on the Light Bird Song, examinations that were not hard but "took forever," and a "horrid" practice teaching lesson during which the children with whom she was working "acted like fury" while she was being observed by Boston kindergarten director Laura Fisher.[20]

As the number of public kindergartens grew, demand for trained kindergarten teachers increased. In 1912 353,456 children—approximately 9 percent of the children of kindergarten age—were enrolled in public kindergartens in the United States, a 133 percent increase from 1902. In 1922 the number was 500,807, and by 1930 there were 777,899 children enrolled in public kindergartens. The number of public normal schools offering kindergarten training increased apace, from 40 out of 175 in 1903 to 71 out of 146 in 1913. Though public programs continued to gain in numbers, however, private training programs still graduated more than half the kindergartners (1,100 of 2,000 kindergartners graduated in 1912, for example) because of their larger sizes.[21]

The shift to public kindergarten training signaled a concomitant change in pedagogy. Graduates of public kindergarten training programs learned more about instruction in "music, art, literature, and nature study—the lines of work which the kindergarten shares with the grades," Nina Vandewalker observed. They were better able to understand the relationship of the kindergarten to the elementary school and could "doubtless articulate their work with that of the school more easily than those who have taken courses of a different character," an ability of "unquestioned value." But, as Vandewalker and others realized, there was also a downside to this shift. With their focus on the schools, public kindergarten training programs tended to leave out the equally, or even more important, relationship between the kindergarten and the home and community. Vandewalker suggested that public training programs include training that was more "sociological in character" and applauded the links that some programs were forming with child welfare agencies in their communities. She also praised private kindergarten training programs for setting high standards of "conspicuous" community service "that few public training programs can reach" and for their ability to experiment freely with programs and pedagogy in ways that public programs could not.[22]

Not surprisingly, public school administrators supported public training programs, and some principals thought private kindergarten training lacked academic rigor and was overly narrow. These concerns led the National Kindergarten Association, the International Kindergarten Union, and the kindergarten office of the U.S. Bureau of Education to collaborate on a suggested curriculum and entrance requirements for the two-year kindergarten course. The curriculum, published in 1916, consisted of two thirty-six-week years of course work (4), including student teaching and observation; general education in educational psychology, child study, and history and philosophy of education; kindergarten education; and "related professional subjects" such as art, music, nature study, child and school hygiene, physical education, primary education, and English and children's literature (51–55).

The curriculum comprised several "ideals in kindergarten training," a set of values and attitudes toward life, learning, and children that defined the professional ethics of kindergartning. Underlying these ideals, which encompassed considerable knowledge of child study, were the principle that a kindergarten teacher was to be "an educator, not merely an instructor"; a conceptualization of kindergartning as a "life of service to the mothers of their children, to the school of which the children form a part, and to the community in its various forms of cooperative effort"; and a commitment to developing through kindergartning "a fuller realization of the meaning of life in its varied relationships" (55–62).

This commitment to kindergartning as a way of life for both children and their teachers was apparent in the eleven special programs developed by graduates of the California Kindergarten Training School. The elaborate programs, each complete with suggested games, songs, gift work, and occupations, related to a different central theme such as "The Garden," "The Sea," "Harvest Time," "The Family," "Our Friends in Feathers," and "The Wind" and emphasized what today would be called core values of respect for life and harmony with the universe.[23]

Not all was high seriousness, however; some kindergartners could make fun of both themselves and the men who often made fun of them. In a speech at the first alumnae gathering of California Kindergarten Training School graduates in 1883, Kate Douglas Wiggin claimed to have held back tears of joy at being with thirty of her former students because "the scene would inevitably appear in the morning papers, with characteristic head lines of black: 'Weeping Kindergartners'—'Sorrowful Sisterhood'—'Sobbing Simpletons.' *Item:* 'The educational dinner at the Occidental was doubtless a feminine success; the entire company dissolved in tears at the first toast, and declared they had a perfectly lovely time.' *Item:* 'The Kindergartners of San Francisco and vicinity met in high conclave last night. It *was a wet season!!'"* Spoofing the male view of herself and her Froebelian colleagues, Wiggin went on to joke about how a kindergartner would describe a present from a male acquaintance as "Harry's '*Fifth Gift'*—a breastpin consisting of a rhomboidal prism of onyx, studded with elliptical pearls." And parodying a kindergartner's reply to a boyfriend's declaration of love, Wiggin mimicked, "Oh, Timothy, I do indeed love you, but we have quarreled often in the past, and are you sure that marriage would be a 'reconciliation of our contrasts,' for I have sworn to follow Froebel, and that is his law."[24]

Within the confines of the supportive circle of female colleagues at the 1883 reunion, Kate Douglas Wiggin's sister Nora Archibald Smith felt free to express her views of men's intrinsic worthlessness except as potential kindergarten donors. Sounding like a modern ecofeminist and antismoking advocate, Smith accused the opposite sex of being endowed with "a dictatorial manner and imperious temper, an uncontrolled self-will, a desire to witness bloodthirsty sports, an ignorance of spring bonnets, and a fondness for a narcotic and poisonous substance known as tobacco." Among men's various "uses," about which she was "not enthusiastic," she mentioned as "the highest" men's "ability to give large, generous and perpetual contributions toward the support of our beloved Free Kindergartens." Otherwise, Smith warned kindergartners to stay away from men, as she apparently intended to do, because their relation to women as husbands was "an uncertain one, and better avoided," though she knew some in the audience might disagree.[25]

The remarks of Sarah B. Cooper, an honored guest at the California Kindergarten Training School banquet, continued the womanist theme. Cooper began by stating that the "woman question" was "one-half of the human question," though she acknowledged that she "was going to say it was two-thirds." Women had been counted "out as the *half of mankind,*" making the world like "a laborer at work with one arm paralyzed or bound up— very tenderly, very lovingly, but still very *firmly* in a sling." Cooper went on to condemn the concept of separate spheres because it confined women and therefore constrained human culture as a whole. Limiting a woman to a separate sphere "simply because of sex" was "to rob her of her birthright." "That is *no* sphere," Cooper continued. "It is not even a hemisphere. It is a cranny, a corner or an angle. The barbarian of the past attempted to carry on the world after this fashion, and failed," she concluded.[26]

Speeches such as these show how the sentimentalized rituals of Froebelianism could serve as both a vehicle and a mask for much more radically feminist political views. Though prospective kindergartners were preparing to work in a quintessentially female occupation deep within the protective maternalistic confines of "woman's sphere," some were also listening to self-supporting women like Sarah B. Cooper decry the narrowness and even the very existence of such separation. And while graduates may have sung the "Kindergartners' Hymn," in which they asked God to give them "a cheerful spirit, that our little flocks may see it is good and pleasant service, pleasant to be taught of Thee," many were also imbibing Nora Archibald Smith's distinctly uncheerful views of men and being encouraged to consider rejecting marriage. In fact, one of the attractions of kindergartning for some women may have been its extreme isolation from the world of men, coupled with the opportunity it provided to rear young children without having to bear them first. For other women, of course, kindergarten training was attractive as preparation for motherhood.[27]

Private women's liberal arts colleges and colleges of education at private universities began adding kindergarten training courses in the late 1880s and 1890s. Kindergarten trainers also began collaborating with men in college and university departments of education, men who in some ways altered the agenda of kindergarten research and changed the topics of kindergarten discourse. But if the entrance of the kindergarten into the more elite world of academia marked the final acceptance of kindergartning as an occupation for women and of research on the education of young children as a valid subject of intellectual pursuit, it did not guarantee it academic status. Anything smacking of professional education was suspect unless individual faculty could win the support of their colleagues in the traditional liberal arts disciplines. At some elite colleges, the tendency was to offer a special series of lectures on kindergartning instead of a course for academic credit. At Radcliffe, for example, Laura Fisher, director of kindergartens in the Boston Public Schools, gave eight well-attended kindergarten lectures in 1898.[28]

At Wellesley College, teacher education enjoyed a typically contradictory position. Supposedly central to the college's stated mission of educating women for lives of service rather than being served (*"Non ministrari sed ministrare"*), it was relegated to an academic backwater as an extracurricular subject initially offered by a professor in the German Department. Indeed, Carla Wenckebach, whose German background gave her familiarity with Froebel and other European pedagogues whose writings were included on her syllabus, began teaching "Pedagogics and Didactics" as an unpaid overload. Shortly thereafter, an arrangement was made for Wellesley students to supplement their academic study of education with practice teaching in the Brookline Public Schools. When Wenckebach retired in 1902, Anna McKeag, a former secondary school teacher and seminarian from Pennsylvania with a Ph.D. from the University of Pennsylvania, was hired to replace her. McKeag, who had studied under G. Stanley Hall, added courses in child study and experimental pedagogy requiring "written reports of statistical and experimental inquiries," quizzed students on their knowledge, among other things, of "the nascent periods in the life of the child" and of "investigations of fatigue in school children," and asked them to "describe the school building and schoolroom that could be regarded as ideal from the standpoint of hygiene."[29]

Interestingly, the first training specifically in kindergarten methods was initiated by a man, Arthur Norton, who became chair of the renamed Education Department in 1912. Having studied under Harvard Graduate School of Education dean Paul Hanus, who was interested in kindergarten education, Norton encouraged the development of a model kindergarten on campus. With the strong backing of Wellesley professors Katharine Lee Bates and Katherine Coman, who were also staunch kindergarten and settlement house supporters, the Anne L. Page School was opened in 1913 to provide kindergarten instruction for children in the town of Wellesley and kindergarten training for Wellesley College students. The school was headed by Anna White Devereaux, who also taught kindergarten courses in the Education Department. The number of students who received kindergarten training at Wellesley remained quite low, however, until the 1930s, with the advent of the nursery school movement.[30]

It was in the new schools of education in public and private universities that kindergarten training really took hold in academia. The center of curricular reform in preschool education had shifted from Chicago to Teachers College at Columbia University in the first part of the twentieth century. The college had grown out of the Kitchen Garden Association, the domestic and manual training organization started by Emily Huntingdon in 1880. In 1887 the renamed Industrial Education Association, of which Nicholas Murray Butler was president and Grace Dodge a key member, became the College for the Training of Teachers, with a kindergarten department headed by Angeline Brooks. At the same time, President Barnard of Columbia University began suggesting that education be offered as a topic of university study. In 1892 Teachers College and Barnard College became formally affiliated with Columbia University.[31]

The final showdown between orthodox Froebelianism and progressive kindergarten pedagogy took place in the Kindergarten Department at Teachers College. Susan Blow had been lecturing on the kindergarten at Teachers College since 1896. In 1904 Patty Smith Hill, whose innovative practices in Louisville had attracted national attention, was invited to be a lecturer by Dean James Russell, who was set on making Teachers College the center for debate on kindergarten curriculum and pedagogy. Blow and Hill gave a series of public lectures on the kindergarten and for a while taught rival courses and divided responsibility for kindergarten training. But Blow became increasingly frustrated by the direction kindergarten training at Teachers College was taking and correctly felt she was losing influence to the much younger Hill. After getting her old mentor, William Torrey Harris, to intercede unsuccessfully on her behalf, Blow left Teachers College in 1909 after Hill's course had been made a requirement and dissatisfied students had pressed the dean to curtail Blow's own lecturing. Blow had lost her battle to maintain Froebelianism as the knowledge base of American kindergartning; Hill had won the right to experiment even further with merging pragmatism and behaviorism in kindergarten pedagogy.[32]

Hill immediately took advantage of her position at Teachers College to develop new preschool theory and practice that applied psychology to education. Her own educational philosophy was an eclectic blend of child study, pragmatism, and behaviorism. During the many years she taught at Teachers College, she was particularly influenced by the associationist, behavioristic psychology of Edward L. Thorndike, the founder of learning theory, and she and classroom teachers at Teachers College's Horace Mann laboratory school began experimenting with Thorndike's principles of learning with the kindergarten children in their care. In 1923 they published *A Conduct Curriculum for the Kindergarten and First Grade*, which consisted primarily of a "Habit Inventory," a lengthy list of kindergarten activities and the behavioral outcomes they were expected to produce. An item in the category of paperwork, for example—which contained three groups of fifteen activities with the learning outcomes for each—was the activity "cutting paper," next to which were listed the outcomes "pleasure in activity" and "learning how to use scissors." Kindergarten teachers accustomed to the minutely detailed instructions of older Froebelian guides responded similarly to the specificity of the "Habit Inventory," and Hill's curriculum became very popular, particularly for use in evaluating and reporting on individual children.[33]

In an interview late in her life, Hill recounted how she learned to modify traditional kindergarten whole-group teaching methods in ways very similar to those prescribed by today's theories on cooperative learning. For instance, during her early days in Louisville, when "Howard" had asked her to whom she was talking when she led full-group discussions and presented thematic content to the children in a circle, Hill realized that young children understand information best when it is presented to them in naturalistic conversations. "After this," Hill said, "I did my talking with individual children and little groups who came to me to discuss matters of genuine interest." Similarly, Hill learned from observing a little boy in the Teachers College kindergarten that even very young children can organize small-group sessions when they are genuinely interested in discussing a subject. After watching "Jack" organize a group of children to decide on the name for the new class canary, Hill observed that he "had taught us something about kindergarten organization that we needed to know: the small, spontaneous group is the natural unit for work with little children. A common interest is the only basis for calling together a large group. Given such an interest, a large group can function simply and spontaneously, and through it the children gain experience as parts of a social whole."[34]

Hill developed curriculum materials that eventually replaced the Froebelian "gifts." In 1898 she had studied with Dr. Luther Gulick from whom she got the idea of designing "a new set of building blocks on a scale sufficiently large to enable children to play in the houses, stores, and barns they built" (509). Hill worked for twelve or thirteen years on these blocks, heavy wooden precursors of the hollow cardboard blocks now used in kindergartens and nursery schools, before perfecting a set that was then mass-produced and successfully marketed to preschools. She also revolutionized the teaching of music to young children by introducing bells, triangles, horns, and other simple instruments that allowed children to experiment with sound rather than being regimented into rote choral singing. And early in her kindergarten work in Louisville, Hill had realized that young children should be allowed to draw freely rather than being taught to repeat successions of horizontal and diagonal lines as had been the practice until then. "Psychologists from all over the country," Hill noted, were "astonished by the observation, imagination, and technique developed through this freer expression" (523).

In the process of developing her new materials Hill had considered and rejected the sensorially based materials of Dr. Maria Montessori then being introduced to American children. The decision was not taken lightly. In fact, Hill went to Rome in 1912 to observe Montessori's methods firsthand. Though she was impressed by much that she saw, she was troubled by the lack of emphasis on cooperation, group activities, and social development. Young children at Montessori's *Casa dei Bambini* spent a great deal of their time individually manipulating educational objects such as graduated wooden cylinders and small color chips rather than playing together as they did in Froebelian kindergartens. Too, Hill thought Montessori's carefully constructed and sequenced materials were overly structured. Like Teachers College psychologist William Heard Kilpatrick, who was primarily responsible for blocking the widespread importation of the Montessori system to this country, Hill condemned Montessori's "whole scheme" as being "too rigid and artificial" and dismissed "the psychological principle of the 'transfer of training' upon which Mme. Montessori's entire plan is based" (509).[35]

The Kindergarten Department at Teachers College remained under Patty Smith Hill's control for thirty years, and her efforts succeeded in rationalizing and modernizing kindergarten training and practice. Though many improvements were made, particularly the new emphasis on spontaneity and free play, some important insights about inspiration and aspiration may have been lost in the process. During Hill's tenure at the college, the kindergarten faculty was increasingly dominated by male academic psychologists, few if any of whom had her experience with, sensitivity to, or respect for the small but important events of young children's daily lives in classrooms and homes. Science replaced spirituality as the authorized source of information about preschool education, and masculine-model analysis replaced female intuition as the prescribed guide to interactions with young children.

Battles for Control of the Kindergarten

When the establishment of kindergartens in public schools around the turn of the century brought kindergartners into contact with the world of male politicians and administrators, a battle began for control of the kindergarten. Kindergartners also continued to fight among themselves over curricular issues. Internal curricular battles were especially acute at meetings of the International Kindergarten Union (IKU) in the years immediately following Patty Smith Hill's defeat of Susan Blow.

An outgrowth of the Kindergarten Department of the National Education Association, the IKU was an umbrella organization like the NKA but focused primarily on issues of internal coordination rather than external political organizing. In 1903 the IKU appointed a committee of influential kindergartners to reach a consensus on curricular matters. Unable to agree, the Committee of Nineteen eventually submitted three separate reports: a conservative report authored by Susan Blow, a progressive report written by Patty Smith Hill, and a liberal-conservative report coauthored by Lucy Wheelock and Elizabeth Harrison. Though chairwoman Lucy Wheelock in particular tried to put a positive spin on this dissension by equating it with Froebel's law of contrasts, the committee's inability to reach consensus was representative of the new plurality in kindergarten pedagogy.[36]

In the decades after the turn of the century, many different methods competed to fill the vacuum left by the decline of Froebelian orthodoxy. While the views of Progressives like Hill prevailed in academia, no single model replaced Froebelianism in the classroom. The concentric program, which tied activities to daily and weekly themes such as the home, community helpers, transportation, and food production, became popular, as did other approaches such as John Dewey's industrial curriculum, in which children made useful objects rather than symbolic designs; William Heard Kilpatrick's project method; nature study; and literature, music, art, and seasonal programs. In 1920 Julia Wade Abbot described this burgeoning variety of kindergarten subjects: making "paper borders of pumpkins and grapes at Thanksgiving time, pictures of Christmas trees and holly at Christmas, flags and soldiers at Washington's Birthday, and flowers and rabbits at Easter," to name but a few educationally valuable experiences, could all be linked to handwork that expressed thought. "Life in the kindergarten," Abbot exclaimed, provided "an inexhaustible supply of things to be talked about."[37]

The most radically open-ended approach to kindergartning was the free play curriculum that provided for time periods during which children were allowed to participate in activities of their own choice. In a yearlong study conducted in public kindergartens in Santa Barbara, California, in 1898, Superintendent of Schools Frederic Burk, a student of G. Stanley Hall, and Caroline Frear Burk, found that, when given a choice, young children did not play with Froebelian materials at all but preferred dolls, swings, bean bags, and other toys. The problem with the kindergarten, the Burks declared, was that children had not been "particularly consulted either in the choice of material, or in the use to be made of it." The "natural reaction toward these materials" of the "docile little puppets who furnish the background in the drama of the gifts and occupations" was thus "hard to determine." The Burks proposed instead that children be given two free play periods, called "recesses," and encouraged teachers to become more aware of children's intrinsic interests.[38]

Changes in kindergarten teaching methods resulted both from pressures within school systems and from academic research. As university psychologists and teacher trainers became increasingly receptive to the demands of parents, teachers, and school administrators for useful information about children's education, new curricular approaches evolved. A particularly successful collaboration occurred at the University of Chicago, when Alice Temple, former director of the Chicago Free Kindergarten Association, and elementary curriculum specialist Samuel Chester Parker cowrote a textbook on combined kindergarten and first-grade teaching methods.

Temple and Parker's *Unified Kindergarten and First Grade Teaching* (1925) showed the influence of Thorndike and the measurement movement but was even closer to Dewey in its focus on community life and social experience. Also new was its emphasis on linking kindergarten and first grade. More an explication of underlying principles than a manual or guide to methods, Temple and Parker's book tried to unify kindergarten and first-grade curricula in a way the authors stated would be "continuous and delightful." Though they sympathized with the desire of kindergartners to bring "more enjoyment" into children's lives, they saw "no necessary conflict" between Froebelian idealism and the teaching of basic skills, which they argued could be done in a gradual, developmentally appropriate manner. Their broad curriculum linked social and cognitive skills, such as "good will" and reading, with recreational activities, study of community life, health activities, and "civic and moral habits." They included examples of model lessons on topics such as the post office and the farm; a yearly calendar of seasonal themes; a list of habits important for children to develop, such as getting to school on time and saying "please" and "thank you." The book concluded with a section on the "general spirit" of "happiness, freedom, orderly habits, obedience, courtesy, independence in thinking and acting, and confidence in and affection for the teacher" that should pervade the kindergarten and first grade.[39]

The internal curricular battles that resulted in stalemates or pastiches like Wheelock and Harrison's liberal-conservative report and Temple and Parker's wildly eclectic "unification" of kindergarten and first-grade pedagogy were mirrored by less publicized but equally fierce turf fights between mostly male politicians and public school administrators and mostly female kindergarten supporters and supervisors. These power struggles took place in the arena of municipal politics where, beginning in the 1870s, women's groups began trying to get women elected to city school boards. In fact, the kindergarten was one of the reasons women fought to gain the vote: they wanted to vote *for* public kindergartens and other maternalist programs for children, women, and families.

The New England Women's Club succeeded in getting six women elected to the Boston School Committee in 1875. Among the new committee members were Lucretia Hale, an early supporter of public kindergartens who helped Pauline Agassiz Shaw start her network of charity kindergartens, and Lucretia Crocker, who eventually became a powerful supervisor and kindergarten advocate within the Boston public school system. In 1880, women in Boston won the right to vote in school board elections, and in 1888 they turned out in force to elect Pauline Agassiz Shaw's kindergarten supervisor Laliah Pingree to the School Committee. Pingree in turn voted to establish public kindergartens in Boston. After 1905, however, few women were elected to the Boston School Committee until the 1960s. Moreover, even when women in Boston were winning power at the polls, within the school system itself they were losing it to male school administrators who were rationalizing and entrenching a hierarchical bureaucracy.[40]

Getting additional funding for public kindergartens was a major impetus in the campaign for municipal suffrage for women in New York City. An

1895 article in the *Kindergarten Magazine* condemned the lack of financial support for the few existing public kindergartens in New York, asserting that it was "not possible that such a state of things could exist very long, if women had even a restricted right of suffrage, with a power to sit on school boards and to control legislation within narrow limits." Arguing that corrupt male party bosses had kept women from serving on school boards, the author said women would be a "revolutionary influence" who would act to protect the "neglected lambs" who were left to roam the streets for lack of adequate funding for public kindergartens. In fact, the author stated, "Those who are champions in the general field of woman's rights might well limit for a time their efforts to this single object of municipal franchise, and the placing of women on our school boards."[41]

But the biggest fights took place in school systems where the administrative styles and educational philosophies of female kindergarten supervisors differed drastically from those of male school administrators. Though job descriptions varied from system to system and often depended on the personalities and relative power of the people involved, large public school systems generally had separate kindergarten departments administered by female directors who were responsible for most aspects of the programs they supervised. As a 1918 U.S. Bureau of Education study documented, in most cities directors made decisions about class size and promotion of children, ordered supplies and materials, ensured that there would be opportunities for outdoor and gardening activities, helped plan the kindergarten curriculum, provided for what today would be called in-service education, and supervised kindergarten teachers. Larger issues such as the amount of money to be allocated for kindergarten budgets, teachers' salaries, and the architectural planning of new kindergarten rooms were not within their purview, however, and neither did they determine the number of sessions a day or their length. And since many kindergarten supervisors had been directors in free kindergarten associations before working in the public schools, they still identified more with the kindergarten movement than with the school bureaucracy and often tried to use their power to protect the embattled interests of their staff.[42]

Differences were most evident in the characteristics kindergarten directors said they looked for in teachers. The qualities mentioned most frequently by kindergarten directors in the Bureau of Education survey were "sympathy, understanding, seeing from the child's standpoint," and "play-spirit."

"Grade teachers," by contrast, were "trained to consider and deal with the child as a *learning* being, and not primarily as a feeling, doing individual." Public kindergarten directors and public school principals also differed on how they supervised teachers. While some kindergarten directors provided teachers with a curriculum outline or handbook, and a few required teachers to submit weekly or monthly lesson plans, most said they saw their job as communicating "essential principles" rather than defining the daily program of activities, which they thought was the responsibility of individual teachers. Principals, on the other hand, frequently checked for a specific list of items and often felt they should and could make minute classroom decisions for teachers, much as a foreman would manage hands in a factory (38).[43]

Of course, female supervisors only permitted teachers freedom within the context of the lingering Froebelian tradition of prescribed curricula, which often left little latitude for teacher autonomy. Nor were relationships between supervisors and teachers completely free of tension; indeed, some public kindergarten teachers felt they did not need a supervisor at all. Public school superintendents, who may have had their own axes to grind, also criticized kindergarten directors for being too rigid and dogmatic, especially with younger teachers. Concern was also expressed that kindergarten teachers were indirectly forced to "cater to the supervisor's whims for the sake of good standing." Nevertheless, kindergarten teachers in the early twentieth century were probably freer to design and implement their own curricula in public school kindergartens than primary and elementary school counterparts were and than they themselves had been in private kindergartens where senior kindergarten directors supervised individual teachers directly and daily.[44]

In any case, tensions between public school kindergarten directors and kindergarten teachers were minor compared to the conflicts between public school superintendents and principals and kindergarten directors. Some superintendents sought to curtail the power and independence of kindergarten supervisors or do away with kindergarten supervisors altogether, bringing kindergartens under the administration of principals. But superintendents and principals were hampered in this effort by their ignorance of kindergartning and their reluctance to become involved with the emotional, messy, noisy, and sometimes noisome aspects of daily classroom interaction with young children. This gulf between the culture of young children and that of the school in general undoubtedly exacerbated the endemic tensions between kindergarten directors and public school administrators.[45]

Of all the conflicts between male school superintendents and principals and female kindergarten directors, none was more fierce than the debate over the shift to double sessions. In the years after 1900, superintendents under growing pressure to accommodate larger numbers of children became increasingly concerned about the cost of kindergartens. Because of their generally smaller sizes and special materials, kindergartens were more expensive than primary classes were. One solution to this fiscal problem was to have kindergartners teach two sessions, as William Torrey Harris had discovered in St. Louis in 1875. A 1915 Bureau of Education survey reported that by the 1911–12 school year, 546 of 867 school systems had instituted morning and afternoon kindergartens. Though schedules, class sizes, session lengths, and rationales for the assignment of children varied considerably, most sessions were from two to two and a half hours long. In cities with single sessions, kindergartners were increasingly asked to help other teachers and engage in other in-school activities in the afternoons.[46]

Most kindergarten directors and teachers adamantly opposed the change to double sessions. Like free kindergartners, public school kindergartners believed that home visits and mothers' meetings were critical to the success of the kindergarten program. Since double sessions reduced the amount of time teachers could spare for this community and family work, they would limit their ability to make the home-school connections that were the essence of the kindergarten's unique function as a bridge between the private domain of the home and the public world of the school. As one public kindergartner put it, the kindergarten was "the link that unites the school and the family," and children needed to "feel the bond of sympathy which exists" between mother and teacher (24). The director of kindergartens in the New York Public Schools stated that the kindergartner had a dual role: she was "not only a teacher, but a social worker," and a balance had to be struck between her teaching and social welfare activities. "If it is more important to accommodate large numbers of children, then the double session may be introduced; but if the kindergartner is to take her rightful place in the community as an influence in the home as well as in the school, . . . then she must have some afternoon hours free" (2).

Another issue in the debate over double sessions was job comparability and respect. Because kindergarten teachers' hours of in-class time were usu-

ally shorter than those of primary grade teachers and because the children
with whom they worked played rather than doing traditional academic work,
other teachers sometimes said kindergartners' jobs were easier. Kindergartners themselves were convinced they worked as hard as other teachers and
wanted this to be understood. "Kindergarten work is not more difficult, but
takes more time," one kindergartner reported. Some even felt teaching young
children was more difficult than teaching older children, because "it is more
of a strain on the nerves and requires more patience." A kindergarten teacher
who taught double sessions would have "two sets of children the same size
as the primary teacher" and so would have to "respond to many differing
personalities" (23).

Pay was also clearly a factor in the battle over double sessions. The
smaller number of hours kindergartners spent in the classroom compared
with primary teachers was the main reason for their lower salaries. Public
school bureaucracies forced kindergartners to choose between hours and
program quality. As kindergarten teachers in most public school systems
were gradually assigned two sessions, their pay rose. A National Education
Association report stated that by 1923 most kindergartners were paid about
the same as primary teachers, with kindergartners in smaller towns, who also
served as kindergarten directors, being paid somewhat more than primary
teachers and those in larger cities, where there tended to be separate kindergarten directors, being paid somewhat less.[47]

Public school kindergarten teachers gradually came to accept the need for
double sessions. As class sizes had increased, some realized that double sessions might even be better in the long run because they would reduce the
number of children in each class, thus making it possible for teachers to
continue using the more effective individualized and small-group teaching
styles young children needed. Kindergartners also viewed the change as the
price to be paid for acceptance of the kindergarten. As one kindergartner
put it, "The double session promotes a general feeling on the part of the
community, the teaching body, and the teacher that the kindergarten is a
vital, integral part of the school system and not a luxury, exceptional in its
organization and privileges."[48]

Some kindergartners adapted readily to being part of the public schools,
some resisted, and still others took a cautious wait-and-see approach. Patty
Smith Hill, who supported institutionalization, nonetheless posited two
equally unfortunate results of incorporation into the public system: some

kindergartners would respond to the tendency of schools to reward teachers who were didactic disciplinarians; others, especially those who clung to Froebelianism, would see schools as "always in the wrong" and reject any form of compromise. Distrust was often mutual, as some school people were very critical of kindergartners. Boston public kindergarten director Laura Fisher tried to make the best of it, comparing kindergartners and school personnel to a family in which criticism was actually an act of acceptance. But Fisher was also exasperated with all the resistance, saying, "The school reserved and meant to exercise its special right of freely criticising us forever."[49]

Initially many public kindergartens functioned like separate programs, their environments, philosophies, and methods so different from those of schools that kindergartners and school personnel alike worried that the gap between kindergarten and first grade might cause difficulties for young children. As one kindergartner stated, "the home and the kindergarten are sometimes felt to be more closely united than the kindergarten and the next grade of the school." These differences seemed so pronounced that a student attending one of Laura Fisher's kindergarten lectures in 1898 asked, "How can a child, beginning with such an education, go into the ordinary primary school without feeling a tremendous break and consequent revolt?"[50]

This discontinuity led to a movement to adjust the kindergarten and first grade. Not surprisingly, however, a 1915 Bureau of Education survey found considerable disagreement over what and how any adjustments should be made. Superintendents, principals, and primary teachers thought kindergarten children were too dependent during handwork periods, needed "constant help and supervision," evidenced "unnecessary communication and ill-timed play," and recommended that kindergartners provide less assistance and enforce more quiet. They also suggested that first-grade teachers introduce more handwork, permit greater freedom, discipline less strictly, use movable furniture, have smaller classes, and assign more creative paper-and-pencil exercises.[51]

The kindergartners surveyed were asked how kindergarten prepared children for first grade and how first grade should be adjusted, not how kindergartens should be changed. In answer to the first question, kindergarten teachers ranked reading and writing last and described instead the preparation in color and shape discrimination that kindergarten activities provided (14). When asked how closer contacts should be formed between kindergarten and first grade, they suggested training courses in primary methods, observation of first-grade classes, and joint conferences but did not recommend altering the kindergarten program (17). Kindergartners made the same suggestions for changing the first grade as superintendents, principals, and primary teachers did, reiterating the importance of the "play-spirit" for young children (18).

As the twentieth century progressed, battles between female kindergarten supervisors and male school administrators continued. Though the 1918 Bureau of Education survey on kindergarten supervision reported "a good spirit of cooperation" and "democratic" relationships among kindergarten supervisors, teachers, principals, and superintendents, the power of kindergarten supervisors gradually lessened. Without strong supervisors looking over their shoulders, kindergarten teachers probably gained more autonomy in their individual classrooms, but the price was marginality. Kindergartners were left more or less alone to develop and implement their own pedagogy, but they were ignored and undervalued. Isolated and denied recognition of the worth of the kindergarten, kindergartners did not produce the evaluation results required to rationalize funding decisions in American public education. School administrators continued to complain about the costs of kindergartens, and some school systems and states were slow to institute kindergartens because of their expense.[52]

Despite this increasing marginalization, public kindergartens had an impact on primary education. At a kindergarten conference sponsored by the University of Chicago in May 1897, Superintendent of Schools Ella Flagg Young described the incorporation of the kindergarten into the public schools as part of a larger rethinking and restructuring of American education. The primary, grammar, and high school model was giving way to a new elementary and secondary school model in which teachers of the first three grades were no longer responsible only for the teaching of reading. The kindergarten, according to Young, was the opening wedge in this transformation. "First busy work from the kindergarten was used to relieve the children from so much slate work," Young stated; "then gradually better conceptions of both primary and kindergarten work prevailed."[53]

The kindergarten may have influenced the upper grades in other ways as well. In 1902 Harvard University president Charles W. Eliot gave a speech on the positive influence of the kindergarten, saying that the most important reform it had brought about was the emphasis on treating each child as an individual, which had led to a reduction in kindergarten class size. This in turn, Eliot said, had caused a movement to reduce class size at all grade levels, "the main educational reform now before the American public." Another positive influence of the kindergarten was that it demonstrated the importance of using teaching assistants so that students could learn by doing in smaller groups, a practice that universities had adopted only recently. Eliot also praised the kindergarten's use of real objects for nature study, something he said he had missed out on at Boston Latin School and Harvard College, where he had had "to learn a natural science out of a book, without one particle of laboratory practice, without seeing any of the objects of study except on the professor's table." Eliot also commended the kindergarten for its recognition that "healthy children are restless, and that their attention cannot long be held to a single subject." This attention to students' actual attention spans, Eliot thought, was helping to shorten periods in elementary and high school classes from an hour to forty minutes, something that universities should also consider, Eliot argued, because after "a few minutes the minds of many [college students] are entirely absent from the scene." Finally, Eliot asserted, the kindergarten was on the right track pedagogically because kindergarten teachers showed children how to do things and gave them physical practice, something that Eliot himself was grateful for whenever it occurred.[54]

Observational studies conducted at Teachers College in the late 1920s and early 1930s documented the infiltration of kindergartning methods into the primary grades. But, as Ella Flagg Young noted, this was a two-way street. Kindergartners, too, had changed their methods, "though not always wisely," introducing "work in elementary science beyond the children's grasp" and directive physical exercises "better adapted to the sixth grade." Worksheets appeared in kindergartens, and "reading readiness" and other skill-oriented assignments were added to kindergarten curricula, reducing the time available for play and other nonacademic activities. Teachers were increasingly trained in both kindergarten and primary pedagogy, as U.S. Bureau of Education reports on adjustment, training, urban kindergartens, and kindergarten-primary education recommended. Though kindergarten and first-grade teaching methods continued to differ in important ways, and even an untrained classroom observer would probably have been able to distinguish one from the other, twentieth-century curriculum guides, U.S. Bureau of Education surveys, and other descriptive and prescriptive literature on kindergarten teaching all provide evidence that the public kindergarten was in danger of becoming a new first grade.[55]

Some kindergartners were worried about this potential problem but attributed it more to the influence of science than to the effects of institutionalization. The author of a Bureau of Education kindergarten report wrote in 1914,

> Those who are watching the trend of school practice cannot yet decide whether the kindergarten teacher stands in peril of losing just that quality which has been so potent a factor in modifying school theory and practice. That quality, not easily described, grows out of the motherly, nurturing character of the kindergartner's work. It is not "an artificial pose of motherhood," but a genuine necessary element of the teaching relationship, lacking which all teaching becomes flat, dull, inert. Scientific it may be, but it fails to be humanized.

Most modern educational historians argue that the kindergarten did indeed lose its potential to be "a factor in modifying school theory and practice" but tend to blame the bureaucratic, hegemonic nature of public school systems for this and other changes in public kindergarten ideology and practice. Marvin Lazerson, for instance, describes the "delicate balance" between freedom and order that characterized earlier private and charity kindergarten practice and argues that the essential conservatism and social control functions of public school systems tipped this balance inexorably toward order. But although some public kindergartens may have been more focused on order and more coercive than private kindergartens, not all private and charity kindergartens were as free as Lazerson has characterized them. Moreover, considerable evidence suggests that the tension between freedom and control did not disappear when kindergartens entered the public schools. In fact, Nina Vandewalker has argued that kindergartners' "faith in creative self-activity as the fundamental article in the kindergarten creed" was never shaken, and in some cases the balance may even have tipped the other way, as the Burks' public school "free play" curriculum attested.[56]

Kindergartners themselves freely admitted, however, that preparation for first grade gradually replaced social reform as a goal in public kindergartens. In her history of the American kindergarten movement, Nina Vandewalker lauded this change as positive evidence of the improvements in kindergarten training and the increased standards for kindergartning as an educational profession. The greater emphasis on academics may also have been due to a belief that the lower-class children whom many public kindergartens served needed to be better prepared if they were to succeed in school and in society—on its face, not an inherently reprehensible goal. In any case, despite their new emphasis on academics and school preparation, kindergartners still continued to value nurturance and to employ child-centered teaching methods. And though female kindergarten supervisors were overshadowed by male school administrators, public kindergarten departments remained one of the last strongholds of female power within school systems.[57]

The institutionalization of kindergartens in the public schools hastened the breakdown of Froebelianism. Kindergartners now had license to search for pedagogical ideas from a variety of sources and even to invent their own curricula—or, even more radical, to allow the children to do it for themselves. But even without the Froebelian program, twentieth-century kindergartens became quite uniform. Most teachers turned to psychology for theories and guidance about kindergarten practice and used a version of what was called the "reconstructed program," a combination of free play and teacher-directed activities, such as counting, color and form discrimination, and letter recognition exercises. Most favored projects with seasonal motifs and curriculum units on the home, community, nature, and other topics considered to be of interest to young children. Kindergarten methods remained different from those in the upper grades, but kindergartners, teacher educators, and psychologists created a new orthodoxy, a canon for young children, which became the dominant pedagogical model for American preschool education.

Even with all the changes from 1860 to 1930, the relationship of kindergartning to the larger culture and to schools remained fairly constant. The Froebelian gifts, occupations, songs, and games, which supposedly corresponded to universal forms and laws of development and replicated nature and traditional German family life, were replaced by similar, if less rigidly patterned, sensory discrimination exercises based on modern scientific concepts of children's development, reading readiness activities, and thematic units on the seasons and middle-class American life. Character training through the inculcation of morals and models was replaced by habit formation and an equally pervasive emphasis on correct social attitudes and good behavior. None of these changes affected the basic socialization process that was the main societal effect of kindergartning. Kindergartning continued to be as normative and class-biased as other forms of education.

In the process of universalization, public kindergartens inherited the bureaucracy and other burdensome traditions that many educational historians have attributed to public schools but also gained more funding and an ideology of universal access. They lost some of the unique, reformist, needs-oriented aspects of free kindergartens but also shed some of the patronizing characteristics of charity kindergarten work. The campaign to enfranchise the educational rights of five-year-olds had been won.

Chapter 7   "A Place for Children in

the Modern World"

Private Nursery Schools in

the 1910s and 1920s

After their success establishing public kindergartens for five-year-olds, preschool educators began experimenting with schooling outside the home for two-, three-, and four-year-olds in a new kind of institution: the nursery school. Designed to be "a place for young children in the modern world," as one preschool advocate put it, nursery schools were more future-oriented than the kindergarten. Though some kindergartners, especially Patty Smith Hill, provided leadership for both movements, in general the crusade for nursery schools belonged to younger women who had enjoyed the benefits of formal higher education themselves and had professional training in psychology and the social sciences. Nursery school leaders participated actively in psychological studies, took pride in implementing the latest research, and distanced themselves from older, less scientific, less objective forms of charity work with young children. Men also played an increasingly important role in the nursery school movement. This was no longer Progressive Era "social housekeeping" dominated by concepts of voluntarism and "women's sphere"; it was the beginning of modern, professional early childhood education and child welfare work.[1]

Nursery schools were part of a broad new configuration of fields and professions dealing with children and families. Following World War I, children became a central concern not only of parents, educators, psychologists, and physicians but also of social workers, juvenile court authorities, home economists, parent educators, and a growing number of other so-called experts who formed a public-private network (or, better, patchwork) of child welfare programs and organizations. In fact, as Steven Schlossman has suggested, some of the most important educational efforts of the 1920s were focused on the relationship between families and these other institutions and organizations, rather than on schools. Nursery school educators were more closely allied with these advocates than they were with kindergartners, who were now part of public school systems and increasingly looked upward toward the grades rather than downward and outward toward young children and families.[2]

Much of the impetus behind the interest in young children and families came from newly organized, foundation-based private philanthropy, especially the Laura Spelman Rockefeller Memorial. All six of the prototypical private nursery schools described in this chapter received funding from Rockefeller director Beardsley Ruml's assistant, Lawrence K. Frank, who administered the foundation's programs for children and families. A great believer in the ability of science to solve social problems, by 1925 Frank had directed more than a million dollars of Rockefeller funding to selected child study, child development, child guidance, child welfare, parent education, and nursery education projects and done much to make young children a legitimate topic of academic research.[3]

Nursery schools reflected the multiplicity of new psychological and sociological ideas about children and families. Unlike most kindergartners, nursery educators experimented with pedagogical methods, viewing the nursery school as a source of empirical information about what environment and educational procedures were best for young children. Unlike most nursery schools today, which are primarily morning programs for affluent children, nursery schools in the 1920s had diverse schedules and hours, served varied populations of "normal" and "problem" children, and focused on such goals as liberating, educating, researching, and guiding young children, as well as on educating parents and remediating family pathology.

Like the infant school and kindergarten movements, the nursery school movement had European origins. In 1907 the Consultative Committee of the English Board of Education recognized the need for a new kind of program to educate the large numbers of unhealthy, under-school-age children left alone during the day. Shortly thereafter, Rachel and Margaret Mc-Millan, who had been campaigning for school health inspections, women's suffrage, and other causes, started a school clinic in Deptford, a depressed slum of London. After her sister's death, Margaret McMillan started an open air nursery school in Deptford in 1913 for children from one to six years of age. In 1918 Parliament passed the Fisher Act, which enabled local education authorities in England to establish nursery schools for children between two and five years old.[4]

Margaret McMillan's nursery school philosophy derived from a variety of political, pedagogical, and psychological sources. A member of the Independent Labor Party, McMillan wanted to create a model environment "that would not only lengthen the period of working-class children's education, but would enrich and refine the nervous system in the formative period" and thus even up the "gross injustice" in the early backgrounds of rich and poor children. Another influence on McMillan's educational thought was the sensory psychology of Edouard Seguin, who had worked with Jean Itard and the wild child of Aveyron. Like her contemporary, Maria Montessori, McMillan developed a physiological, sensorial pedagogy in which young children learned through their bodies' physical actions on objects.[5]

McMillan's educational work focused most closely on young children's health. She abhorred dirt and placed great emphasis on good ventilation and outdoor play. The first children's environments McMillan designed were not fully enclosed, hence the name "open air nursery schools." As Patty Smith Hill wrote in 1921, the buildings were "little more than 'shacks' or shelters set in a garden of flowers and trees overlooked by tenements of the lowest order." Sometimes the children even slept outside. This emphasis on fresh air and hygiene dominated the training program McMillan started at Deptford in 1914, which, like kindergarten training programs earlier, began attracting young women from upper-class backgrounds from England and elsewhere, including the United States.[6]

But American educators were doing pioneering work with young children before the introduction of the British nursery school to the United States in the 1920s. In 1906 Cora Bussey Hillis began organizing efforts that would lead to the creation of the Iowa Child Welfare Research Station at the State University of Iowa in Iowa City. Arnold Gesell started a small clinic to treat young children with school adjustment problems when he arrived at Yale University in 1911. And Caroline Pratt, Harriet Johnson, and Lucy Sprague Mitchell began working with poor and immigrant children and with the sons and daughters of the radical intelligentsia in the years before World War I in Greenwich Village, where they developed a radical preschool pedagogy designed to counteract what they saw as the psychologically and politically oppressive environment of the private family.

The new emphasis on young children's oppression stemmed in part from an ongoing sexual revolution in American psychology and society. Though the analytic psychology of Sigmund Freud would not become popular in this country until later, a small avant-garde of preschool educators in the 1910s and 1920s were influenced by the theory of infantile sexuality and Freud's concept of children's stages of psychosexual development. For them, childhood was no longer the period of innocence idealized by the romantics but a time of sexual lability in which young children enjoyed the oral pleasures of sucking and then learned to master their bodies' anal functions. But though no longer innocent, young children were blameless because much of their development was thought to be either instinctual and unconscious or the result of what had been done to them by their mothers. With this move from Froebelianism toward Freudianism, the focus changed from unifying mothers' and children's interests to liberating children from their mothers, a shift that was to have a profound impact on preschool policy and pedagogy.

Technological, economic, and social changes were giving some mothers more time to focus on raising their children. In addition, as more women pursued higher education and as sexual, social, and technological revolutions made birth control more available, birth rates dropped rapidly, and families became smaller. But even with more time to devote to child rearing, middle- and upper-class mothers worried more about it, and experts deemed them to be less successful at it. Warnings about mothers damaging their children were especially apparent in the new behavioristic psychology of John Watson, which became popular in the 1920s and 1930s and greatly influenced the nursery school movement. In Watson's view, the role of parents and preschool teachers was to instill correct habits in children. Though operating from an environmentalistic viewpoint entirely opposite from Freud's psycho-organicism, Watson was even more pessimistic about the destructive potential of mothers. In his 1928 treatise *The Psychological Care of the Infant and Child*, he questioned whether children should live in "individual homes" or "know their own parents" at all. "Never hug and kiss them, never let them sit in your lap," Watson told mothers, advising them instead to treat their children like young adults. If a mother was "tempted to pet" her child, Watson said, she should remember that "mother love is a dangerous instrument . . . which may inflict a never healing wound."[7]

In the face of such ominous advice, modern mothers increasingly sought help from psychologists and preschool educators, who took it upon themselves to give authoritative information on children and intervene in family matters. Working together in laboratory nursery schools, child guidance clinics, and child welfare institutes, psychologists and preschool educators produced an extensive new literature on child rearing and early education. Psychologists Bird Baldwin, Arnold Gesell, George Stoddard, and Helen Thompson Woolley collaborated with nursery school directors on studies of young children, examining and recording in detail their every attribute, habit, preference, and taste. (Their subjects, who for the most part lived on or near college or university campuses, became the new exemplars of American normality.) Psychologists and nursery educators also focused their attention on young children who were abnormal and began preschool mental hygiene programs, habit clinics, and guidance nursery schools to prevent delinquency and deviance and provide treatment for young children with problems.

The more research nursery educators became involved in and aware of, the more problems they saw, and the more they turned to science for solutions. A few researchers, such as Ethel Puffer Howes and Abigail Eliot, tried to reunite mothers and children in positive ways and to come up with practical techniques to help women be better mothers. More common, however, was concern about mothers' lack of ability and about so-called problem parents. Nursery educators did not think all children developed in the same way, but they did think all parents needed help with child rearing. The universal theme of the nursery school movement was that all parents, rich and poor, could become better parents through the application of scientific educational principles and the enrollment of their young children in nursery school. But the promise of science as a solution to messy human problems proved illusory and even harmful, as some nursery educators reluctantly began to discover in the 1930s.

Liberating Young Children: Caroline Pratt's and Harriet Johnson's Nursery School Experiments

Of the numerous experiments in Progressive education in the late nineteenth and early twentieth centuries, Caroline Pratt's Play School, which opened in New York City in 1913, was one of the most radical. Born in Fayetteville, New York, in 1867, Pratt taught briefly in a one-room school in a small farming community near Syracuse before attending Teachers College in 1892. As she described in her remarkable autobiography *I Learn From Children* (1948), Pratt did not like the kindergarten courses she took from "a little, plump woman" (probably Susan Blow) who commanded the class of "big-boned Westerners and decorous New Englanders and up-State country girls like myself" to follow her around the room fluttering like butterflies. Nor did she approve of the rigidity or "mystical fol-de-rol" of kindergarten methods. Pratt astutely observed, "You taught children to dance like butterflies, when you knew they would much rather roar like lions, because lions are hard to discipline and butterflies aren't," and with this realization, dismissed the kindergarten as an institution designed to get children "ready to be bamboozled by the first grade."[8]

Pratt discovered her vocation through experiences with young children, not through formal teacher education. After leaving Teachers College she went to Philadelphia to work in a manual training school for girls. There Pratt met Helen Marot, a young Quaker who was to become her lifetime companion and whose socialistic political ideas greatly influenced Pratt's work. After helping Marot investigate the exploitation of seamstresses in the custom-tailoring trade in Philadelphia, Pratt returned to New York, where she taught manual training in a small private school and in two settlement houses. Then, like Elizabeth Peabody, Lucy Wheelock, and so many other preschool educators whose lives were changed by observing individual children at play, Pratt was transformed by a chance experience watching the "inventive and ingenious" six-year-old son of a friend building a toy railroad system. As she stood "pressed against the wall of that nursery so as not to get in the way of the busy miniature world he had created there," she realized this was how children learned about the world: "He had observed for himself, had gathered his facts, and was here, before my eyes, writing the perfect child's textbook of what he had seen" (23). Pratt concluded that this happy little boy's play activity could be "developed into an ideal means of teaching young children" (24).

Eager to put her new ideas to work, Pratt resigned from her manual training jobs and began designing educational toys called "Do-Withs," which were not financially successful. In 1913 she started a playgroup at the Henry Street Settlement's Hartley House, to which she hoped to attract the children of the immigrant and working-class families who lived around Washington Square, rather than the children of the cultural rebels who flocked to the Village in the period before World War I. But not many working-class parents were willing to enroll their children in Pratt's school. Pratt thought they "were afraid the children would not be ready for public school later, and they were not far wrong" (39). "We had no intention of pushing the three R's on the children until we thought they were ready" (40), Pratt asserted. The artists and writers were willing to take risks with their children, however, and this was the community that supported Pratt's unconventional program, which gradually grew into the progressive, private City and Country School in Greenwich Village.

Pratt's pedagogical experimentation began to attract attention. Harriet Johnson, a visiting teacher with the Public Education Association, brought Lucy Sprague Mitchell to see the school. Excited by what she saw, Mitchell, the former dean of women at the University of California at Berkeley, offered Pratt space in a converted garage in MacDougall Alley behind her Washington Square home. In 1916 Mitchell organized the Bureau of Educational Experiments, a unique educational coordination and research institute of which Pratt was a founding board member. Mitchell taught in Pratt's school until 1928, helped develop curriculum materials for it, sent each of her four children there, and supported the school financially even after she and Pratt had a falling out over money in 1930.[9]

The early 1920s were heady days for Pratt. She resisted formulating any kind of "system" and insisted that the curriculum be based only on the "experiences offered to the children." Pratt called her philosophy of education "creative pedagogy" and equated teachers with artists. "Artist teachers" as Pratt called them, were "rebels" against the institutional methods of traditional schooling. Young children were artists, too, if educated properly, Pratt argued in her foreword to Lucy Sprague Mitchell's 1921 collection of stories, *The Here and Now Story Book*. Good teachers unleashed the creative artistry within children; good schools helped children "to compose and to create," not just "to appreciate and reproduce." And like art, Pratt felt, good teachers' work should be accepted and appreciated unconditionally.[10]

This aesthetic, liberationist view of education permeated Pratt's dealings, or lack thereof, with parents. There were "no bad children, only bad parents," she stated confidently; children's problems were all home problems. Half of the time she wondered why parents "sometimes gave so little of themselves to their children . . . and the other half of the time" she was "convinced that children would be better off without them altogether." Maybe in part because she was not a mother herself—she never married and lived with Helen Marot until Marot's death in 1940—Pratt deprecated mothering. A mother's main job, in Pratt's view, was to help her child become independent. The "good mother" helps her child "by setting him gradually free among his equals" (168). The nursery school, a "democracy in miniature," provided the critical "first step" in the child's "emancipation from the home."[11]

Not surprisingly, some parents resented Pratt's dismissal of their importance in their children's lives. According to the accounts of friends and colleagues, Pratt had a difficult, autocratic personality and made no attempt to hide her criticisms. In her autobiography she wrote that she had been "accused to my face of hating parents, of wishing all children could be born orphans" and admitted to having avoided parents by walking around the block "so as not to meet them, for the truth was that I was afraid of them" (188). Pratt saw parents as obstacles to their children's education, not as partners. Rather than trusting parents to want what was best for their children or to be open to discussion about this critical topic, she was afraid they would try to subvert what she and the teachers were trying to do.[12]

Pratt was sympathetic, however, to the difficulties parents encountered in trying to raise liberated children. "This new freedom for children is not easy for all parents, nor indeed for any parents all the time" (199), she wrote. Pratt gave parents credit for trying "mightily, though with uneven success, to make the leap from their own traditional childhood to the freedom they have approved in principle for their children" (193). The struggle to become a good parent was especially difficult for modern women, she felt, "so many of whom have careers outside of the home" (194). To these women, who had "a profound dilemma to solve when they have children," Pratt offered "no censure," no matter what they decided to do, though she did quote approvingly a mother who decided to stop working while her children were young (197).

Pratt's experimentation with preschool education was extended to even younger children by Harriet Johnson, who directed the Bureau of Educational Experiments nursery school located next to Pratt's City and Country School. Born in Portland, Maine, in 1867, Harriet Johnson trained as a nurse at the Massachusetts Homeopathic Hospital and at Teachers College and worked at Hartley House, where she became interested in the educational problems of schoolchildren. Johnson became the head of the visiting teachers' program started by the Public Education Association; she was a staff member of the Psychological Survey, a group conducting investigations in public schools; and in 1916, along with Caroline Pratt and Lucy Sprague Mitchell, she helped organize the Bureau of Educational Experiments (BEE).[13]

Begun in 1919, the BEE nursery school admitted children from as young as fourteen months to three years of age. Though the school enrolled some children from poor and working-class backgrounds and provided care from early in the morning to late in the afternoon, its principal purpose was research. As Lucy Sprague Mitchell emphasized, the BEE nursery school was not like the "English type of Nursery School" that was concerned with meeting "social and economic need" and aiding "working or professional mothers." Rather, Johnson's main concern was to create an educational environment that maximized the objects and events with and from which young children could play and learn.[14]

In particular, Johnson popularized the hardwood blocks that are still in use today. In a lucid little book called *The Art of Block Building,* she sketched out the stages of children's block building, in a manner that foreshadows the work of Howard Gardner and other psychologists studying children's use of different artistic media. What was really "dramatic" about the young block builders, Johnson wrote, was "not their mastery of techniques but their attitude toward the material."

> It is essentially that of the artist. Even when they do representative building it is the essence, not the bald form, that they make alive. We adults are prosaic in the use of our skills. We learn to speak or write, and thereafter practice these arts in a strictly utilitarian and unimaginative fashion. . . . The child speaks with his blocks. He says in his own way what he has to say. It may be fanciful or humorous. He may express a resemblance or a parallel in his building, or a symbol may stand for a complex conception.[15]

Johnson was also concerned with socializing young children for life outside and after nursery school. The "successful human being," she wrote, "was one equipped to grow and to do, with a maximum of satisfaction to himself and to society." Though Johnson was opposed to early toilet training or to teaching young children formal manners, there were rules in the BEE nursery school: Toys were community property with possession "established by use"; if misused, they were taken away. Children were not allowed to push each other or endanger other children; if they did so, they were removed from the group. Indeed, the punishment for "any behavior" that was "opposed to the social good" was exclusion from the group. "Most of all," she was "concerned with [children] developing an attitude of readiness to act" that was "characteristic of the creative, dynamic personality."[16]

Like Pratt, to whose school most of the BEE children went when they were three or four, Johnson believed that young children's main need was to be liberated from their parents and society. Though she thought children needed to adapt to certain standards and situations and thought adult authority was necessary to keep them safe and free from aggression from their peers, it was an undeniable fact, Johnson asserted, that children lived in a world in which they were "dominated either by adults, by social conventions, or by the circumstances of their inferiority in strength, maturity, and judgment" (42). Johnson's views on mothers, however, were considerably more sympathetic to women than Pratt's were. The problem with mothers, particularly middle- and upper-class mothers, according to Johnson, was that many did not find "a continuous return in affection or companionship" in their marriages and so turned to their infants for emotional sustenance, creating an unhealthy dependence. Young children needed to spend time away from their mothers in a nursery school, an environment centered on all children, not just themselves. "When the family is reunited" at the end of the day, Johnson declared, "they come together as individuals each from his own group with his own interests, and the child comes to realize that the life of the mother as well as that of the father includes concerns beyond the circle of which he is the center."[17]

Like Pratt, Johnson had a permanent relationship with a woman, Harriet Forbes, a nurse involved in settlement work with whom she lived until her death in 1934. Unlike Pratt, however, Johnson did know what it was like to be a parent, which may partly explain why her writing contained none of the hostility toward parents apparent in Pratt's work. Harriet Johnson and Harriet Forbes adopted a baby girl, of whom Johnson became the legal parent because of New York state laws forbidding adoption by women living as couples. This firsthand experience contributed to Johnson's understanding of the difficulty of being a mother. For example, Johnson thought mothers needed to be away from their children, too. Some women found motherhood and housekeeping had "no charms," she observed. Even if a woman liked mothering, she needed to keep up her outside activities and interests; otherwise, being at home would "lose its attractiveness." And if a woman had a career that marriage had "temporarily interrupted," she would have "the same impatience to get back to it that a man would have in a like situation," Johnson asserted.[18]

Caroline Pratt's and Harriet Johnson's experiments in preschool education in Greenwich Village before World War I provided enormous quantities of information about educational environments for young children. Their extensive observations of children's play, particularly with blocks, and the learning materials they developed became the basis of modern nursery school curricula that focus on free expression and creativity. This influence grew steadily through the training programs and other materials published by the Bank Street College of Education in New York City, one of the main centers of preschool education today.

Promoting Parent Involvement: Abigail Eliot and the Ruggles Street Nursery School and Training Center

Though the writings of most other researchers and nursery educators in the 1920s and 1930s echoed Pratt's and Johnson's estimation of the private family as an environment unsuitable for raising emotionally healthy children, Abigail Eliot's work with parents and children in the slums of Boston was a model for modern views on the importance of parent involvement in young children's education. Born in 1892, the daughter of a Unitarian minister and a well-educated mother who knew all about Froebelianism and was a personal friend of Lucy Wheelock, Abigail Adams Eliot went to the progressive Winsor School, to Radcliffe College, and to Oxford University for a year. After working for a while as a social worker with the Children's Mission, Eliot was receptive when Elizabeth Pearson, a family friend and member of the Women's Education Association, asked her if she would like to go to London to learn about nursery education. In 1921 the association sponsored Eliot's six-month stay at McMillan's open air nursery, with the understanding that she transform its own day nursery into a nursery school on her return.[19]

At times Eliot found working in McMillan's nursery school "exhausting." One incident, which confirms modern findings concerning the importance of limiting group sizes in programs for young children, stuck in Eliot's mind. At the end of a long day, McMillan had left Eliot in charge. A thick London

fog rolled in. Then "the two-year-olds got to fighting over toys or something, and we couldn't see them because of the fog! My student helpers
were paralyzed, not knowing what to do. Somehow we managed to get the
situation in hand without any major accident but I've always called that a
'panic time.'" From this harrowing experience Eliot learned never to "put
32 two-year-olds together in one room—no matter how large the room or
how many adults there are to take care of them."[20]

Eliot also found McMillan's focus on physical hygiene extreme, docu-
menting that much of the teachers' time was spent bathing three- and four-
year-olds in "large common outdoor baths" and "the two-year-olds in individual tubs." She wrote home to her Boston sponsor that McMillan's
trainees were "carried away by the health aspect, but at the same time do
not seem to see the social significance of it." Eliot was also disturbed by
McMillan's rigidity and petty rivalry with Maria Montessori, whom McMillan
refused to allow even to visit Deptford. But what most concerned Eliot was
that McMillan "made very little of the contact with the families," a weakness
Eliot would attempt to remedy in her own nursery school work in Boston.[21]

Despite such criticisms and her disappointment with Margaret McMillan's
lack of "scientific spirit," Eliot was impressed by what she had seen in
general and encouraged by contacts with other nursery educators. She visited
the Manchester nursery school run by Grace Owen, the sister-in-law of
Teachers College psychologist James McKeen Cattell and a Teachers College
graduate herself. She found Owen to be scientific and "broad minded" and
enjoyed their conversations enormously. On her way home from England,
Eliot stopped in New York and met with Patty Smith Hill, who recommended she also visit in New Haven with Arnold Gesell at Yale. She finally
returned to Boston in 1922, enthusiastic about starting her own nursery work
with poor children.[22]

On January 22, 1922, when Abigail Eliot first walked into the Women's
Education Association day nursery at 147 Ruggles Street in Roxbury, she
saw her main challenge the creation of a stimulating educational environment. The Roxbury section of Boston, which then included more white
children than now, was for the most part very poor. In Eliot's view, however,
the principal problem was the pedagogical poverty of the program. The old
day nursery was "spotlessly clean but oh! so dull and uninteresting." What
equipment there was, including Montessori materials, was stored on high
shelves out of the children's reach; the tables were covered with white oil-

cloth; there was no rug on the floor. Eliot and her helpers soon transformed the place by adding "low tables and chairs, blackboards, blossoming plants on low window sills, boxes of 'mighty blocks,' piano and low shelves." She also raised the entrance age to two and changed the hours from 7:00 A.M. to 6:00 P.M. to 8:30 A.M. to 4:00 P.M.[23]

Fundamental to Eliot's nursery school philosophy and practice was positive treatment of parents. "Without the active cooperation of parents," Eliot said in a report to the National Education Association in Philadelphia in June 1926, the "best possible development of very little children, physically, mentally, and spiritually" could not be achieved. Without parents' interest and help, "no nursery school can do its work really well." Nursery school teachers needed to know about children's "home relationships" so that parents and teachers could work together. This was especially important, Eliot thought, because "each moment" of a child's contact with his parents left "a supremely lasting impression on his development." A child's home was "the greatest influence in his life"; the child spent more time there "even than in an all day nursery school," and "the emotional tie and therefore the emotional drive is incomparably greater."[24]

Eliot's methods of involving parents were not new; it was the positive way she treated them that was unusual. At Ruggles Street, where parents were burdened by poverty and the need to take care of many children, conferences were often "casual"; if a mother could not come to the school, the teacher went to the child's home. Mothers were invited to visit, observe, and help at the nursery school whenever they could. And informal mothers' meetings were held at which the mothers talked about topics "connected directly with little children" and contributed examples of what they did with their children at home (185). Eliot admitted that these methods were "an old, old story to kindergartners," but she thought that nursery educators needed to learn that the key to being effective was "establishing mutual confidence between school and home" (187). Parents had "to feel sure" that the nursery school was "working for the good of the children," Eliot emphasized, and for this to occur, teachers had to feel "that every mother loves her child and truly wants to do her best for him" (188). Teachers at Ruggles Street found the parents "ready to learn and eager to help," Eliot asserted (184). She had no problem getting the school's black and white parents together for integrated parents' meetings, and some mothers became so involved they decided to become professional nursery school teachers themselves.[25]

In 1926 Ruggles Street became the Nursery Training Center of Boston, offering one- and two-year courses in nursery education for high school and college graduates, programs that included course work at Simmons College, Boston University, and the Harvard Graduate School of Education. That same year Eliot received her master's degree from the Harvard Graduate School of Education; a doctorate followed in 1930. Eliot lectured and taught about nursery education at other institutions in the Boston area, including Wheelock, Wellesley, and Lesley colleges. In 1954 the Nursery Training Center became the Eliot-Pearson Department of Child Study at Tufts University in Medford, Massachusetts, a leading center of preschool research and training today. Well before her death in 1992, Eliot saw her focus on parent involvement become the hallmark of effective modern early childhood education programs.[26]

Promoting Preschool Mental Hygiene: Arnold Gesell and the Yale Psycho-Guidance Clinic Nursery School

Psychological theorist, organizer and administrator, and practitioner-researcher, Arnold Gesell was to the nursery school movement what William Torrey Harris, G. Stanley Hall, and John Dewey were to the kindergarten movement. Like these other psychologist-educators, Gesell grew up in a small rural town and began his career as a schoolteacher. Born in 1880 in Alma, Wisconsin, he attended the Los Angeles State Normal School, where he worked with Lewis Terman and others involved in the testing movement that was sweeping American psychology and society. He then went to Clark University, where he obtained a doctorate in psychology in 1906 under G. Stanley Hall. Much influenced by Hall's genetic psychology, Gesell began formulating his own theories about the role of maturation in development and looked increasingly toward organic rather environmental causes of behavior. This turn toward organicism led Gesell to attend medical school until 1911, when he was summoned to Yale to be an assistant professor in the new Department of Education. Remaining at Yale until his death in 1961, Gesell produced a prodigious amount of research on young children's development, including his *Atlas of Infant Behavior*, with photographic documentation, and a trilogy of well-known books describing twenty alternating "inward-outward" stages of children's development between the ages of eighteen months and sixteen years. He also investigated many environmental factors affecting development and designed preventive programs and intervention models.[27]

Gesell's work linked the nursery school movement and kindergarten to the mental hygiene and child guidance movements that had been growing since the turn of the century. In 1896 Lightner Witmer had opened a clinic at the University of Pennsylvania to treat children with school problems. In 1899 Hull House member Julia Lathrop had helped start the first juvenile court in the country in Chicago and in 1909 got funding to establish the Chicago Juvenile Psychopathic Institute, a clinic to treat court-referred juvenile delinquents. Psychiatrist William Healy directed the Chicago clinic until 1917 when he went to Boston to head a similar program, the Judge Baker Guidance Center for children. Sponsored by grants from the Commonwealth Fund, other guidance clinics opened in St. Louis, Los Angeles, Cleveland, and elsewhere in the 1920s, and the movement spread rapidly. Working together, psychiatrists, psychologists, and social workers at these clinics did case studies of school-age "problem children" referred to them by juvenile courts, child welfare agencies, or parents; made recommendations and arrangements for treatment; and collaborated on broad-based prevention programs with other community agencies.[28]

Arnold Gesell was the first to recognize the importance of child guidance work for younger children and to popularize the idea of the primacy of the preschool years. For Gesell, the preschool period was of paramount importance in overall human development "for the simple but sufficient reason that *it comes first.*" But this critical time of physical and psychological plasticity was also, in the 1920s, the most neglected. G. Stanley Hall had drawn attention to adolescence, the child study and child guidance movements had added much information about elementary-school-age children, but the preschool years were a "'No Man's Land' in the field of social endeavor" and scientific investigation, in part because toddlers and preschoolers were less accessible for research.[29]

Much of Gesell's early clinical work was carried out in public schools and kindergartens in the New Haven area. In 1915 he finished his M.D. at Yale and was appointed professor of child hygiene at the Yale Graduate School on condition that he also accept the post of school psychologist for the Connecticut State Board of Education, the first such position in the country.

While studying deviant or exceptional Connecticut school children, Gesell decided that school failure was primarily due to developmental unreadiness. Settling on dentition as the best index of school readiness—the eruption of the "sixth-year molar," he stated, was a "convenient punctuation point in the development of a human being" (1)—Gesell recommended that young children be given a battery of health, psychological, and educational tests, including a dental evaluation and psychological observation, before entering school and suggested they be held back if they were not ready, a practice that was to have an enormous and sometimes problematic impact on children's lives. Pointing out that kindergartens were the agencies most "strategically situated" to detect readiness and prevent problems caused by the lack of it, he said they could serve as "a kind of vestibule or induction school" (84) where children would remain until they were developmentally ready to do traditional academic work (57).

Gesell was afraid that kindergartners were worrying too much about coordinating with the primary grades. Instead, he thought, they should be looking downward to and connecting with work being done in the fields of infant health and child welfare. He proposed a "reconstructed kindergarten" that would concentrate on four main functions: "1. the developmental education of normal children from three to six years of age"; "2. parental guidance and training"; "3. educational provision for handicapped pre-school children"; and "4. hygienic regulation of school entrance" (205–8). Gesell also described community-based models for linking health and educational services for young children (toward which advocates of comprehensive, coordinated children's services in America are still working today) (189–96) and addressed the problem of medical versus educational control of preschool hygiene, arguing that "conjoint and cooperative methods of attack must be evolved by both medical and educational agencies" (185).[30]

But Gesell's focus, like that of the child guidance movement generally, gradually shifted from preventive community- and public school–based programs serving children from poorer families to clinic-based models providing individual treatment for children from families who could afford to pay privately for the services of children's specialists. In 1920 the small Juvenile Psycho-Clinic Gesell had begun in 1911 moved and became the Yale Psycho-Guidance Clinic; in 1926 a grant from the Laura Spelman Rockefeller Memorial enabled the clinic to move again and expand its services. In 1930 the clinic changed its name to the Yale Clinic of Child Development and moved into an even larger, more elegant facility. In 1940 financial overruns and Gesell's retirement ended the clinic's association with Yale and marked the conclusion of this phase of academic involvement in practical clinical work with young children.

In its heyday, the Yale Psycho-Guidance Clinic ran a unique nursery school designed to treat problem children. Founded in 1926, the Guidance Nursery School had no fixed enrollment, instead serving individual children referred on an as-needed basis while they were being studied and treated by the clinic. As Gesell described in a 1929 national survey of preschool and parental education, the Yale nursery school varied its activities "from week to week and even from day to day" and grouped children on the basis of "special social and guidance needs" rather than age. Problem children were placed "for a period of reeducation" into a small ongoing "Regular Group" of about five normal children who attended the school for free in return for their "services" to the clinic.[31]

The curriculum of the Guidance Nursery School was determined by the specific problems and needs of the individual children attending at any given time. "Thus," as Gesell described, "a child who is referred on account of certain problems in relation to the feeding situation may be served luncheon in the nursery alone or with other children; one who is over-dependent upon the presence of the mother may have to undergo separation; or a child who is given to disobedience or temper tantrums may be faced with situations which bring out these responses." The key to solving problems, according to Gesell, was for the child's mother to sit in a hidden observation alcove and watch the nursery staff deal with the child effectively. The staff would then discuss the observation with the mother so that she could learn to modify her guidance of the child at home.[32]

Though Gesell's clinic was apparently very successful at helping problem children, in some cases the advice of experts much like those on its own staff appears to have caused the problems in the first place. Gesell described the case of "Richard," for instance, whose serious eating disorder seems to have been caused by his mother's rigid force-feeding as a result of "misinterpretation of her doctor's instructions" about the importance of regularly scheduled feeding times (171). According to Gesell, the clinic nursery school was able to help Richard and other children like him by giving mothers detached perspectives on their children's behavior and increasing their confidence in their own mothering ability. Recognizing the role of the so-called expert's advice in Richard's problem, Gesell observed that by the time mothers brought their children to the clinic they had "completely lost confidence in their ability to handle the problems presented by their children" (168). What Gesell did not see, however, was that his own widely published research on what constituted children's normal behavior may have unintentionally diminished maternal self-confidence by providing mothers with expert and highly specified norms against which to measure their own children's development and behavior.

Douglas Thom was the other clinical psychologist whose work focused on mental hygiene and guidance of preschool-age children. Thom's habit clinic in Boston was one of the major centers for habit training, the psychobehavioristic reeducation technique popular among nursery educators in the 1920s. A mélange of psychoanalytic and behavioristic psychology, habit training was used to treat problems such as feeding difficulties, enuresis, masturbation, temper tantrums, aggressiveness, shyness, delinquency, personality disorders, convulsions, psychoses, and retardation. Sponsored in part by the Community Health Association of Boston, by 1923 Thom was operating six habit clinics in Massachusetts, most of which served children from very low income families. The clinics dealt with families facing such difficult problems, including child sexual abuse, domestic violence, and extreme poverty, that Thom realized some parents were unable to carry out the advice he gave them. One mother, for instance, was not able to take her little girl to the bathroom the two or three times necessary every night to stop her bed-wetting because doing so would wake the neighbors.[33]

Like Gesell, Thom thought preschool teachers were in a "particularly strategic position" to deal with difficult family problems. He worked closely with nursery educator Grace Caldwell, to whose Play School for Habit Training he referred children. Begun in 1922, Caldwell's small nursery school in Boston's North End claimed success in changing the problematic habits of the poor, mostly Southern Italian immigrant children and families it served. Caldwell's reports contain troubling stereotypic references to the children's parents and home environments, however, and in some cases her methods seem to have caused unintended side effects. She was able to stop the temper tantrums of one child, for instance, but then the little boy developed a stammer, an outcome whose desirability Caldwell herself questioned: "In view of the development of stammering, was the temper tantrum, with its release of emotion, better at his age than regulated group pressure toward more stable behavior?" Like Gesell, Caldwell seems to have been unable to see the implications of this observation for her own practice.[34]

Arnold Gesell had an enormous impact on the nursery school movement. His normative studies of children's development and behavior provided guidelines that were used for years to come. His conception of school readiness was to have a long-lasting and powerful influence on school entrance age, placement, and retention policies. His recognition of the need for developing a comprehensive collaborative model of preschool education and health care remains a goal of children's advocates today. By the end of the 1920s, however, Gesell's work, like that of the child guidance movement generally, was limited primarily to clinic-based, fee-for-service private practice for upper-income families. The nursery school, too, was becoming a program for children from families who could afford to pay for private preschool education.

Educating Parents of Young Children: Edna Noble White and the Merrill-Palmer School

Parent education had changed radically since the days when kindergartners like Susan Blow would give mothers lectures on topics such as Greek philosophy and classical literature along with Froebelianism. Where kindergartners stressed culture, moral education, character training, and socialization for voluntary participation, nursery school educators emphasized psychology, mental hygiene, social adjustment, and habit training. Kindergartners encouraged mothers to be concerned for the public good and take responsibility for "other people's children"; nursery school educators focused primarily on private child rearing and on how mothers could be more effective with their own children.

The clientele for parent education changed as well. Though some parent educators in the 1920s focused on poor, immigrant, and African-American families and the adequacy of lower-class parents was a topic of much concern, most nursery school–based parent education programs were directed at middle- and upper-class parents. Not surprisingly, the main audience for parent education programs and literature was college-educated mothers. Unlike the first generation of college women, many of whom had remained single and become leaders of the social programs that grew out of "woman's sphere," the second generation of college-educated women often married, had children, and stayed home while their children were young. In lieu of listening to their mothers and other traditional sources of information about child rearing, these college-educated women turned to women like themselves, who, though they were not mothers, took it upon themselves to popularize modern scientific ideas about mothering.

These college-educated professionals saw ineffective parenting as a social problem of major proportions. Nursery school educators helped run parent education programs and produced an enormous new parent education literature. By 1928, parent education programs existed in twenty-five states and the District of Columbia, and between 1922 and 1928 fifty-three national conferences of various organizations included discussions of preschool and parental education.[35]

Preschool educators played important roles in the two main national parent education organizations: the Parent Teacher Association and the Child Study Association of America. The Parent Teacher Association, which originated in the kindergarten movement as the National Congress of Mothers, was dominated by the ideas of G. Stanley Hall and grounded in Progressive notions of social reform. The PTA was led by second-generation kindergartners such as Lucy Wheelock, who in 1920 published a parent education book. Exemplary of this older, kindergarten-style parent education, Wheelock's book, *Talks to Mothers*, emphasized maternal caring rather than psychology and told mothers they did "not need any scientific training . . . only the loving, watchful observation of one who wishes to know the meaning of all that she sees."[36]

The Child Study Association of America also grew out of the kindergarten movement but promoted a more modern style of parent education, espousing the usefulness of academic psychology research rather than common sense in child rearing. Started in the 1890s as a small cooperative kindergarten and mother's study group run by and for middle-class German-Jewish women in Felix Adler's Ethical Culture Society in New York City, the Child Study Association was led by Sidonie Matsner Gruenberg and her husband Benjamin Gruenberg. By the 1920s the Child Study Association of America had become an influential national organization that sponsored conferences, classes, study groups for parents, and publications, including the popular journal *Child Study*. Some of the association's efforts focused on reaching lower-class mothers, and its Inter-Community Child Study Committee, established in 1929, formed and coordinated separate African-American child study groups.[37]

Recognizing the immensity of the need for parent education, in 1925 the Child Study Association of America started the National Council of Parent Education to coordinate parent education groups nationwide, appointing Edna Noble White as its chairwoman. White's background in home economics, another of the new women's professions that assiduously applied science to domestic issues, lent additional expertise to her work in nursery and parent education. Born in 1879, White graduated from the University of Illinois in 1906, taught high school, became a member of the home economics faculty at Ohio State University, and distinguished herself during World War I through her Council of National Defense work as director of food conservation in Ohio. In 1919 White was named director of the Merrill-Palmer Motherhood and Home Training School in Detroit, a unique private institute begun with a three million dollar bequest in the will of Lizzie Merrill Palmer, the wealthy, childless wife of Ohio Senator Thomas W. Palmer.[38]

At the core of Edna Noble White's ambitious plans for the new Merrill-Palmer School was the establishment of a model nursery school. Like Abigail Eliot, White went to England in 1921 to study nursery education with Margaret McMillan and others, but, unlike Eliot (whom she met in England), she found that McMillan's emphasis on children's physical health fit well with her own training in home economics and nutrition. For the nursery school that opened at Merrill-Palmer in 1922, White hired an English head teacher who followed McMillan's practices, including "daily inspection by a nurse each morning as a safeguard against the spread of infection; the glass of water; the tomato juice and cod-liver oil; the toilet, the dinner; the nap; the round of daily duties; the monthly weighing, measuring, and occasional visit to the dentist or other specialist." The Merrill-Palmer program served fifty-five physically and mentally normal children from "many types of family background within the wide range of the so-called 'middle class.'" The children, who ranged in age from eighteen months to five years, were divided into two groups, one including the whole age range and the other made up of younger children, and attended school from 8:00 A.M. to 3:00 P.M.[39]

The special mission of the Merrill-Palmer School, as set out in Lizzie Merrill Palmer's legacy, was to train young women for motherhood. Though Edna Noble White was not a mother herself—she lived with her sister and acted as foster mother for her brother's two sons—she cared deeply about the problems of families and felt that families needed individual counseling in addition to the group mothers' meetings advocated by the kindergarten movement. This "shift in the focus of attention from the individual child to the whole family" and the concomitant "shift from group discussions with parents to consultation on an individual basis" were White's main contributions to parent education. The nursery school collected and disseminated enormous amounts of information about young children and their families. New parents were interviewed and filled out lengthy questionnaires about their children's developmental histories. School lunch menus were sent home weekly, and parents were asked to send in information about what their children ate at home. Home visits, individual family counseling sessions, monthly parent meetings, and special courses on behavior problems and training methods rounded out the parent education program.[40]

Under White's direction, Merrill-Palmer became world famous as a center for parental and preparental education. Through cooperative arrangements with colleges and universities, undergraduates took courses for credit at Merrill-Palmer, and there was a special year of study for graduate students on topics in child development and nursery and parent education. During 1924–25, for instance, ninety college seniors and twenty graduate students from eighteen different colleges and universities were enrolled at Merrill-Palmer, along with eight students doing nursery school training. All these students also worked in the Merrill-Palmer nursery school.[41]

White extended Merrill-Palmer's original mission to include the study of child development as well as parent education, and in 1921 she hired Helen Thompson Woolley to direct the nursery school and head up research. Woolley, who was one of the preeminent female psychologists in America when she came to Merrill-Palmer, had studied philosophy and psychology at the University of Chicago under John Dewey and James R. Angell and done extensive research on child labor while working for the Bureau of Investigation of Working Children in Cincinnati. At Merrill-Palmer, she began conducting research on young children's personalities and development. Concentrating on children's mental and emotional development, she found evidence to support the benefits of nursery education. For example, when testing children attending the Merrill-Palmer School and a similar group of children on the waiting list, Woolley found that the intelligence quotients of the children enrolled at the nursery school were "going up at a spectacular rate as compared with the children on the waiting list."[42]

Like others in the first generation of college-educated career-marriage advocates, Woolley saw nursery schools as a benefit to mothers as well as to children. "What the nursery school does for the child is important," she told the participants of a parent education conference sponsored by the Child Study Association in 1925, "but it is by no means the whole story." Having mothers and children "together all of the twenty-four hours a day up to five years of age" could be bad for both; she knew, she said, because she had tried it. The "emotional pitfalls" and intensity of the mother-child relationship created overdependence that could be problematic, Woolley stated. Conscientious, "executive"-style mothers ended up "bossing and dominating" their children, while "nervous and fearful" mothers worried about everything that could go wrong. Removing young children from the home for part of the day diminished the potential for these emotional problems.[43]

Woolley did a series of classic individual case studies on the emotional development of three young children that showed how nursery school attendance could improve personality problems. "Agnes," according to Woolley, was a "dominant personality in the making" whose "intense egoism and selfishness" was channelled into healthier paths at the Merrill-Palmer. A bright, active child of middle-aged parents, Agnes was used to getting enormous amounts of adult attention. After a year at nursery school, her IQ went up twenty-one points, a gain Woolley considered "not at all unusual," and though her behavior regressed over the summer when she was home alone with her parents, Agnes was learning to take turns with other children. Woolley predicted that Agnes would continue to be an "independent, executive type" but that after attending nursery school her dominance problems would lessen and might even be converted into a strength.[44]

Woolley also analyzed "Peter," a four-year-old boy who attended Merrill-Palmer for only nine months whom Woolley thought was a juvenile court problem in the making. The son of an abusive, alcoholic father and an abused, neurotic mother, Peter, according to Woolley, witnessed family violence at home, cringed from teachers at school, and had a "crafty," evasive, dishonest personality. After a short while at the nursery school he became more emotionally stable, but his personality problems recurred, and his IQ dropped when his family moved away from Detroit. Woolley was convinced that Peter's probable delinquency could have been prevented and his "antisocial tendencies corrected" had he stayed at Merrill-Palmer longer. "Peter could be at least an average and well-behaved child," she sadly concluded, but she feared the likelihood was small that he would turn out well.[45]

Woolley's third case study, "David," provided the most dramatic evidence of the child-saving potential of the nursery school. David, who had spent the first two years of his life in an orphanage and then been adopted by a well-to-do businessman and his college-educated wife, arrived at Merrill-Palmer at the age of two and a half with the mental abilities and behavior of an eighteen-month-old. He could barely talk, and the staff was unable to get him to complete any of the items on the Stanford-Binet intelligence test. After about a year in nursery school David had progressed but was still noticeably behind; his IQ was eighty-five, and he had become difficult to manage. The nursery school staff thought he was retarded and informed his mother, who was greatly distressed. The head teacher then began working with David intensively to teach him how to complete tasks. With special help he began to progress more quickly, and by the time he left Merrill-Palmer he had an average IQ score, and all that remained of his retardation was his continuing passivity and inability to take initiative. After just 423 six-hour days in the nursery school, David was a normal child.[46]

While engaged in this casework at Merrill-Palmer, Woolley saw the need for better tests to assess young children's development, and, with Elizabeth Cleveland, who became Woolley's close friend and companion after her husband left her in 1924, she developed the Merrill-Palmer Scale of Mental Tests, a graduated sequence of tasks for young children based on Maria Montessori's sensory materials. Cleveland's *Training the Toddler* (1925) documents Woolley's research and provides an example of the somewhat invasive, maternalistic Merrill-Palmer approach to parent education. Cleveland began by positing the right of the state to intervene in the private family to protect the rights of the child. "The modern state," Cleveland wrote, "in its exercise of power of guardianship, asserts with confidence and emphasis its right to intervene between parent and child to protect the rights of the child in behalf of the citizen of the future." But the state waited too long before intervening, Cleveland argued. There were untrained parents in American cities whose "unfortunate babies" could be seen "late at night falling asleep in crowded street cars, or pitifully wide-awake at the movies." And even middle-class mothers neglected their preschool-age children, Cleveland stated, by turning them loose in the yard and ignoring them.[47]

Parenthood and childhood needed to be standardized, Cleveland argued, and the goal of Merrill-Palmer's parent education programs was to provide this necessary standardization. Cleveland then described standards for ensuring children's optimal physical, mental, emotional, and social development, emphasizing that absolute regularity was the key in all four areas. Healthy physical development, for instance, required an "unrelenting regularity" in which parents kept a "constant and careful watch" over diet and habits. "No guesswork is tolerated, no irregularities in daily schedule are allowed," Cleveland insisted (36). Moreover, mere compliance was not enough; this "regimen" had to be "practiced with willingness and joy" (55).

The nursery school could provide this "unrelenting regularity" better than the home (92). An adamant behaviorist, Cleveland blamed parents for all of children's problems and warned against "the danger of excessive affection" (98). She described cases of young children who acquired phobias from unthinking parents who did not understand the importance of maintaining "a cheerful atmosphere" and an "unflinchingly pleasant emotional tone" (104). In conclusion, Cleveland stated that the only two failures she had ever seen at the Merrill-Palmer nursery school were caused by mothers, not by the school. "In both cases," she asserted, the mothers could not "be brought to see or admit the difficulties, but continued to excuse and explain and deny without any real attempt to cooperate" (145).

Helen Thompson Woolley served as vice-president of the American Association of University Women from 1923 to 1925 and was instrumental in moving that organization toward greater involvement with issues concerning parenting and preschool-age children. Edna Noble White chaired the National Council of Parent Education for twelve years and was Lawrence K. Frank's special adviser for parent education. In 1925 Woolley left Merrill-Palmer to head the new Institute of Child Welfare at Teachers College, the flagship of Rockefeller's parent education efforts, which Patty Smith Hill helped organize. But it was not to be. Separated from her husband and in poor health, Woolley suffered a breakdown and turned over her position to Lois Hayden Meek, the young psychologist who had headed the AAUW's child study campaign. Though it operated two nursery schools, produced some research, and was instrumental in the founding of *Parents Magazine*, the Institute of Child Welfare never fulfilled Rockefeller's hopes for integrating parent education into academia. In 1930 Lawrence Frank left Rockefeller, funding was cut, and the parent education movement dwindled. Edna Noble White continued at Merrill-Palmer, but parent education gradually became mostly an adjunct to suburban and campus nursery school programs.

Studying Young Children's Development: The Preschool Laboratories at the Iowa Child Welfare Research Station

The other main strand of research that influenced preschool education was more descriptive than therapeutic, though most nursery schools in academic settings combined these functions to a greater or lesser extent. The primary purpose of the Preschool Laboratories located at the State University of Iowa in Iowa City was to provide baseline data on normal young children the better to enhance their development, not to cure their problems. Unlike Yale and other guidance clinic nursery schools, Iowa admitted children "on the basis of physical and mental normality" (director Bird Baldwin called them normal and "superior" children) rather than exceptional children with problems or children from poor or pathological families. In addition to being a site for research in child development, the Iowa Child Welfare Research Station was also committed to the dissemination of information about young children and sponsored extensive, statewide parent education programs.[48]

The Iowa Child Welfare Research Station was the brainchild of Cora Bussey Hillis. The daughter of a Civil War general and wife of the mayor of Des Moines, Hillis was involved in all manner of child welfare causes, including the Child Study Association, the National Congress of Mothers, and the founding of the first children's hospital ward and juvenile court in Iowa. The experience of raising her severely handicapped younger sister and the deaths of three of her own children gave her a strong personal motivation to seek information about improved child care and education. After wading "through oceans of stale textbook theory written largely," she guessed, "by bachelor professors or elderly teachers with no actual personal contact with youth," Hillis came up with the notion of a program to study children scientifically "by the same research methods that we give to crops and cattle." In 1901 she began presenting her plan to a succession of state university presidents. Finally, in 1914 Dr. Thomas H. MacBride, president of the University of Iowa, said yes. Psychologist and dean of the graduate college Carl Emil Seashore also supported the idea. After much pressuring of the state legislature, in 1917 a bill appropriating fifty thousand dollars was passed, and the Iowa Child Welfare Research Station was organized, finally opening in 1919, after Bird T. Baldwin returned from Washington, D.C., where he and other psychologists had been developing the first army intelligence tests used for screening recruits.[49]

Before receiving his doctorate in psychology from Harvard in 1905 Baldwin had been a teacher. He had studied in Germany with Wilhelm Wundt and made the pilgrimage to Froebel's birthplace. Like so many American psychologists in the 1920s, he was obsessed with testing and measuring human characteristics. But Baldwin believed that IQ was not the only important index of children's development and worried that it was being overused. "We cannot afford to promote the children on their I.Q.'s alone as is being advocated in this country in a very broad fashion," he warned a group of kindergarten teachers. He thought children should be assessed in six "parallel and inter-related" ways—chronologically, physiologically, mentally, pedagogically, socially, and morally—averring that in normal children these different "ages" were usually nicely balanced. Baldwin and his colleagues conducted multitudes of tests on the children in the Iowa Preschool Laboratories to test this hypothesis, reporting their findings in 1924 in *The Psychology of the Preschool Child*. Translating this mountain of data into useful information for parents and preschool teachers did not prove to be an easy matter, however, as they and other researchers began to discover.[50]

Funded in part by a grant from the Laura Spelman Rockefeller Memorial, the Iowa Child Welfare Research Station sponsored a number of parent education projects to disseminate information they had gathered. Beginning in 1924 it helped organize supervised child study groups around the state. Radio lectures on child study were begun in 1925 and expanded to include broadcasts of child study group sessions in 1933. An annual state conference on child development and parent education was begun in 1927, and numerous books, pamphlets, and journal articles were published. Issues of the *University of Iowa Studies in Child Welfare* reveal, however, that researchers found it increasingly difficult to provide the kinds of direct applications of psychology to practical problems that Cora Bussey Hillis had hoped they would. A study of factors in the home, for instance, began by stating "much more will have to be known about the home and many more factors will have to be isolated and experimented with before either the status or contribution of the home environment in relation to the influence and development of the child's personality can be determined." And a study of 166 preschool parents' knowledge of and attitudes toward corporal punishment, preschool education, thumb-sucking, the use of praise as a means of control, and children's self-expression concluded only that "analysis of the data indicated that a significant number of parents did not recognize the implications of the generalizations as applied in the tests."[51]

The Iowa Child Welfare Station's Preschool Laboratories provided more practical information to nursery school educators and parents. Administrative supervisor Ruth Updegraff's *Practice in Preschool Education* (1938) was used as a textbook in preschool education courses nationwide. Updegraff's approach tended to be experimental and questioning rather than dogmatic and certain. She did, however, describe in detail the programs and practices of the Iowa Preschool Laboratories. There were four nursery school programs enrolling about a hundred children from eighteen months to five years old divided into groups by age. All the children attended half-day sessions, except for a special Preschool Home Laboratory mixed-age session begun in 1925 that ran from 9:00 in the morning to 3:00 or 4:00 in the afternoon. Like most other nursery school educators, Updegraff emphasized that the Iowa preschool programs were "a supplement to the home, not substitute for it." Parents had to be ready to rearrange their plans at the last minute as the children were examined each morning by a nurse and sent home if there were "any suspicious signs . . . a nasal discharge, a red or irritated throat, or a persistent cough or sneeze." Inspections such as this were routine practice in nursery schools in the 1920s and point up the general orientation of preschool education toward meeting the needs of young children first and of their families second.[52]

This primacy of children over parents was exemplified by the gradual shift of nursery schools from full-day to half-day schedules, a trend encouraged by George Stoddard, who took over as director of the Iowa Child Welfare Station when Bird Baldwin died in 1928. In 1932 only about a quarter of nursery schools were half-day programs, the other three-quarters ranging in length from three-and-a-half to twelve hours. Stoddard's advocacy of half-day rather than full-day preschools appears to have been primarily economic, but it reflects the relatively small number of middle- and upper-class mothers in the workforce in the 1920s, as well as the presence of lingering concerns about fatigue and maternal deprivation and a lack of understanding of women's interests. Stoddard stated that taking care of young children privately at home was the most economical arrangement because although a mother might hypothetically use this time to earn money, child care usually took over a "low pressure area in her scheme of things previously occupied by excessive attention to small duties and pleasures." Half days at preschool were sufficient for young children's educational needs, and they were better overall because they were "simpler," cheaper, and avoided "any danger of overstimulation or fatigue." The "ideal arrangement," Stoddard concluded, would be "a half-day for mother and child together in the home, with the child in the nursery school for the other half, while the mother is free to add to the family budget, or her own enjoyment as opportunity and preference dictate."[53]

Nursery schools were also started at numerous other public universities and state colleges in the 1920s and early 1930s. Most of these programs, among the better-known of which were the laboratory schools at the University of California at Berkeley and at Los Angeles and at the University of Minnesota, served as sites for both teacher training and research. Though the South was generally slower to adopt educational innovations like the kindergarten and the nursery school, nursery schools for white children were started in the 1920s at the University of Georgia and at George Peabody College in Nashville, Tennessee. Some of the historically black colleges in the South also sponsored nursery schools. African-American educator W. McKinley Menchan argued that if black colleges were to build even higher, they had "to go further downward in order to lay a firmer foundation"; it was thus "incumbent upon the Negro college to take the lead in establishing this most worthy institution . . . for children of the Negro group." Menchan himself started one of the first nursery schools for African-American children in the South at Alabama State Teachers College in Montgomery in 1930. A psychologist who went on to write a popular book on child development and parent education, he did not consider the nursery school at Alabama State "a mere child-parking place for mothers who are employed, nor is it a dumping place for mothers who desire a few hours of daily freedom from the care of their young children"; the program enrolled children from twenty-two months to five years of age for daily six-hour sessions. Laboratory nursery schools for black children were also started at Spelman College in Atlanta, at Grand View State College in Texas, and at Hampton Institute in Virginia. Unlike the Alabama State nursery school, however, which Menchan described as a model "baby-size world" in a specially constructed building, the nursery school at Hampton was housed in a foods laboratory, shared space with the home economics department, and sounds as if it may have been as oriented toward vocational training as Hampton's kindergarten program was.[54]

The research of academic psychologists such as Bird Baldwin and George Stoddard at the University of Iowa Child Welfare Research Station provided much of the groundwork for modern developmental psychology. Ruth Updegraff's and Beth Wellman's documentation showed how academic researchers and preschool educators collaborated in the 1920s and early 1930s to produce exemplary nursery school programs and preschool education texts and guides. But the efforts of researchers at laboratory preschools at Iowa, UCLA, and elsewhere also showed the divide that was developing between basic and applied research.

Coordinating Women's and Young Children's Interests: Ethel Puffer Howes and the Smith College Cooperative Nursery School

The cooperative nursery school Ethel Puffer Howes started at Smith College in 1926 was part of an ambitious program to research ways of coordinating women's interests with those of their children. A focus on the legitimacy of women's needs was unusual in the nursery school movement, which generally required mothers to subordinate their interests to those of their children. Howes's ultimate failure to institute a way of maximizing mothers' and children's interests was prophetic of the dilemma working mothers still face in America today. Ethel Puffer Howes's own life and career made her acutely aware of the difficulties facing the new generation of college-educated women and mothers trying to combine their personal and professional interests. Born in Framingham, Massachusetts, in 1872, Howes graduated from Smith College in 1891, studied aesthetics in German universities, and then completed work for a doctorate in psychology under Hugo Münsterberg at Harvard in 1898. In 1899 she was asked to join the Harvard psychology faculty, where she taught as an assistant, though her name was not listed in the catalog. Knowing that Harvard would not award a doctorate to a woman, Howes wrote to Radcliffe, which offered her and three other women doctorates in 1902.[55]

One of a small but growing number of career-marriage advocates, Howes was determined to continue working after her marriage in 1908 and subsequent motherhood. Having been turned down for jobs because she was married and facing enormous difficulties combining career and motherhood, she decided to concentrate her considerable intellect and energies on helping other women solve the problems she faced. To this end, she began promoting home-making and child care cooperatives, an idea that socialists and feminists such as Melusina Fay Pierce, Marie Stevens Howland, and Charlotte Perkins Gilman had advocated in the 1870s, 1880s, and 1890s. Howes chaired a committee of the American Association of University Women on "Cooperative Home Service," and in 1925 with the award of a grant from the Laura Spelman Rockefeller Memorial, she convinced her alma mater to let her experiment with putting into practice her ideas about integrating women's interests.[56]

Howes's novel program, the Institute for the Coordination of Women's Interests (ICWI) was designed to find ways of helping well-educated women continue to use their educations after marriage and motherhood. Howes thought educated women were wasting their education if all they did after becoming mothers was stay home and raise children. Like Harriet Johnson and others, she was also convinced that being solely a mother was unsatisfying to many women. The "disuse after marriage of special powers which it has cost much in money, time and effort to achieve," she asserted, was a "source of much personal regret, in some cases mounting to unhappiness." This was what Howes called the "mother's basic problem" in an address to the Child Study Association in 1925, "the conflict between the traditional, invariable, and therefore generic demands of wifehood and motherhood" and a woman's own individual self-fulfillment. In fact, Howes thought that women's "suppressed desires" and "suppressed powers" were the cause of many personal problems and "instability." The purpose of the ICWI was therefore the "conservation of valuable social material"—that is, women's lives and productivity—and promotion of the mental health and liveliness of educated women.[57]

Howes focused on two approaches to solving the problem of waste and unhappiness: providing new services that would make it possible and easier for mothers to work outside the home and promoting new part-time careers. Socialistically oriented, though less radically so than were Pratt and domestic revolutionaries like Charlotte Perkins Gilman, Howes had studied the cooperative nursery school organized by faculty wives and students at the University of Chicago in 1916 and was very impressed by the Merrill-Palmer nursery school, which she had visited. This research convinced Howes that the solution to women's problems lay in their banding together to care for their families communally. To this end, she designed two special programs to help working mothers. The Home Assistants Service, directed by Esther Stocks, provided mothers of children in the nursery school with trained home helpers. Howes and Stocks carefully distinguished the helpers' role from that of servants or home economists; though she helped with laundry, housecleaning, child care, and cooking, the helper was "an apprentice to family life."

The Cooked Food Supply Experiment, directed by Doris M. Sanborn, supplied nursery school families with inexpensive healthy dinners that they could pick up or have delivered to their homes. Families were charged fifty cents per portion, were given a menu from which to choose, and could even get "special cakes, cookies, or muffins, and so forth" if they ordered in advance. The food service was so popular that it was expanded to include Sunday as well as weekday dinners. And for a small fee of two dollars, families could have the food service plan their meals and provide a week's worth of nutritionally sound appetizing menus for them to cook themselves.[58]

The ICWI's first experiment, however, was to start a cooperative nursery school based on the philosophy of parents being responsible for their young children's education as a group. Howes cited Robert Owen's communitarian child-rearing experiment in New Lanark and recommended use of Margaret McMillan's book as the primary source on nursery practice. In the summer of 1925, she explained the idea for the cooperative nursery school to a group of local parents. After a series of organizational meetings, the nursery school opened in the fall of 1926, with Dorothea Beach, a graduate of Simmons College and former head of home economics at Temple University, as its principal and Dorothy Williams, a graduate of Columbia University who had been a student assistant at Merrill-Palmer, as its head teacher. One mother was hired to prepare meals for the children, and another, a nurse, examined the children's throats each morning. Each of the other mothers assisted for one morning every other week. The parent advisory board raised money to buy equipment and, by the end of the first year, took over operation of the school under an agreement with Smith's Education Department.[59]

Howes saw the parents' assumption of responsibility as proof of the success of the cooperative nursery school experiment and documented how the nursery school had achieved its goal of freeing women for work or other endeavors. Of the twenty-four mothers whose children were enrolled for the 1926–27 school year, nine worked for pay (six full-time and three part-time), one volunteered in community service, and one received "needed release from overwork, and the mothers who did not work outside the home found the nursery school to be a great benefit to their mental health. As the president of the parent organization, Mary Thayer Bixler, reported, most of these women shared the sentiments of one mother who said, "I don't seem to have acquired any free time and I haven't made any intellectual contributions and I haven't developed my talents, and I haven't earned any money . . . but . . ." The big "but" was that they had regained their "serenity"; their lives had become "less complicated." This was the goal Howes had hoped to accomplish: allowing mothers to lead more "balanced well-integrated" lives and somehow "keep the thread" of their outside interests while married.[60]

The other important measure of success was that Howes, the teachers, and the parents felt the nursery school was good for the children. The school was open from 8:30 in the morning until 4:30 in the afternoon. Some of the children, who ranged in age from two to five years old, stayed all day; others stayed just for the morning. They played indoors and out, ate, took a nap, and then played outdoors again until they were picked up. Though habit training was practiced at the nursery school, the prevailing atmosphere appears to have been relatively relaxed. The plan, according to Howes and Beach, was to leave the children "as free as possible" so they could develop "initiative, self-reliance, imagination, concentration, and cooperation."[61]

Despite Howes's glowing reports of success, the ICWI experiment was short-lived. Howes, who commuted from her home in New York, was not perceived as part of the Smith academic community. Some faculty saw the ICWI as peripheral and vocational and may have been alienated, as Dolores Hayden argues, by Howes's remarks in a 1922 *Atlantic Monthly* article that women's education was a "solemn farce" because most female college graduates ceased professional or scholarly endeavors after marriage. Howes may also have been marginalized by her age; at fifty-six, she was part of an earlier generation whose style and values were at odds with those of Smith's younger faculty members. Despite her training in psychology, Howes was no longer engaged in the kind of "scientific" psychological research that was the *raison d'être* of the nursery schools that became popular on the campuses of Vassar, Yale, Iowa State University, and elsewhere, where academic research increasingly took precedence over other functions. Money was also a problem, of course; Rockefeller funding was not renewed, and most of the ICWI's activities were discontinued in 1931. The official reason was that, as Lawrence Frank of the Laura Spelman Rockefeller Memorial put it, the Smith faculty had found it "unintellectual and unacademic." The nursery school survived, however, and remains in operation at Smith today, though not as a formal cooperative.[62]

Nursery schools were also opened at other women's colleges in the 1920s. One was begun at Wellesley in 1926 by Education Department chairman Arthur O. Norton, who said it was designed for children whose mothers are "in business or preoccupied with housework." The head teacher, Pauline Hoadley, was a graduate of Mount Holyoke, the Wheelock School, and the Ruggles Street Nursery Training Center. Modeled after the simple cabinlike structures of the progressive Shady Hill School in Cambridge, Massachusetts, the nursery school building cost four thousand dollars to construct and had windows that could be lowered "to form an open-air room." A more ambitious nursery school project was begun at Vassar College in Poughkeepsie, New York, where in the 1920s an interdisciplinary curriculum reorganization was under way to integrate the college's courses around the concept of "euthenics," or "the idea of improving the individual through improving his environment." Dr. Smiley Blanton was brought from the Minnesota Child Guidance Clinic to head the new child study department, and Lovisa C. Wagoner, who earned her doctorate in psychology at Iowa State University, headed the nursery school. Named for a Vassar graduate whose wealthy textile manufacturer father donated the money, the Mildred R. Wimpfheimer Nursery School opened in 1927 in a handsome gray stone building in "the style of the English Manor House." The school, which enrolled children from twenty-one months to four-and-a-half years of age, who attended from 8:45 A.M. to 3:15 P.M., was the site of much child development research under psychologist Joseph Stone and is still in operation.[63]

Other cooperative nursery schools were established in the United States in the 1920s and 1930s, but none had Howes's specific focus on women's interests. Instead, programs concentrated on parent involvement as a beneficial and necessary aspect of preschool education, as Abigail Eliot had defined it. In fact, one of the first parent cooperative nursery schools in America was started in 1923 when a group of mothers from Cambridge, Massachusetts, visited Eliot's Ruggles Street school and were impressed by what they saw. "If this is good for children from this kind of home, why shouldn't it be good for ours?" they asked Eliot, who agreed that it would be. Mothers whose children attended the Cambridge Nursery School volunteered in the classroom at least half a day every week, either from 9:00 to 12:00 or from 2:30 to 5:00 (the children went home for lunch and an early afternoon nap). The "on duty" mother could either help the head teacher (who had come from Ruggles Street) or observe, depending on her skill and the children's needs, and had to provide a substitute if she could not come on a given day. Mothers who refused to participate were asked to withdraw their children. There were also Saturday workdays for fathers, and parents were responsible for the school's governance. All of this required a major commitment of time and many meetings. As a child in a cooperative nursery school was overheard to observe, "My mommy is a nice mommy but when will she not go to meetings . . . meetings . . . meetings . . . meetings?"[64]

Parent cooperative nursery schools were popular in both this country and Canada, becoming a grassroots "folk movement," as the leader of the cooperative nursery school movement, Katharine Whiteside Taylor, called it, much like homeschooling today. There were 285 parent cooperative nursery schools documented in the United States by 1950, many of them located in academic communities like Cambridge, Northampton, and Berkeley, California, where Taylor started the Children's Community in 1927. But without the food kitchens, home assistants, and other supportive adjuncts Howes designed, involvement in a parent cooperative nursery could become a full-time job in itself; indeed, even with extra help, some of the "coordinating wives" at Smith found this to be true.[65]

By the end of the 1920s nursery school educators felt their experiments had proved the worth of educating young children outside the home. Many hoped that private nursery schools might be universalized and incorporated into public school systems much the way the kindergarten had been. As E. Mae Raymond from Teachers College told the first annual Conference of Nursery Schools, which Patty Smith Hill organized in Washington, D.C., in February 1926, nursery schools should be "an integral part" of the American educational system. Nursery school educators, Raymond said, should do everything possible to prevent the nursery school from going through a long and costly wait and "guard against the needless waste suffered by the earlier movement." At the same conference, Arnold Gesell and Patty Smith Hill both urged downward extension of the school into the nursery years and more coordination among nursery schools, kindergartens, and primary grades. But the academic establishment, public school administrators, and the American public were not convinced, and the nursery school had to wait.[66]

Raymond and others understood that extending "the range of public education two years longer" would be tremendously expensive. The only "justification," other than the rationale that "the child of two or three years of age has the right to the best education that can be provided," would be "the belief that there would be a saving of something which could be weighed in the balance with that cost and at least enable the public to see that cost item with a new sense of value," Raymond stated. To find out more about exactly how much nursery education cost, George Stoddard of the Iowa Child Welfare Research Station did a study in 1933 of sixty nursery schools nationwide. He found that the median annual tuition paid was $100 per child for full-day and $58 for half-day nursery school, while actual costs per child ran about $370 a year. "Running a nursery school," Stoddard concluded, was "an expensive business" that required philanthropic, university, or public support, as parents could not be expected to meet these costs by themselves.[67]

Costs were not the only obstacle to the universalization of the nursery school. By the 1920s child welfare advocacy had convinced most Americans that poor and abnormal children needed nursery education, but two long-standing traditional arguments contested the notion that all young children would benefit from nursery education. First, nursery schools aroused old fears about precocity and hothousing. As David Snedden from Teachers College wrote, nursery schools would create "a kind of 'institutional fussiness' over babies that will be as bad in its way as the 'fussiness' of one pampered pet." Why rush children, Snedden asked, when by the age of five they would accomplish all the things they do in nursery school on their own anyway? Sounding much like Amariah Brigham and G. Stanley Hall before him, Snedden worried that nursery schools might become "moral, intellectual, aesthetic, social, and even physical forcing stations, eager to do with much solicitude for the three-year-old that which will come most naturally at five."[68]

The other old argument against the universal provision of nursery schools was that it was not a good idea to take young children away from their mothers and place them in control of the state. As a 1926 article in the *New Republic* noted, Americans simply did not accept that a "school for babies" was needed; it did not fall within "the ordinary American conception of education nor of any category of the state's functions." Though Harriet

Johnson, Helen Thompson Woolley, Ethel Puffer Howes, and others did all they could to overcome this argument, the boundaries between the private family and public society in the 1920s were impassable for any but poor or abnormal children, who were seen as already being partly wards of the state.[69]

Given their costs and this resistance, it is not surprising that the number of nursery schools in the United States grew slowly after their introduction in the 1910s. A 1928 survey by the National Society for the Study of Education listed 84 nursery schools in twenty-three states and the District of Columbia; an Office of Education survey documented 262 nursery schools in the United States by 1930. Robert Tank estimates that by 1932 there may have been as many as 500 nursery schools nationwide "enrolling between 10,000 and 14,500 students" out of a total preschool population of about 16 million. Private nursery schools gradually shortened their hours, becoming half-day programs that no longer tried to meet families' or women's needs or desires for child care. By the beginning of the 1930s, foundation support for nursery education was dwindling; psychologists were retreating to their laboratories and clinics; and nursery school educators were left increasingly alone to cope with the growing problems and daily concerns of young children in America. Only the national emergencies of the Depression, World War II, and the 1960s' War on Poverty would reverse the retreat to privatization of preschool education.[70]

Chapter 8   Public Preschools

Much of the push to make the education of young children a
public responsibility originated in the women's settlement house
networks at the turn of the century. As the story goes, the idea
for a federal children's bureau first came up in a conversation
between Lillian Wald of New York's Henry Street Settlement
(where both Harriet Johnson and Caroline Pratt had worked)
and Florence Kelley of Chicago's Hull House (which sponsored
a kindergarten and a nursery school), both of whom were in-
dignant that boll weevils drew more federal concern and research dollars than children did. Participants in the first White
House conference on children in 1909, which Wald and Kelley
helped organize, supported the idea of establishing a children's
bureau, and Julia Lathrop, another Hull House activist, was appointed director of this first federal agency for children, which
started in 1912.

Like the Bureau of Educational Experiments and many other
early twentieth-century social reform organizations, the Children's Bureau's main purpose was research and dissemination of
information. The bureau had a very small budget, but Lathrop
focused on programs that gave it high visibility. In particular,
the bureau published *Prenatal Care* (1913) and *Infant Care* (1914).
That these pamphlets became instant bestsellers is evidenced in
the hundreds of thousands of letters the bureau received shortly
after publication from women asking for advice on child rearing.
However, though most of the replies to these letters were reasonable and helpful, the bureau's advice givers do not appear to
have recommended preschool education, possibly because they
thought it was either unavailable or unaffordable to the majority
of families. A California mother of an active two-year-old, who
said she did not see how she was going to be able "to live until
he gets old enough to go to school or kindergarten," was sent
a reading list and the advice that it was "not necessary that a

child should have someone to amuse him all of the time," not the suggestion that she find a nursery school or start a neighborhood cooperative or playgroup.[1]

The fact that the Children's Bureau was able to organize a national children's year during World War I shows both its growing political strength and the way the war helped promote concern for children. The shocking results of army physicals showing how unhealthy many recruits were lent support to the campaign for improving children's health and welfare. Women, like men, also gained organizational expertise from the war effort. These events, followed by the ratification of the Nineteenth Amendment in 1920, culminated in the passage in 1922 of the first federal "women's bill," the Sheppard-Towner Maternity and Infancy Protection Act, which provided funds for visiting nurses and encouraged other types of parental education and well-baby care.

But Sheppard-Towner was a short-lived victory for the Children's Bureau though there was a trend toward the assumption of public responsibility for the welfare of mothers and children. The Children's Bureau had struggled against conservative resistance since its initiation. At least one congressman decried the idea of unmarried, childless women like Julia Lathrop dispensing advice on child rearing. And some mothers, particularly older, foreign-born, African-American, and Native American women resisted the bureau's advice and the invasiveness of Sheppard-Towner nurses, who promoted some of psychologist John Watson's ideas about not hugging, rocking, or feeding children on demand. The greatest resistance, however, came from the American Medical Association and doctors who saw Sheppard-Towner as encroaching on their professionalism. This powerful lobby eventually won over Congress, and the act was allowed to expire in 1929. And although later Children's Bureau directors Grace Abbott, Katherine Lenroot, and Martha Eliot (Abigail Eliot's pediatrician sister) designed provisions for maternal and child health programs and mothers' pensions that were incorporated into the 1935 Social Security Act as Aid to Dependent Children, this major federal program of public support for children was not given to the Children's Bureau to administer.[2]

The 1930 White House Conference on Child Health and Protection highlighted the tenuous position of women's and children's interests at the federal level and the concomitantly low status of preschool education before the depths of the Depression. President Hoover made a medical doctor with a record of opposition to Sheppard-Towner chairman of the conference. The conference's Committee on the Education and Training of the Infant and Preschool Child, however, was directed by John E. Anderson, head of the University of Minnesota's Child Welfare Institute, and included Edna Noble White from Merrill-Palmer and Helen Thompson Woolley, then at the Child Development Institute at Teachers College. George Stoddard from the Iowa Child Welfare Research Station and Douglas Thom from the Boston Habit Clinic were also on the committee, along with three other kindergarten and nursery school educators. But despite this representation, the committee's report recommended increased support for public kindergartens but stopped short of proposing universalization of nursery schools. Though the nursery school was "not a fad" and should be encouraged, the report stated, it was still experimental, and "any attempt to standardize it would be premature at the present time."[3]

The committee's two extensive surveys of nursery education and of young children in the home documented how few American children attended any kind of nursery school in 1930. Though 29.1 percent of the 403 five-year-olds surveyed attended kindergarten, only 7.3 percent of the 620 three-year-olds counted attended nursery school. Data collected on socio-economic backgrounds found that kindergartens were attended primarily by middle- and upper-class children; lower-class children (but only 1.4 percent of all children) attended day nurseries. The committee also collected data on African-American children and found striking evidence of racial bias in preschool attendance. Because universalization of the kindergarten had already begun, a somewhat higher percentage of African-American children attended kindergarten than nursery school, but racial discrepancies in attendance were still sharp. The survey documented that only 8.2 percent of African-American children under age five attended kindergarten, as compared to almost 30 percent of white children, and only 1.6 percent of African-American children attended nursery school or play school, as compared to 6.4 percent of white children surveyed. The survey also documented the beginnings of segregated preschool education, finding that more African-American than white children (2.2 percent as opposed to 1.2 percent) attended day nurseries. That African-American parents, if given the choice or the resources, might have strongly preferred the more educationally oriented curriculum of a nursery school to the generally more custodial conditions of most day nurseries in the early twentieth century is suggested by the fascinating finding that 13.2 percent of African-American children were being taught to read by their parents before they reached age five, as compared to only 7.6 percent of white children. But more young white children were being taught to count (60 percent of white children were counting before age five as compared to 44 percent of African-American children).[4]

The Depression of the 1930s affected the education of young children in this country much more than it did programs for elementary- and secondary-school-age children. A U.S. Office of Education survey reported that by 1928, right before the Depression, about 32 percent of American cities provided public kindergartens. Then, from 1931 to 1933, 19.8 percent of American cities reduced or cut kindergartens, more than reductions in music, art, or physical education. According to U.S. Office of Education figures, the number of public kindergartens dropped from 723,443 in 1930 to 601,775 in 1934. Moreover, kindergartens did not recover as quickly from the Depression as some other programs did. There were even fewer public kindergartens in 1940—594,647, to be exact—though by 1944 the number of public kindergartens had almost returned to the pre-Depression high.[5]

This decrease in public support for the education of young children did not go unnoticed or unchallenged. In an article on the kindergarten and the New Deal, Patty Smith Hill noted that the cuts in public support for kindergartens were being initiated by businessmen and local school boards, not by superintendents or educators who knew how important kindergartens were. To the business community, Hill explained, those "aspects of education farthest removed from the problems of manufacture and commerce" were the "least understood or appreciated." Since young children would not contribute to the economy for a long time, their education was expendable. Hill, however, thought the early childhood period was the least efficient to ignore, arguing "[this] period may be the one we can least well afford to neglect," a view now supported by much current medical, psychological, and educational research. Elsewhere, in a classic statement of maternalist policy, Hill argued that cutting kindergartens was also inherently undemocratic. Reporting that there was "*more* protection of infants and young" in Russia and Austria than in the United States, she decried the fact that "communistic and socialistic governments" did better by young children than America did. When "one whole age level . . . is ruthlessly, and often wholly cut out of the benefits of its share of the school tax, while elementary and high school boys and girls are either wholly protected, or only partially sacrificed, one's sense of justice and fair play is both shocked and outraged," she stated vehemently. If some kindergartens had to be cut, Hill suggested a fairer way to do it: kindergartens for poor children should remain open, and those for wealthier children should be turned into parent education programs with smaller staffs. Worried that some teachers of the upper grades might guard their own jobs and salaries rather than accept equitable, across-the-board reductions, Hill implored parents to help save the kindergarten.[6]

At least some parents agreed with Hill. When the School Committee in the town of Wellesley, Massachusetts, threatened to suspend "all kindergartens including seven teachers," the PTA stepped into the fray. The local newspaper carried an article by a concerned citizen saying that in "dollars and cents alone" the kindergarten was cost-beneficial because it reduced the likelihood of children being kept back in later grades, thus saving the town money. The writer, identified only as an "interested economist" (possibly a faculty member at one of the colleges in town), said that kindergartens were "as indispensable as the first or any other grade" because they promoted children's "mental, emotional, social, and physical welfare" and taught reading and numerical readiness skills necessary for success in school. In addition, because kindergartens were "such an acceptable part of the public school system now," they raised property values in communities that supported them. When the Wellesley Town Meeting convened on March 13, 1933, fifteen hundred voters showed up and stayed until past midnight to protest the cuts. The School Committee got the message and voted to maintain kindergartens in Wellesley. Not all parents were so organized, however, and many communities cut or reduced their kindergartens during the Depression. Last in, first out was the rule.[7]

Some mitigation of the inequities in public funding came during times of national emergency, but not because of concern for children's needs or rights: employment for adults, child care for the war effort, or combating poverty was the motivation. The only exception was programs for young children in dire need, but even poor or disabled children received only limited public support. And even during national emergencies, if there was not enough money to provide services, support was not guaranteed. If a program was full, new spaces were not added; young children simply had to wait until they were old enough to go to school.

Public Nursery School Experiments in the 1920s

There were a few experiments with public nursery schools during the heyday of the nursery school movement in the 1920s. Like kindergartners, many nursery school educators were initially wary of universalizing programs for two- to four-year-olds, believing that the value of nursery education had not yet been proved scientifically. Still, there was some support for the idea of establishing nursery schools in the public schools on an experimental basis. Just as Pauline Agassiz Shaw had financed a network of charity kindergartens in the Boston Public Schools, women's clubs in the Chicago area sponsored nursery school experiments in public schools, and elsewhere a few public schools and other organizations started nursery school programs as well. A U.S. Office of Education study documented 13 public nursery schools in 1931–32, out of a total of 203 nursery schools responding. All were demonstration programs, and most received outside private funding or charged tuition because state laws restricted the amounts of public school monies that could be spent on children under four.[8]

The first of the early public nursery school experiments began in the Franklin School in Chicago in September 1925 under the auspices of the Chicago Women's Club, which had operated the first public kindergartens in Chicago under Alice Putnam's guidance in the 1880s and 1890s. The idea for starting the school came from Rose H. Alschuler, widow of prominent Chicago architect Alfred S. Alschuler and mother of three sons and two daughters. Mrs. Alschuler, who was also an active supporter of the Chicago Child Study Association and the Chicago Association of Day Nurseries, was concerned about the low quality of Chicago's day nurseries. In a letter to the Chicago Day Nursery Association in 1925, she spoke of the "need to introduce higher standards and an educational program" and helped organize a fund to send "Play Leaders" to day nurseries in the city. She saw public school involvement as a way to raise educational standards for young children, not as a threat to quality or as academicization. From the beginning, Alschuler envisioned the nursery school "as a future addition to public-school education" and considered the Franklin Public School Nursery an experiment "to learn whether it was feasible and wise for a nursery school to operate within a public school."[9]

The Franklin Public School Nursery was a public preschool mental hygiene program that appears to have provided many of the child guidance services Arnold Gesell and others had hoped public schools might undertake. Different child welfare agencies in Chicago collaborated to serve the two- to four-year-olds enrolled, who were referred by social workers. The Elizabeth McCormick Memorial Fund provided health care, and the Institute for Juvenile Research served as mental health consultant. The twenty children, who came from Italian- and German-American working-class backgrounds, spent the six-and-a-half-hour school day in a twenty-seven-by-twenty-eight-square-foot classroom. Rose Alschuler hired Christine Heinig, a 1916 graduate of Elizabeth Harrison's National College of Education, to be head teacher, and there were two student teachers as well. The program received national attention and had visitors "almost daily," which may partly explain why Alschuler decided to cut the number of children enrolled to seventeen and warned other public schools interested in starting nursery schools to limit "the number of children in the group and the number of children per director."[10]

In 1927 Alschuler began coordinating a similar public nursery school experiment in nearby Winnetka. Sponsored by the Winnetka Women's Club and with the continued collaboration of cooperating agencies from Chicago, this program served sixteen two- to four-year-olds in an even smaller classroom. Like Harriet Johnson and other nursery educators, Alschuler took these space limitations very seriously and designed special indoor climbing apparatus and other equipment to maximize play opportunities. But though the small room caused difficulties—some of the children had to be sent home for naps "because there was not room enough to place and separate 16 cots"—Alschuler felt that a nursery school was "decidedly more dependent upon the personnel of its staff and the underlying philosophy and sense of organization of the Directors than upon any physical properties."[11]

The Winnetka experiment had the active support of superintendent of schools Carleton W. Washburne and was so successful that in 1933 Alschuler and a group of teachers and parents involved with the program published a handbook for other parents and teachers of young children. Intended to be a practical guide, *Two to Six* was a nursery school version of the older kindergarten manuals. In it, Alschuler denounced the tendency of modern parents and teachers to "sit lazily by and allow children to be satisfied with some sort of 'canned' home and school life" filled with "stories and songs furnished by the phonograph" and the "poor stuff which comes over the radio and which is offered in the movies." She emphasized the importance of giving children plenty of "raw materials" like clay, paints, and crayons, reprinted directions from the Bureau of Educational Experiments for how to make Harriet Johnson's unit blocks, and listed other "good" play materials, books, and phonograph records for young children, including a Mozart minuet from "Don Juan" and various classical marches and dances. The book also included a lengthy section on habit training, in which Alschuler stressed the importance of gaining the child's cooperation. "The purpose of habit training," Alschuler emphasized, was "to further the child's development as an independent and self-sufficient being." Simply forcing habits on young children was ineffective and caused resistance; parents should enlist the child's voluntary participation. The young child's "desire or 'will' to do things," Alschuler insisted, was "our greatest asset in working with him— his 'won't' is our greatest liability."[12]

Most public preschools, like the one in Highland Park, Michigan, associated with Merrill-Palmer, were run by high-school home economics departments as preschool laboratories for preparental education. Others, like those in Chicago and Winnetka, served poor children with emotional or behavior problems and were associated with child guidance facilities or county and municipal welfare programs and hospitals. A few public school nurseries, however, served normal children regardless of their economic backgrounds. In Grand Rapids, Michigan, for instance, three half-day nursery schools were started in the 1920s, two located in public school buildings. These experimental projects were explicitly designed "to demonstrate to parents and teachers the values of nursery education." Supervised by the kindergarten and primary supervisor, the "junior kindergarten" at the Harrison Park School, which opened in 1925, enrolled twenty four-year-olds and "operated on the nursery school plan, with an equipment which encourages freedom of activity and good physical growth." The nursery school at the Kensington School, which opened in 1926, enrolled two-and-a-half- to three-year-olds from the local school district, and parents from other school districts could also send their children if there was space. But though the Grand Rapids Board of Education was convinced that their public nursery schools were "worth all they cost in acquainting the public with the value of early education," they did not extend the apparently successful experiment to the other thirty-five elementary schools in town. The board of education knew that the high per-pupil cost of nursery education was prohibitive without the financial support of parents, something that was unlikely to be forthcoming in the early 1930s, in the depths of the Depression.[13]

Public Preschools during the New Deal: The WPA *Emergency Nursery Schools*

After a decade of experimentation, nursery school educators were ready when the Federal Emergency Relief Agency announced in 1933 that it was going to establish public nursery schools as part of President Franklin D. Roosevelt's New Deal to end the Depression. Though there are conflicting accounts of how the idea for federal emergency nursery schools originated, the subject apparently came up in a conversation between a staff member from the office of Harry Hopkins, administrator of the Federal Emergency Relief Agency, and Lois Meek Stolz, who had succeeded Helen Thompson Woolley as director of the Institute for Child Development at Teachers College. Supposedly, while waiting in Stolz's office, the staff member watched young children from the institute's two nursery schools playing and then talked with Stolz about starting nursery schools for poor children, asking, "Who could you employ? Nutritionists, maintenance workers, all kinds of people besides teachers!"[14]

The dual goals of helping the economy and helping young children, in that order, were clear from the outset. Assistant FERA administrator Jacob Baker was explicit about this when he wrote to Children's Bureau director Grace Abbott about the new program. Harry Hopkins's announcement of the emergency nursery schools to state relief administrators on October 23, 1933, stated that "the rules and regulations of the Federal Emergency Relief Administration may be interpreted to provide work relief wages for qualified and unemployed teachers and other workers on relief who are needed to organize and conduct nursery schools under the control of the public school systems."[15]

Nursery educators heard about the new program a few days later during a conference of their new professional organization. The National Association of Nursery Educators (NANE) had started in 1925 when Patty Smith Hill had called a group of twenty-five nursery school and parent educators and psychologists to a meeting in New York. Hill was appointed chair of this National Committee on Nursery Schools, which met again in Washington, D.C., and New York City in 1926 and 1927. The committee formed NANE in 1929. Along with educators and psychologists, public nursery school ad-

vocates were invited to join. Rose Alschuler from the Franklin Public School
Nursery was named secretary-treasurer and donated five hundred dollars to
the group.[16]

The issue of public support for nursery education came up frequently at
NANE conferences and meetings, as did the issue of hours. In fact, the possibility of twenty-four-hour-a-day nursery schools was discussed at the 1927
conference in New York City. Margaret Wylie from the Cornell University
nursery school described five cases of children with mental hygiene problems
who had stayed at the nursery school around the clock for periods ranging
from ten days to eight weeks. In her summary of this session, Rose Alschuler
referred to half-day programs but termed full, five- to six-hour-a-day programs "more usual," though the question of program length was by no
means as resolved as Alschuler's remarks implied.[17]

The remarks of NANE president-elect George Stoddard at the Philadelphia
conference in 1931, two years before the FERA announcement, reveal the
readiness of nursery educators to begin experimenting with public preschools. Stoddard said nursery school workers should be proud that because
of their pioneering efforts the question of whether nursery schools should
be "established in this country under *any* conditions" had been tested scientifically and the results seemed to be positive. Now it was time to marshal
public opinion and gain major financial support for public nursery schools.
"If we are serious about this matter of universal nursery education," Stoddard declared, "we must be prepared to recommend expenditure of possibly
half a billion dollars per year on the systematic education of five million
preschool children." Prophetically, Stoddard even suggested that a large-scale
program of public nursery schools might stimulate the economy and create
jobs. A national program of nursery schools could "lead to new construction,
new employment, new careers." Nursery schools "could be made permanent
and beneficial," with nursery educators contributing all their "research and
experience" as a "dowry." Of course, such a plan would involve "a major
economic readjustment," but such bold measures were needed. Stoddard
concluded pessimistically, however (unduly, as it turned out), saying, the
"whole scheme is so beautifully logical that I very much fear it will not be
carried out for a long time."[18]

Stoddard's visionary comments may explain in part why there was so little
resistance when Mary Dabney Davis of the U.S. Office of Education announced the federal emergency nursery school program at the beginning of

the NANE conference in Toronto on October 26, 1933. The announcement gave "an overtone of reality and seriousness" to the proceedings, and a committee was immediately formed "to draw up a statement for recommending desirable organization and procedures for the development of the program." Like most nursery educators, Davis emphasized the potential of the new schools to benefit young children, not their economic effects. The emergency nursery schools, as they were soon called, would provide an environment in which "children for whom the school system is not now responsible, that is children under five years of age," would be "so normal and happy that they shall be relieved of the tensions of worry and despair which are found in many homes which are suffering financial insecurity or overcrowding, due to the depression," Davis said.[19]

Though NANE members responded positively to Davis's request for support, nursery educators were worried about how quality could be maintained with the large numbers of children the program was to serve. They knew that "only with the greatest care could a large number of new groups be started without danger to the standards of nursery school aims and procedures for which we have worked so earnestly during the course of our existence." Recognizing that it would have to become personally involved in the program to ensure quality, the group formulated a set of recommendations requiring teacher training, parent education, and other provisions. The NANE committee concluded that this was their chance to experiment on a large scale and "an opportunity to broaden its services to the field of public education." They wanted to do everything possible to see that this public nursery school experiment went well (91).

Though from the U.S. government's point of view, the WPA nursery schools were primarily an emergency job program, not a public preschool experiment, this was not to be desultory make-work or unregulated custodial child care. Staff were to be drawn from the growing numbers of school and health personnel on relief. As a report on the emergency nursery schools for 1934–35 documented, a little more than half of those hired were teachers; the rest included nurses, nutritionists, cooks, janitors, and other service workers. Eligibility guidelines for children were specific as well. They were to be between two and five years of age and to come from families who were on relief. Importantly, the emergency nursery schools were called "schools" and were to be controlled by state and local education agencies. Most of the schools were housed in public school buildings, though some were in settlement houses, health centers, or other locations. Schools or other local agencies paid for rent and utilities. Most emergency nursery schools kept public school hours and were open from 8:30 or 9:00 A.M. to 3:00 P.M.[20]

Preschool educators were actively involved in the WPA nursery schools from their inception and ignored their internal disagreements to support this emergency program. Leaders of the three main preschool organizations, NANE, the Association for Childhood Education International, and the National Council of Parent Education organized the National Advisory Committee on Emergency Nursery Schools (NAC), which exercised power through a network of twenty-one regional supervisors. These supervisors, who included Rose Alschuler, Abigail Eliot, George Stoddard, and Edna Noble White, were paid out of private funds, possibly from Rockefeller, and volunteered time beyond their official hours. NAC also raised private funds to support Mary Dabney Davis, on loan from the U.S. Office of Education, to serve as the director of the emergency nursery school program at FERA. The government began paying Davis's salary in 1934, the second year of the program, when state commissioners were also allowed to hire some professional preschool specialists and teachers who were not on relief.[21]

Nursery educators sometimes found themselves at odds with the WPA. Supervisors stressed issues like staff training and parent education, while the government was concerned with expanding the program and opening more nursery schools. NAC's quality control efforts focused particularly on staff training, conducting numerous training courses and conferences at institutions such as Teachers College and the Nursery Training School of Boston and organizing in-service workshops and professional meetings for WPA staff. Another way of raising quality was to monitor the age of the children enrolled. In Massachusetts, for instance, Abigail Eliot convinced Commissioner Smith not to accept two-year-olds. Remembering her near-disastrous experience with children that age at Margaret McMillan's open air nursery school in London, Eliot told Smith that putting "people who are out of work who have been teaching high school with two-year olds seems to me very dangerous." "Two-year olds are very sensitive . . . if you do the wrong things with them, you're going to hurt them badly," she said to Smith, who agreed to set the entrance age for the emergency nursery schools in Massachusetts at three.[22]

Eliot thought the education and supervision of elementary and secondary school staff by preschool educators was the key to maintaining acceptable quality in the emergency nursery schools given the scale of the program and its rapid growth. Even though, as Robert Tank notes, the WPA nursery schools enrolled only a fraction of the some two million eligible preschool-age children with unemployed parents, one source documented that 2,979 emergency nursery schools enrolling 64,491 children opened during the first year of the program. In 1934–35, the program was consolidated into about 1,900 schools serving some 75,000 children. This was a staggering increase from the 200 or so nursery schools Mary Dabney Davis had surveyed in 1930. Abigail Eliot, who supervised the 346 emergency nursery schools in Massachusetts—more than twice as many as in any other state—said she and other preschool educators found the size of the program "so big and so frightening" that "some people said it would kill the movement." But preschool educators worked hard to keep this from happening. Eliot warned graduates of the Nursery Training Center of Boston that it was "not going to be easy and you're going to find schools that make you sick but you are going to try to get them to improve."[23]

The detailed field reports of emergency nursery school specialist Grace Langdon, a nursery educator from Teachers College whose salary was paid with private funds, document just how hard it was to maintain an acceptable level of quality. In her many trips around the country, Langdon saw high teacher turnover that made it difficult to maintain consistency. She also saw an overall teacher-child ratio of approximately one to nineteen. Inadequate space and equipment were problems, too, though community agencies and local businesses contributed supplies and materials. Langdon concluded that despite all the hard work of preschool specialists and supervisors and the "care taken by the states," "many units probably exist under the name of emergency nursery schools which in no way even approximate a good nursery school."[24]

Langdon was especially worried about some of the pedagogical practices she saw. Not surprisingly, with about 17 percent of emergency nursery school teachers having originally taught elementary or secondary grades and about 52 percent having taught unspecified older students generally, many did not understand the importance of play, and some saw their job as baby-sitting. Langdon kept being asked how the nursery schools differed from the play centers run by the recreation section of the WPA. Her answer was that there was "no distinction" between recreation and education and that it was her "philosophy that all work with young children should be on a sound educational basis." It is not clear her audience understood what she meant.[25]

The 35.57 percent of the emergency nursery school staff with no prior teaching or employment experience presented problems as well. One former emergency nursery school teacher who had been a kindergarten teacher in New London, Connecticut, described the harsh discipline an untrained staff member meted out to the young children in the emergency nursery school where she worked during the Depression and World War II. On one occasion, she recalled, this teacher forced a little girl to finish her meal against her will on a hot day and then reacted angrily when the child proceeded to throw up. Because the former kindergarten teacher had been forced to leave her job when she married, she had low status even in the emergency nursery school program and could do little to prevent such inappropriate treatment.[26]

Langdon also saw problems with pedagogical rigidity. On a trip to Wisconsin in April 1940, for instance, she visited an emergency nursery school that she thought was using habit-training techniques in a manner "more formally and directly than is consistent with the development of two and three year old children." At a conference for local supervisors in Milwaukee she stressed the need to help teachers "see how to work out a flexible informal program and to do away with the formal teaching of music, literature, etc." Langdon said she "tried to help the supervisors see how they could help the teachers to think of music, books, pictures, etc. as experiences rather than as definite steps at fixed or formal periods in the day when the children were supposed to be 'taught' how to enjoy these different experiences." Again, however, it is not clear the local supervisors or staff understood the pedagogical distinctions Langdon was trying to make between preschool and elementary and secondary education. After visiting the Community House Nursery School in Sioux City, Iowa, for instance, Langdon reported that most of the teachers' time was spent planning how to move groups of children from one activity to the next in an organized but overly strict fashion. "I missed, almost entirely," she wrote, "the free, easy, spontaneous activity on the part of both children and teachers which is one of the marks of a good nursery school."[27]

Despite these problems and pedagogical shortcomings, however, Langdon and other supervisors did not see the emergency nursery schools as a failure. Though quality varied enormously, there were some real successes. Jessie

Stanton, who had worked for the Bureau of Educational Experiments nursery school with Harriet Johnson, described the positive effects of the eighteen emergency nursery schools in New York City, where in addition to performing their educational duties the staff helped families obtain food and health care. Stanton also provided anecdotal evidence of the kinds of transformations free kindergartners had described a half century earlier. One three-year-old bilingual boy's stutter "almost disappeared," for instance, after the emergency nursery school teacher explained to the father during a home visit how hard it was for the boy to learn English and Italian simultaneously and convinced him to stop hitting the child. And working in the emergency nursery school was also changing the lives of those women teachers who had never worked before. "I never knew before that it was fun to work," one staff member exclaimed. Stanton made special mention of "Pete," the janitor who had become very involved with the children. "Pete is one of our best teachers!" she declared.[28]

Though the emergency nursery schools were meant to be temporary, nursery educators saw them as a universal preschool experiment and hoped they might become permanent. Grace Langdon frequently referred to a study by John Anderson, director of the Minnesota Institute of Child Welfare, showing that the emergency nursery schools were serving children from families that "were very nearly a cross-section of the general population [except for farmers] so far as occupational status is concerned." This implied, nursery educators thought, that public preschools were not just for the poor but for all children. But while some states interpreted the eligibility requirements more liberally than did others, figures compiled by the National Advisory Committee on the second year of the program show that 64.81 percent of the children came from families receiving some sort of federal relief aid; 23.61 percent were from families in need but not on relief; and only 11.56 percent were from families not in need. Enrollments did reflect the general population racially, however, with 10.85 percent of the children coming from African-American families, 4.5 percent from other nationalities (Native-, Spanish-, Chinese-, Japanese-, and Mexican-American), and 84.65 percent from white families.[29]

Grace Langdon thought there was a real chance that emergency nursery schools might become permanently established within the public schools. When speaking at a supervisors' conference in St. Louis in February 1940, she said, "Care should be taken to keep the staffs of the nursery school such as are reasonably possible should the time come when the nursery schools would go into the public school system." When asked about the future during a visit to Wisconsin in April 1940, Langdon said that it was the responsibility of supervisors "to carry on a program of such a high caliber that school superintendents in time may wish to take it over." And when asked the same question at a conference in Milwaukee the following May, she said there "was no guarantee but that it has been the policy from the beginning of the program to continue carrying on the program as if it were going on indefinitely."[30]

George Stoddard, who had become an adamant advocate for public assumption of responsibility for preschools, declared the WPA experiment to be a success. After reviewing the evidence on the emergency nursery schools, he estimated that the true cost of nursery education "need not be more expensive day by day than high school or college instruction" and argued any saving by not funding nursery schools was a "delusion" because "for what we save we must subsequently spend in patching up children who were off to a poor start." If preschool educators believed in the value of nursery schools, then they had to see that they were funded and made permanent. "We have before us the hard task of welding, once and for all, the needs of five million preschool children to the great body of public education," Stoddard declared in 1935.[31]

At least a little temporary welding of the emergency nursery schools and the public school systems that housed them did take place. Grace Langdon reported that in Kalamazoo, Michigan, the local kindergarten and primary grade supervisors met monthly for dinner and discussion with everyone on the nursery school staff. (What she did not add was that Kalamazoo was one of the few towns that had sponsored public nursery schools even before the Depression, so the tradition of public support and cooperation may already have been in place.) And a public school representative in Wisconsin told Langdon that they were "very much interested in building up, throughout the state, an attitude toward the nursery schools which may insure their eventual inclusion in the public school programs."[32]

But in general no real welding occurred. In fact, by 1942, when the emergency nursery school program was nearing its end, there were only 944 nursery schools enrolling 38,735 children, down from a high of almost 3,000 schools with about 500,000 children earlier in the program. Bess Goodykoontz, Mary Dabney Davis, and another U.S. Office of Education specialist involved with emergency nursery schools later concluded that though the program convinced the public that nursery schools were good for all children, that they were educationally serious and belonged in the public schools, and that the federal government had a stake in providing educational services to young children, three obstacles blocked their establishment in the public schools. First, local community agencies may have preempted the public schools in controlling programs for young children. Second, because the emergency nursery schools had their own separate staffs, they did not leave "a unit ready to continue as an integral part of an elementary-school organization" when the relief-linked funding ended. Last and most problematic was the stigma of emergency nursery schools as poverty programs for poor children only. And, of course, there was the problem of costs. The emergency nursery schools "left the double impression that nursery schools were good things for the economically underprivileged but that they were a service which local schools could not undertake without federal aid."[33]

Once again, George Stoddard had foreseen this. Noting that the state spent enough on "passenger cars alone to pay its educational bills many times over, that such incidentals as cosmetics or tobacco taken separately will pay the costs of a state's complete educational program," Stoddard thought the problem was willpower. The resources existed, but people were not willing to reallocate them to pay for the education of young children. He also suggested another possible obstacle to public preschools: "Resistance to nursery schools, like war, begins in the minds of men; presently in the mental habits of the male administrative animal," Stoddard told a UNESCO conference in Paris in 1949.[34]

The Wartime Children's Centers

Strangely, war is what it took to refocus public attention on the needs of young children and keep the emergency nursery schools from extinction, although, as before, the federal emphasis was on the war first and young children second. Preschool educators, of course, reversed this priority, as indicated by the order of topics in a 1942 article by Abigail Eliot on the welfare of young children during wartime. This article, which emphasized preventing emotional problems, planning for evacuation, and providing care for the children of working mothers, shows the increased concern for and interest in children's emotions among preschool educators in the 1930s. In academia, Freudian psychology was making inroads into behaviorism as the promises of environmentalism began to appear more elusive. In preschool education, habit training was giving way to an interest in ensuring that young children were happy.[35]

The new message that preschool educators communicated to parents during the war years was that young children needed lots of love and the opportunity to express their fears. In her 1942 book *You, Your Children, and War,* Dorothy Baruch, professor of education and director of the preschool at the Broadoaks School of Education at Whittier College in California, told parents to forget earlier behavioristic advice and, in an explicit rejection of Watsonian child-rearing methods, advised mothers to hug their children and feed them on demand. "If only I had known," Baruch quoted a mother as saying, "how much babies do need to be cuddled, I certainly would have done plenty of it. I wanted to. But I'd been warned, 'Now, leave your child alone. Don't touch him any more than you have to.'" Young children needed "a lot of affection to live with stamina in a world at war," Baruch said. She even went so far as to argue that children's talk of killing and other warlike themes was actually "disguised talk of hostility toward family members," possibly caused by deprivation of maternal affection. She did not intend this as criticism of mothers who had simply done what experts had told them to do; she merely wished to encourage them to begin to express their feelings of love now and to warn them that their children might sometimes respond with hostility.[36]

According to Baruch, who worked on the committee that planned wartime nursery schools, teachers and schools also had an important role to play during the war. She suggested that teachers use pedagogical techniques such as directed discussion and journal writing to encourage children to express their thoughts and to help them see the difference between hating the oppressor and hating the oppressed. Class sizes needed to be smaller so that there would be time for these activities. Baruch also included a very disparaging description of a regimented kindergarten class in which the teacher had all the children make identical snowmen out of clay and then forced them to put the clay back into the can, destroying what they had made. "What were the children learning about originality and inventiveness which have marked American progress?" she asked. "Nothing except to look down on these" (114). All children needed to experience more informal nursery school teaching methods, she asserted, and she exhorted parents to "rise up and demand that more instead of less be spent on education." Teaching loads needed to be reduced, and education had to "be more universally provided in the early years," she concluded (123).

As war broke out abroad, changes on the home front affected the lives of women and children. Migration to the cities, the return of full employment, and the sharp increase of women in the labor market transformed family relationships. Almost half of all American women held jobs at some time during the war, and mothers of young children joined the workforce in great numbers for the first time, increasing by 76 percent (to 1.47 million) between 1940 and 1944. This rapid entry of mothers into the workplace caused an immediate need for child care. Though most young children were looked after by relatives and neighbors, horror stories abounded about children being left home alone, locked up, or harnessed to posts while their mothers worked. But despite studies of the defense industry showing that women's absenteeism to care for young children was a serious problem and a potential threat to the war effort, there was still ambivalence about mothers of young children working outside the home. Paul McNutt, head of the War Manpower Commission, expressed the view of many Americans in his July 1942 policy statement that "the first responsibility of women with young children, in war as in peace, is to give suitable care in their own homes to their children." Women in the federal government, from the head of the Children's Bureau to Secretary of Labor Frances Perkins, concurred. And preschool educators like Abigail Eliot thought it would be better to have four-hour shifts for working mothers, as apparently happened in some British war industries, rather than trying to provide all-day child care. Even the head of the National Association of Day Nurseries opposed the idea of mothers of young children going to work.[37]

Federal policymakers preferred the idea of providing preschool education for young children of working mothers during the war to the alternative of providing child care, which was stigmatized by negative associations with day nurseries. The involvement of preschool educators in the emergency nursery schools had given them an imprimatur as sources of education rather than of custodial care, and since most nursery schools in the 1920s and 1930s operated for six or seven hours a day, they could even meet most child care needs in a limited fashion. This clearly was the view of Grace Langdon when she stated in 1940, "There is no doubt that a new need for day nurseries is imminent, which the WPA can take leadership in meeting." She kept as many of the WPA nursery schools open as she could during the transition from the Depression to the war. Then in 1942 Representative Peggy Norton, a Democrat from New Jersey, got Congress to appropriate six million dollars to expand the program—the first time Congress had officially approved of spending for preschool programs. In early 1943 the Lanham Act, which had been passed in 1941 to provide funding for community facilities in "war-impact areas," was interpreted as extending to child care programs. The WPA ended in 1943, and the nursery schools were transferred to the Federal Works Agency (FWA) and jointly administered by Grace Langdon and Florence Kerr, the head of the War Public Services Bureau. Even though the FWA administered the program, however, local communities had to seek approval from the Children's Bureau and the Office of Education to be certified as war-impacted areas, and because they were required to contribute half of the funding for their programs, almost all children's centers were run under the auspices of the public schools.[38]

There were many similarities between the Lanham Act children's centers and the WPA emergency nursery schools, but although interagency collaboration was mandated, as before, this time it did not work as smoothly. In a series of complicated maneuvers, the Children's Bureau tried to gain power over the children's centers. The War Area Child Care Act, known as the Thomas Bill, which was introduced to the Senate in May 1943, would have transferred the program to the Federal Security Agency, under which the Office of Education and Children's Bureau operated, but the bill did not pass the House of Representatives. Some historians see this as a major defeat for universalization of federal support for preschool education, something like the demise of Sheppard-Towner earlier. The bill was surrounded by controversy and infighting between various children's agencies and advocates, however, and it is difficult to predict what its effect would have been. What is clear is that the bureaucratic confusion and jockeying for control helped create a welter of red tape that made it harder for children's centers to be established and may have contributed to the program's ultimate termination.[39]

As with the WPA nursery schools, preschool educators were actively involved in supervising and running the wartime children's centers, and they raised concerns about the issues of professionalism and standards. Though there was no network of regional supervisors, a National Commission for Young Children similar to the National Advisory Committee on Nursery Schools was formed. The commission, which was headed by Rose Alschuler, served as a clearinghouse for information and administered training courses in colleges and universities. Alschuler went around the country giving lectures and published a book of guidelines for children's centers, based in part on bulletins prepared for the emergency nursery schools.[40]

Alschuler's guidelines make the children's centers sound like nursery schools, and this is clearly how most preschool educators thought of them. Like nursery schools, the children's centers could "give real assistance to parents in the handling of their children." Research showed, Alschuler stated, that the programs could supplement home child rearing and contribute importantly to children's physical, social, and intellectual development. Mothers could be better mothers, she insisted, and enjoy their children more if their children attended children's centers. Only secondarily were the centers to serve as child care; indeed, Alschuler said little about their war-related purpose, simply observing that mothers would be freed "for most of the day so that they can do other necessary work or perhaps they can relax with free minds because they know their children are well cared for." The closest she came to acknowledging that the centers were meant as child care programs was to observe that because "more and more young women with children under five are perforce going into industry," it was "important that they have a feeling that their children are protected and affectionately cared for when they must be away during the day."[41]

Like descriptions of earlier nursery schools, Alschuler's book focused on standards, daily schedules, the design of appropriate space and play equipment, and pedagogy. She suggested two daily schedules, a six-and-a-half-hour day identical to that of most nursery schools and a longer session for working mothers in which children were given supper after the afternoon nap and play period and picked up at 6:30 P.M. (55–56). She also included architectural plans for a children's center designed by her son John H. Alschuler, a senior at the Massachusetts Institute of Technology, and diagrams for how to build playhouses, storage areas, child-sized furniture, blocks, and other equipment (110–11).

The sections on pedagogy revealed the more relaxed attitude toward child rearing and preschool education characteristic of wartime prescriptive literature. Like Dorothy Baruch, Alschuler stressed the importance of young children being able to express their feelings. Habits were mentioned but were not the bugbear they used to be. Young children acquired good habits through experiential learning, Alschuler argued, not through didactic instruction. "Good manners and good habits are rather like measles and creative expression—more easily caught than taught." Eating, for instance, she said, was a "natural process," and "so-called 'good manners' will come quite naturally if children eat together in a calm atmosphere without pressures of any kind" (62).

Also like Dorothy Baruch, Alschuler emphasized that young children needed affection. "The most important thing," she wrote, "is to see to it that children get legitimate and sufficient affectional satisfactions at home and at school" (69). Alschuler's attitudes toward parents were understanding and supportive as well. She recommended that teachers put themselves in parents' places and help them find ways to solve their own problems, rather than just telling them what to do. Most importantly, she did not think there was a single, simple, correct way to deal with young children but a plurality of possible approaches, "several methods that might be tried with equal chance of success." The best hope of success was when parents and teachers trusted one another and could work together. "After all, a given plan is likely to succeed," Alschuler wrote, "not because it is the one perfect idea, but because home and school used some common sense and perhaps some technical skill in making a plan and then have supported one another in trying to carry it out" (73).

The best-known and documented of the wartime children's centers were the quasi-private, industry-based Child Service Centers run by the Kaiser Shipbuilding Company in Portland, Oregon. Portland apparently had resisted seeking Lanham Act funding for child care programs, but recognizing the critical need, Kaiser decided to open its own model programs. Funded with $750,000 of federal money from the U.S. Maritime Commission, Kaiser's programs provided six-day-a-week, twenty-four-hour-a-day education; child care, and other services to children ranging in age from eighteen months to school age. Lois Meek Stolz, who had been the first president of NANE, agreed to be director. She was assisted by James L. Hymes, Jr., who managed the daily operations so that Stolz could continue with her job at the Institute for Child Welfare at the University of California at Berkeley.[42]

The two Portland Centers, Oregonship and Swan Island, opened in November 1943 in specially designed, hub-shaped buildings with playgrounds and other special features. Kaiser was able to commandeer preschool equipment from Educational Playthings in New York and from a Chicago company that Rose Alschuler had persuaded to make complete kits of basic

materials for preschool rooms. The Kaiser centers provided even more services than those Ethel Puffer Howes had organized at Smith. As Hymes put
it, "These are good nursery schools but they are more: They are Child
Service Centers." Extra services included drop-in care for new children when
necessary, an infirmary for children who failed the daily health inspection
because of mild illness, a rental library of children's books, a store where
mothers could buy items like combs, shoelaces, and other children's items,
a mending service, and a food service providing reasonably priced meals.
Hymes and Stolz even dreamed of offering an infant service, a shopping
service, and a barber service. But model programs such as these were expensive, and wartime children's centers generally reached only a few of the
children in need of care. At their peak in September 1944, 1,005 children
were in attendance at the two Portland centers. Even with federal and industry subsidies, parents at Kaiser paid $5.00 a child for a six-day week and
$3.75 for each additional child. And this did not cover costs, as Hymes told
Edgar Kaiser. Moreover, Hymes reported, "It is incorrect to hope that with
increased volume of business a Child Service Center will eventually break
even or show a profit."[43]

The Lanham Act children's centers also charged a fee. Parents paid fifty
to seventy-five cents a day, a relatively high rate for many families in the
1940s. At its height in July 1944, average daily attendance at the 3,102
children's centers in operation was 129,357 children, a figure Robert Tank
estimates to represent only about 10 percent of the children who needed
care. There were various reasons for this. For one thing, some mothers
refused to send their children to the centers. Almost no African-American
children attended the Kaiser centers, for instance, in part, Lois Meek Stolz
speculated, because they had no African-American staff, because African-
American mothers did not think the "grandiose" buildings were really intended for their children, and because of fears that "white teachers would
hit their youngsters." In addition, most mothers still preferred in-home care
or care with relatives, friends, or neighbors when they could arrange it. A
government official also suggested that working women were averse to group
care because "to some it connotes an inability to care for one's own; to
some it has a vague incompatibility with the traditional idea of the American
home; to others it has a taint of socialism." This official concluded that out-
of-home group care "violates the mores and sentimentalism that has grown
up around the young."[44]

As with the WPA emergency nursery schools, preschool educators hoped the children's centers would be models for permanent federal support for early childhood education. Once again, however, they were disappointed. After the war, the Kaiser centers were closed abruptly, and although President Truman extended funding for the Lanham Act children's centers for six months, this was only a temporary measure. In only two localities— Washington, D.C., and California—were the centers continued and only for lower-income children and single working mothers. (Congress continued to support children's centers for poor children in Washington, D.C., until 1953; the California children's centers remain in existence but are not universal.) Still, some progress was made during the war years in establishing enabling legislation for public preschool education. Between 1942 and 1945, sixteen states lowered school entrance age to allow funding for children under six, and thirteen states passed permissive preschool laws. As American mothers of young children started returning to the workforce in larger numbers than ever before, the demand for nursery schools increased, and nursery school places were in short supply. Abigail Eliot noted that with the "withdrawal of federally-sponsored wartime nurseries, private centers are crowded so that each has a long waiting list and only one in this area is able to accept any additional children this year."[45]

The other growing concern in the 1950s was the Cold War. Many parents looked to nursery educators for help in what to say to their young children about the atom bomb. Once again Abigail Eliot had wise words of advice. It was most important, she told parents, "to reassure young children, not to pressure them." "If little Johnny is upset about the bomb," a Boston newspaper article quoted her as saying, "you must tell him flatfootedly and confidently that there isn't going to be any atom bomb dropped on Boston." And, Eliot added, with the concern for larger social issues so characteristic of preschool educators, "then you must say to yourself, 'I've got to work to see that it isn't.'" Unfortunately, however, it took another war, the War on Poverty of the 1960s, to revive public interest in the need for public preschool education.[46]

Public Preschools for the Poor: Project Head Start

Soon after Lyndon Johnson succeeded John F. Kennedy in 1963, he declared a "War on Poverty," a new national campaign to fight poverty with economic, educational, and community action programs. Project Head Start, one of the most popular and lasting of these Great Society programs, was targeted at poor children, for whom it was to provide comprehensive child welfare services including health and nutrition, and at their parents, who were to receive parent education and be otherwise involved in the program. Head Start was never intended as a universal preschool model. Run by primarily male pediatricians, psychologists, and federal administrators from the Office of Economic Opportunity, Head Start was intentionally separate from existing educational institutions and from the early childhood education establishment.

The theoretical basis for Head Start came from three strains of new psychological research that converged on the idea of using preschool education to boost intelligence. The first strain was the resurgent environmentalism of J. McVicker Hunt, whose influential 1961 book *Intelligence and Experience* was the gospel of the early intervention movement. Drawing on the work of ethologists like Konrad Lorenz, Hunt emphasized the importance of optimal early experience and the match between environment and experience. His somewhat speculative views on the incredible power of early environmental experience to modify IQ were much discussed but little debated, in part, psychologist Sheldon H. White suggests, because they served as a useful rationale for liberal social programs such as Head Start.[47]

The arguments in Hunt's book were strengthened by a second strain of research, the work of educational psychologist Benjamin Bloom. Bloom's 1964 *Stability and Change in Human Characteristics*, a study of correlations among IQ test scores at different age levels, posited that about half of human intelligence is determined by age four. Though this radically environmentalistic theory, like Hunt's, provided a good argument for funding social programs, it had an unforeseen downside: The notion of a critical period for optimal stimulation and early learning led to the concept of cultural deprivation, in which whatever was or was not happening to young children from lower-class and poor families was considered deficient, harmful, and in need of remediation. And later, when the scores did not hold up, the implied promise of permanent IQ modification again opened the door to racialist, deterministic views.[48]

The third key influence on Head Start came from the work of Cornell psychologist Urie Bronfenbrenner, whose cross-cultural studies suggested that parent involvement was the most important factor in young children's development. Bronfenbrenner talked about an "ecological" approach to early intervention in which parent and preschool education programs meshed sequentially, a view again in vogue today.[49]

It is unclear how much the theoretical psychological research on environmentalism and IQ modification had to do with the actual inception of Head Start as a social-educational program. (Sheldon White, who helped design some of the early evaluations of Head Start, says that IQ modification theory was not much discussed at the time but then became a "legend" that turned on the program.) It certainly influenced research on the program's effectiveness. A novel provision of Head Start was that scientific evaluation of the program was built in, and this meant collection and analysis of test score data, even though preschool educators complained that test scores did not capture the more subtle, holistic, and important indices of human growth, such as self-esteem and social competency, that preschool programs enhanced. Most of the psychologists associated with Head Start now say that the emphasis on using preschool education to increase IQ was a mistake (and Edward Zigler, one of the founders and directors of Head Start, says he said so at the time); nevertheless, expectations were high that Head Start would have a significant, immediate, and lasting impact on poor children's IQ scores.[50]

In December 1964 Office of Economic Opportunity director Sargent Shriver asked Kennedy family pediatrician Dr. Robert Cooke to appoint a thirteen-member planning committee to design the Head Start program. The committee included only three preschool educators (Bank Street College president John Niemeyer, early childhood specialist D. Keith Osborn, and former Kaiser Children's Center director James L. Hymes, Jr.); otherwise, members—among them, three women—were linked primarily by their association with President Kennedy's Panel on Mental Retardation. Five months later, in May 1965, Lady Bird Johnson held a White House tea to announce Head Start's inception. A decision was made to open as many centers as feasible as quickly as possible, despite potential problems with quality resulting from a shortage of qualified teachers. Dr. Julius Richmond, the pediatrician in charge of Head Start, and his staff (which grew to four hundred in a matter of weeks), along with volunteers, began contacting potential program sponsors immediately.[51]

The cast of characters was very different from the primarily female kindergarten and nursery school educators who for years had staffed the crusade for young children's education in the United States. Male psychologists and pediatricians had taken over the federal initiative in preschool education. Kindergartners, as documentation of Head Start programs in Mississippi and elsewhere illustrates, were now perceived as part of the educational establishment and thus part of the problem, not the solution. Even so, as with the kindergarten movement, influential women were behind Head Start from the beginning. It was a particular favorite of Lady Bird Johnson, who did much to promote the program's popularity with the public. Jeannette Galambos Stone, who in 1963 had taught in a preschool sponsored by the Ford Foundation in New Haven and had been considered for the position of nursery school teacher for the Kennedy children in the White House, was behind Head Start, too. And later other female preschool educators were also involved in training and evaluation for the program.[52]

The history of one of the best-known Head Start sponsors, the Child Development Group of Mississippi (CDGM), shows the importance of the civil rights movement as another component of Head Start and reveals much about the volatile nature of Head Start's intentional lack of traditional educational professionalism. The brainchild of Dr. Tom Levin, a politically radical New York psychoanalyst and social activist, CDGM was actively at odds with the public schools and also had little use for early childhood education experts. As Polly Greenberg describes in great detail in her remarkable 1969 book *The Devil Has Slippery Shoes*, Head Start was "supposed to be a preschool-medical community-action program, not a downward extension of public schools." Further, Greenberg said, somewhat less accurately, it "was known that not nearly enough professionals" existed in the fields of "early childhood education, nursery education, and research based programs for children" to staff Head Start. But CDGM's avoidance of established early childhood education was due to more than a perceived lack of potential staff. The few times CDGM sought help from the professional preschool community the results were unsatisfactory or worse. One Mississippi kindergartner brought in to do training said there was "nothing in the least unique about having a group of totally untrained people pretending to be teachers." Greenberg dismissed this woman as a "white lady kindergarten expert from the state" who "did not visit again, nor did she answer my letter and phone calls."[53]

The grassroots organizing and pedagogy with which Greenberg and others were experimenting in Mississippi had its roots in Open Education, the educational reform movement of the late 1960s and 1970s, but Caroline Pratt and Harriet Johnson would have recognized their free play methods and child-as-creative-artist expressionism in CDGM's philosophy. In fact, Greenberg did include Bank Street in the short list of good preschool programs of which CDGM approved (also mentioned were Montessori, Pacific Oaks in Pasadena, California—where Abigail Eliot taught for a while—and Martin Deutsch's influential preschool program for disadvantaged children in New York City). But CDGM's preschool pedagogy was directly and explicitly linked with radical political activism. Greenberg, for instance, had no difficulty understanding African-American families' push for early literacy: reading was the "key" to "future freedom." CDGM's "living arts project," a traveling improvisational theater workshop, was a typical example of sixties' educational reform. Intended to be an "alternative to stiff, cold 'subject' teaching," the project was conducted by theater types with no experience teaching young children, and some performances were quite crazy and chaotic. Things changed for the better after the arrival of a preschool teacher from New York who understood that "such amorphous structure, boundlessness in terms of time, space, and activity, disorder of events, procedures, and materials . . ." could make children "passive and confused in the sheer effort to keep up with the directions they are supposed to follow."[54]

In addition to the importance of reading readiness, the African-American Head Start teachers and parents Greenberg was training in Mississippi constantly brought up the issue of discipline. These parents and teachers saw a crucial distinction between discipline, which could be taught, and self-respect, which could not. Self-respect, these Head Start staff members felt, could only be learned from positive interactions with adults, not from being mistreated the way African-American children often were in the public schools. Greenberg described a "blond white" "licensed kindergarten teacher" who told a group of Head Start staff to put children who misbehaved in a "bad boy chair." Finally, "an ancient lady stood up and said with toothless passion, 'We Negroes in Mississippi have a mental block. We have been so conditioned that we feel wrong when we speak up. If we don't teach the children anything else, I say let's teach them to speak their mind. Sometimes children speak by acting, doing things. Let them. This is their freedom. Never mind obedience. They'll fit in as they grow. I wouldn't want anyone shaming my grandchildren in no chair.'"[55]

Greenberg provides a rich, idealized portrait of how CDGM served as a conduit for cultural interchange and multicultural understanding, full of heartwarming examples of black and white parents and teachers working together for the benefit of young children. What Greenberg's admittedly biased book does not deal with, however, is some of the thornier issues of race and cultural collision. Stereotypes abound. The white psychologists from New York are all idealistic reformers. The white professional educators (except for the preschool teacher who rescued the living arts project) are all racist conservatives. The black parents and teachers in training are all naturally talented and wise. There is little mention of the insecurity, anguish, and misunderstanding that sometimes accompany cross-cultural communication. Nor does Greenberg fully explain the administrative and management problems that dogged CDGM and contributed to its eventual demise. In August 1965 psychologist Robert Coles was brought in by the Office of Economic Opportunity to evaluate CDGM's operation, in part because of complaints of fiscal irregularities and pressure from conservative Mississippi senator John Stennis. Coles defended CDGM, but Tom Levin was eased out with the help of Marian Wright, then a young civil rights lawyer and active CDGM board member, who thought Levin's somewhat abrasive style was too risky for the good of the program. Levin was angry about how he had been treated and even complained of hostility and a lack of "middle-class amenities" (283).

But if one cannot help wondering whether adult politics and personalities sometimes took precious time away from the more immediate daily needs of the young children in CDGM's care, commitment to quality-of-life issues for young children and their families still comes across more clearly in Greenberg's story than it does in the extensive and expensive battle over Head Start's overall effectiveness. In April 1969 the Westinghouse Learning Corporation released a controversial report that criticized Head Start's summer program but found some modest positive outcomes for the full-year program. Coincidentally and almost at the same time, the *Harvard Educational Review* published Arthur Jensen's notorious article, that began with the sentence "Compensatory education has been tried and it apparently has failed" and went on to argue for a genetically deterministic explanation of IQ and minority children's low test scores. Much of the success of Head Start was forgotten in the ensuing loud and painful rehashing of the nature versus nurture debate. President Richard Nixon and others immediately interpreted the Westinghouse report as signaling the failure of Head Start, and numerous conflicting studies and counterstudies followed. Current accepted wisdom is that Head Start may successfully raise young children's IQ and achievement test scores but that these gains may fade if enrichment is not continued when the children attend elementary school. Though harder to measure, Head Start's positive effects on self-esteem and on parents seem to be more lasting and important.[56]

Some preschool educators expressed concerns about the quality of Head Start programs, as they had about the emergency nursery schools and children's centers. These concerns were allayed somewhat when the Child Development Associate training program was begun in 1972 with the support of the National Association for the Education of Young Children (the successor to NANE) and other early childhood education and child welfare groups. Though the CDA teacher credential has been slow to catch on, by 1994 every Head Start classroom with twenty children is supposed to have at least one staff member with a CDA or an associate's degree in early childhood education.[57]

Meanwhile, others felt Head Start might be doing too good a job in other ways. In a widely read *Harvard Educational Review* article that came out in 1970, for instance, sociologists Stephen and Joan Baratz accused Head Start and programs like it of practicing "institutional racism," "guided by an ethnocentric liberal ideology which denies cultural differences and thus acts against the best wishes of the people it wishes to understand and eventually help." Where Urie Bronfenbrenner thought massive family-oriented parent and home-based education programs needed to begin even earlier, Baratz and Baratz thought changes had to take place not in families but in schools and society. Head Start, according to Baratz and Baratz, was part of a larger "social pathology model" that had "led social science to establish programs to prevent deficits which are simply not there."[58]

Despite these criticisms from both the Right and the Left, the early 1970s was the high-water mark for public responsibility for the education and care of young children. In 1971 a coalition of groups got Congress to pass the Comprehensive Child Development Act, sponsored by John Brademas and Walter Mondale. But the bill, which would have provided federally funded child care and education and referred to establishing a "legislative framework" for the universalization of "child development services," was vetoed in November 1971 by Richard Nixon, who said it would "commit the vast moral authority of the National Government to the side of communal approaches to child rearing over against the family-centered approach." Some feel, however, that the real motivation for Nixon's veto was the bill's cost and the acrimonious debate over control of the new programs.[59]

Dissension over the issue of control arose again in 1978, when President Jimmy Carter tried to transfer Head Start from Health, Education, and Welfare to the new Department of Education. Black civil rights leaders from the South, especially Marian Wright Edelman, were adamant that Head Start remain a social welfare and community action program and not be joined to the public education bureaucracy, even though a substantial number of Head Start programs were run by the public schools. A Children's Defense Fund position paper at the time even stated that Head Start was "not an education program." Evelyn K. Moore, director of the National Black Child Development Institute, also questioned whether linkage with the public schools was a good idea, especially for black children, for whom schools were sometimes "incubators of inequality." A visit to Washington by a delegation of irate Head Start parents clinched the matter, and Head Start remained out of the Department of Education.[60]

Head Start is now considered to be one of the most popular and successful of federal programs. Its reputation was greatly enhanced by the findings of a group of studies that came out in the late 1970s and early 1980s, which showed that Head Start and Head Start–like experimental preschools had potentially lasting long-term effects. Though Head Start's short-term effects in raising young children's achievement and facilitating their transition to school are important, the Consortium on Longitudinal Studies headed by Cornell psychologist Irving Lazar and especially David Weikart's Perry Preschool Project in Ypsilanti, Michigan, have amassed evidence showing the cost-effectiveness of preschool programs in preventing later school failure and any number of other problems, ranging from placement in special education programs to teenage pregnancy, dropping out, and crime. Though some of these reports of changed lives and savings of four to seven dollars for every dollar spent on preschools smack of earlier kindergarten and nursery school transformation narratives, they have helped create a new groundswell of attention and broad-based public support for preschool education.[61]

Arguments about why Head Start is effective and what to do next are likely to continue. As Edward Zigler summarizes, the "snowballing" of children's positive interactions with teachers, the enhancement of young children's health, and the increased self-esteem and advocacy of Head Start parents are all key. The importance of parent involvement in Head Start has been a central theme from the program's initiation. Clearly, Head Start benefits parents, especially mothers. About 35 percent of Head Start staff are current or former parents of children in the program, and a book of "Head Start Success Stories" relates how parents have gone on to obtain degrees and jobs and otherwise improved their lives.[62]

As to the question of Head Start expansion, the passage of national educational goals including that children should enter school ready to learn, bodes well, but, the tensions between quantity and quality remain. To increase quality, teachers' salaries must be raised. As Head Start programs compete for staff with the growing number of public school preschool programs, Head Start will continue to lose teachers to higher-paying public schools, and the odds are that quality will suffer as a result of high staff turnover and less competent personnel. Smaller class size is also critical to maintain quality and to integrate young children with special needs. Providing extended hours and services to even younger children is also under discussion. In the long run, however, quantity is the key to universalizing preschool education, and providing quantity and access will likely mean more public school involvement. Perhaps Head Start's loyal and hard-working advocates and protectors will come to see the universalization of preschool education for all America's children as a good worth fighting for. In the meantime, hopefully Head Start will continue to receive bipartisan support despite the realignment of Congress after the 1994 elections and mood of animosity toward the poor. Children do not choose their parents and should not be punished for being born.

Conclusion

The question that guided this study was, Why is there no universal access to preschool education in America? The answer, or answers, have turned out to be various and to vary over time. European philosophers, pedagogues, and social reformers provided models, guides, and rationales for educating young children outside the home. But just when a few American children began to attend infant schools in the 1820s and 1830s, people began worrying about the potentially harmful effects of extrafamilial education and the dangers of precocity. The responsibility for early education was reassigned to mothers, who were exhorted to become teachers in the "family school" for the good of their children, society, and the new republic. In this first round, domesticity won out over institutionalization.

When a naturalistic romantic form of preschool education that assuaged fears about precocity, mimicked the home, linked women's and children's interests, and employed motherly teachers was introduced to America from Germany in the 1850s, objections to extrafamilial education for young children were overcome. Private kindergartens became popular among the upper classes, and charity kindergartens were started for the young children of the poor. In the 1890s worries about urban poverty and crime, class conflict, the ill effects of city life, and the need to Americanize immigrant children combined with the development of an ideology of children's rights to create conditions for the universalization of the kindergarten for five-year-olds in public schools.

The campaign for public kindergartens was a women's issue and one of the most successful examples of the new social and political power women held in America in the late nineteenth and early twentieth centuries. Once institutionalized, kindergartens gained acceptance as an educational reform and became permanent because female kindergartners worked out compromises with male school administrators that allowed kindergarten practices to continue within a marginalized domain. The kindergarten kept some of its unique, maternalist, child-centered ideology but also became more like school.

Private nursery schools and a few public nursery schools for even younger children were started in the 1910s and 1920s to remediate supposedly problematic parenting and to treat so-called abnormality. But because of negativity about parents, costliness, and the economic problems of the Depression, nursery schools were not universalized. In the 1930s, 1940s, and 1960s the federal government funded public preschools to provide employment and child care for adult workers and to give educationally disadvantaged children and their mothers an economic boost. Again, however, preschools were not universalized, in part because of costs, but also because they were considered to be a temporary response to specific needs and because they were stigmatized as poverty programs. The private family is still primarily responsible for providing or procuring preschool education for three- and four-year-old children in America today.

Another question worth asking is, Why should there be universal access to preschool education in America? Over the years, preschool advocates have provided a number of answers to this question, answers that, with some modifications, remain valid today. First, many families have difficulty educating their young children well. Now, as in the past, this is mostly due to poverty; recently, however, high divorce rates, an ever-increasing number of single-parent families, and other economic and social changes have made it necessary or desirable for most mothers of young children to work outside the home. Another reason for providing universal preschool education is that good preschool education is both beneficial to all children and cost-effective for society. Preschool proponents have stressed this argument for many years, and recent research has strengthened it. Investing in young children, though costly up front, may help prevent undesirable, expensive social problems later. Investing in young children is also equitable from the standpoint of social policy. The social security system has increased the incomes of elderly citizens; meanwhile, the number of children in poverty has been growing steadily since the 1980s, to the point where they are now the most impoverished age group in America. Intergenerational justice demands that young children be treated more equitably.

A final compelling argument is that all young children should have a right to preschool education, the view of kindergarten advocates like Kate Douglas Wiggin since the turn of the century. Though defining children's rights is a complex and politically charged matter, precedents do exist for providing educational services for young children. State and federal legislation already requires the provision of services for handicapped and other categories of children "at risk" under the age of five. In addition, as Anne Mitchell, Michelle Seligson, and Fern Marx document, recently more states have passed legislation enabling public funding of preschool education. Recent school funding cases have interpreted state constitutions as enforcing older children's right to public education, suggesting that a convincing argument could be made for extending the same right to all younger children. Moreover, funding public preschools only for poor and needy children tends to create racially segregated programs, and racial segregation in public education is illegal.

One of the best tests of a just and good society is how it treats "other people's children." But the problem is that there are many competing needs in our society. Simply stating that something is both needed and good is not enough to justify providing it with public funds, especially when the nation is already in debt. Ultimately, Americans must decide which groups in society deserve what amount of society's resources. But why, as Patty Smith Hill asked, should little children always be last in line? Surely their vulnerability and dependence should give them a special protected status even when funding for social services is short?[1]

This book also set out to answer questions about the kind of preschool education that should be provided for young children. First, what should the purposes of preschool education be? Of course, the first purpose of preschool education is to help young children: it should be good for them. But whether it is has yet to be resolved, despite years of experimentation, because of disagreement about what preschool education should be. Indeed, David Elkind's recent book *Miseducation: Preschoolers at Risk*, though phrased differently from G. Stanley Hall's arguments, shows the same concerns about the ill effects of overly formal education on young children. Nevertheless, some consensus has developed over the last century and a half. Most American kindergartners, nursery school educators, and parents think preschools should enhance children's social competence and language skills.

Beyond these important and basic goals, however, there is little agreement. As always, some preschool educators and parents want more free play and opportunities for creative expression, while others want more academics and teaching of cultural knowledge. And though preschool educators and parents have always thought preschools should help socialize young children, in the past as today they disagree as to how and to what norms. Rather than allowing this lack of consensus to hold up provision of public preschool education, as arguably it may have done, we should view these disagreements as healthy, central to our traditions of individualism and democracy. How different families want their young children educated relates directly to critical issues of privacy, freedom, community, and the role of the state. Having a system that permits parents to choose the kind of preschool education their children receive is crucial, even though it risks being a nonsystem, as now.[2]

A mixed public-private system would, with collaboration and coordination, permit parental choice and diversity. However, the history of preschool educators' concerns about quality and standards and recent research on the provision of preschool education suggest that choice models can be very problematic and must be closely monitored. The federal government could provide financial aid for preschool education, something like the Pell Grants that facilitate college attendance for older students. But any such funding mechanism should be studied carefully as it might have other less desirable or unintended effects.[3]

Historically and at present there has been more consensus on what kinds of things young children should have around them than on what they should be doing and when. Preschool educators and parents alike think young children need specially designed environments with plenty of toys, books, art materials, play equipment, indoor and outdoor play space, and child-sized furnishings and bathroom facilities. Everyone agrees these environments should be safe, clean, well ventilated, well heated, cheery, and bright. Unfortunately, however, some of the basements to which young children and preschool programs traditionally have been consigned are a far cry from the model spaces described by Elizabeth Peabody, Harriet Johnson, and Rose Alschuler and from those constructed at Hull House and on some college campuses.

The question of the age at which young children should start preschool remains unresolved, partly because it has important ramifications for later school success. In particular, views on when reading instruction or reading readiness activities should begin have varied enormously over time. Given the strong feelings of different groups of parents and preschool educators on this matter, it seems reasonable to allow some differences in instructional timing to continue. The concept of readiness and the practice of holding children back can be very problematic. Practice tends to go through cycles, pushing young children too hard and too fast and then letting up again in response to adult concerns. Young children cannot be completely protected from these societal swings, but since, as Kate Douglas Wiggin put it, a happy childhood is an "unspeakably precious memory" and, I would add, an intrinsically valuable human experience, it seems better to err on the side of waiting than to rush ahead heedlessly and needlessly. Allowing young children time to be young in a caring, interesting, and secure environment is one of the most important gifts preschools can offer.

As to curriculum and teaching methods, everyone agrees that preschool education should be developmentally appropriate. Providing plenty of time for free play with toys of the right size for little fingers, not forcing children to sit still for long periods of time doing paper and pencil schoolwork, and having teachers who understand young children's emotional needs are basic requirements. Beyond these broad criteria, however, there is less clarity; generations of preschool educators have generated long lists of criteria, yet the National Association for the Education of Young Children continues to try to define what *developmentally appropriate* means. This vagueness has the virtue of permitting much flexibility, which is probably good. After all, one of the hallmarks of preschool education compared to elementary and secondary education is that it has been relatively nonuniform: there are many different kinds of good preschools, just as there are many different kinds of good parents.[4]

Yet the lack of clearness can also lead to problems. Developmental appropriateness can be used to institute uniformity and conformity, for instance; Rebecca Mallory, Bruce New, and Sally Lubeck have pointed out that some preschool programs may not be sufficiently sensitive to multicultural issues, in part because they adhere to rigid, normalized interpretations of developmental appropriateness. Uncertainty about what constitutes developmentally appropriate curriculum has also left room for fads, cant, sentimentality, and commercialism, just as Elizabeth Peabody feared, as well as for unchallenging, uninteresting, and repetitive activities (how many times do young children need to plant seeds in paper cups?). So much room for variation means that, probably even more than at other levels of education, the quality of preschool curricula and teaching depends on the competence and creativity of individual teachers. This makes preschool teacher education very important, yet it has tended to be less demanding than elementary and secondary teacher education, and there is a worrisome trend for preschool teacher education to be marginalized in community colleges and two-year Associate Degree programs.[5]

Where should preschool programs be located? Most parents prefer having their young children physically close to their homes or to where they work, an argument for neighborhood or workplace preschools. Of course, local public schools are an obvious choice for proximity and accessibility, yet many preschool educators remain leery of public school control, in part because of the neglect and lack of understanding they and young children have historically suffered in the public schools. Caution is wise, but public schools have changed, and so have preschool educators. Sharon L. Kagan discusses strategies for "readying" schools to meet the needs of young children and their families. Even staunch Head Start advocate Edward Zigler, who initially rejected the idea of preschool education in the public schools, now advocates a special "School of the Twenty-first Century" that will include a separate preschool and child care wing providing comprehensive, developmentally appropriate, family-friendly programs. Community-based services are another option.[6]

There is also disagreement about how many hours a day preschool programs should operate. But at least the same number of hours as the regular school day seems fair. Like kindergartens, which are gradually lengthening into full-day programs, preschools might start as half-day programs and then be extended. The issue of full-day programming is more critical for preschools than for kindergartens, however, because three- and four-year-olds need naps and more informal playtime in the afternoon, as early nursery school advocates such as Harriet Johnson and Rose Alschuler knew. Zigler and others are recommending all-day year-round programs—what Bettye Caldwell calls "educare"—which meet families' needs for child care and reflect the reality of the inseparability of child care and education for young children. Some communities may prefer making decisions about program hours and length a local option. One alternative is for a locality to provide morning sessions and charge for afternoon and afterschool programs, using a sliding fee scale. The main thing, as Abigail Eliot and other preschool educators have advocated for years, is that parents should be involved in these decisions.[7]

It has been over 150 years since American children first attended infant schools in the 1820s. How much longer must they wait? In the words of psychologist and preschool advocate George Stoddard, speaking before the National Association of Nursery Educators in 1933, "It would be much better if the nursery school movement could evolve as a grand folk enterprise in which millions of people would rise up and demand that the welfare of their children take absolute priority over the profit drives inherent in the capitalist system." When will millions of Americans rise up and make our culture better for young children?[8]

Notes

The following abbreviations appear in the notes: *PKA,* for International Kindergarten Union Committee of Nineteen, *Pioneers of the Kindergarten in America* (New York: Century, 1924); and *NAW,* for Edward T. James and Janet Wilson James, eds., *Notable American Women,* 1607–1950 (Cambridge: Harvard University Press, Belknap, 1971).

Preface

1. For examples of studies and reports on the need for preschool education, see Kenneth Keniston and the Carnegie Council on Children, *All Our Children: The American Family Under Pressure* (New York: Harcourt Brace Jovanovich, 1977); Committee for Economic Development, *Investing in Our Children* (New York: Research and Policy Council of the Committee on Economic Development, 1985); Committee for Economic Development, *The Unfinished Agenda: A New Vision for Child Development and Education* (New York: Committee on Economic Development, 1991); National Commission on Children, *Beyond Rhetoric: A New American Agenda for Children and Families* (Washington, D.C.: National Commission on Children, 1991); and Ernest L. Boyer, *Ready to Learn* (Princeton: Carnegie Council on the Advancement of Teaching, 1992).

2. For more on this theme, see Carol Joffee, *Friendly Intruders: Childcare Professionals and Family Life* (Berkeley: University of California Press, 1977); and W. Norton Grubb and Marvin Lazerson, *Broken Promises: How Americans Fail Their Children* (New York: Basic, 1982; reprint, Chicago: University of Chicago Press, 1988).

3. See Stuart M. Blumin, "The Hypothesis of Middle-Class Formation in Nineteenth-Century America," *American Historical Review* 90 (April 1985): 299–338; Mary P. Ryan, *Cradle of the Middle Class: The Family in Oneida County, New York, 1790–1865* (Cambridge: Cambridge University Press, 1981); David Hogan, *Class and Reform: School and Society in Chicago, 1880–1930* (Philadelphia: University of Pennsylvania, 1985).

4. For the distinction between preschool education and child care, see Bettye M. Caldwell, "A Comprehensive Model for Integrating Child Care and Early Childhood Education," *Teachers College Record* 90 (spring 1989): 404–15; Sheila Rothman, "Other People's Children: The Day Care Experience in America," *Public Interest* 30 (winter 1973): 11–27; and Sonya Michel, "Children's Interests/Mothers' Rights: Women, Professionals, and the American Family, 1920–1945" (Ph.D. diss., Brown University, 1986).

5. Seth Koven and Sonya Michel, "Womanly Duties: Maternalist Politics and the Origins of Welfare States in France, Germany, Great Britain, and the United States, 1880–1920," *American Historical Review* 95 (October 1990): 1076–1108. On gender, women's culture, and public and private domains, see Linda K. Kerber, "Separate Spheres, Female Worlds, Woman's Place: The Rhetoric of Women's History," *Journal of American History* 75 (June 1988): 9–39; Jean Bethke Elshtain, *Public Man, Private Woman: Women in Social and Political Thought* (Princeton: Princeton University Press, 1981); Carole Pateman, "Feminist Critiques of the Public/Private Dichotomy," in S. I. Benn and G. F. Gaus, eds., *Public and Private in Social Life* (London: Croom Helm, 1983), 281–303; and Mary P. Ryan, *Women in Public: Between Banners and Ballots, 1825–1880* (Baltimore: Johns Hopkins University Press, 1990).

6. On reciprocity between preschool education and academic psychology, see Sheldon H. White and Stephen Buka, "Early Education: Programs, Traditions, and Policies," *Review of Research in Education* 14 (1987): 43–91.

7. On the difficulty and complexity of doing historical research on children, see Emily Cahan, Jay Mechling, Brian Sutton-Smith, and Sheldon H. White, "The Elusive Historical Child: Ways of Knowing the Child of History and Psychology," and Glen H. Elder, Jr., John Modell, and Ross D. Parke, "Studying Children in a Changing World," in Glen H. Elder, Jr., John Modell, and Ross D. Parke, eds., *Children in Time and Place: Developmental and Historical Insights* (Cambridge: Cambridge University Press, 1993), 192–223 and 3–21, respectively.

Chapter 1. "The School of Infancy"

1. Philippe Ariès, *Centuries of Childhood: A Social History of Family Life* (New York: Vintage, 1962). On earlier attitudes toward children and their education, see Robert Ulich, ed., *Three Thousand Years of Educational Wisdom* (Cambridge: Harvard University Press, 1947).

2. On Comenius, see, among others, John Edward Sadler, *J. A. Comenius and the Concept of Universal Education* (London: George Allen and Unwin, 1966); and Jean Piaget, "The Significance of John Amos Comenius at the Present Time," in *John Amos Comenius on Education* (New York: Teachers College Press, 1967).

3. Sadler, *J. A. Comenius*, 222–23.

4. John Amos Comenius, *Comenius' School of Infancy: An Essay on the Education of Youth during the First Six Years*, ed. Will S. Monroe (Boston: Heath, 1896), 20.

5. John Locke, *Some Thoughts Concerning Education*, in *The Educational Writings of John Locke*, ed. James L. Axtell (Cambridge: Cambridge University Press, 1968), 166. For Locke, see Axtell, introduction to *The Educational Writings of John Locke*, 18–49; and Maurice Cranston, *John Locke: A Biography* (New York: Macmillan, 1957), 68–81, 214, 239–45.

6. Locke, *Some Thoughts Concerning Education*, 325.

7. I am indebted to Joseph Featherstone for his thoughtful explication of Locke's disciplinary methods. See also John Cleverly and D. C. Phillips, *Visions of Childhood: Influential Models from Locke to Spock* (New York: Teachers College Press, 1966), 15–18.

8. John Locke, letter to Mrs. Clarke, February 1685, in Axtell, *The Educational Writings of John Locke*, 344–46.

9. Locke, *Some Thoughts Concerning Education*, 325.

10. Jean-Jacques Rousseau, *Emile*, trans. Barbara Foxley (New York: Dutton, Everyman's Library, 1977), 9, 44.

11. See P. D. Jimack, introduction to Jean-Jacques Rousseau, *Emile*. See also, among others, Maurice Cranston, *The Noble Savage: Jean-Jacques Rousseau, 1754–1762* (Chicago: University of Chicago Press, 1991); John Sturrock, "Well on the Way to Paranoia," review of Cranston, *The Noble Savage, New York Times Book Review,* July 28, 1991, 12; and Allan Bloom, "The Education of Democratic Man: *Emile,*" William Kessen, "Rousseau's Children," and Joseph Featherstone, "Rousseau and Modernity," all in *Daedalus* 107 (summer 1978): 135–92.

12. On Rousseau's views on the education of women, see Jane Roland Martin, "Sophie and Emile: A Case Study of Sex Bias in the History of Educational Thought," *Harvard Educational Review* 51 (1981): 357–72; and idem, *Reclaiming a Conversation: The Ideal of the Educated Woman* (New Haven: Yale University Press, 1985), 70–102.

13. Pestalozzi's journal quoted in Roger de Guimps, *Pestalozzi: His Life and Work* (New York: D. Appleton, 1909), 40, 45 (also quoted in Gerald Lee Gutek, *Pestalozzi and Education* [New York: Random House, 1968], 28, 29); Johann Heinrich Pestalozzi, *How Gertrude Teaches Her Children: An Attempt to Help Mothers to Teach Their Own Children,* trans. Lucy E. Holland and Frances C. Turner (Syracuse: C. W. Bardeen, 1900), xvi (also quoted in Gutek, *Pestalozzi and Education,* 11).

14. The main source on Pestalozzi's life is Kate Silber, *Pestalozzi: The Man and His Work* (London: Routledge and Kegan Paul, 1960). Other sources include Michael Haefford, *Pestalozzi: His Thought and Its Relevance Today* (London: Methuen, 1967); and Robert B. Downs, *Heinrich Pestalozzi: Father of Modern Pedagogy* (Boston: Twayne, 1975).

15. Johann Heinrich Pestalozzi, *Samtliche Werke,* 1:143, quoted in Downs, *Heinrich Pestalozzi,* 24–25.

16. Johann Heinrich Pestalozzi, "The Evening Hours of a Hermit," quoted in Lewis Flint Anderson, *Pestalozzi* (New York: McGraw-Hill, 1931), 21.

17. Johann Heinrich Pestalozzi, *Leonard and Gertrude,* trans. Eva Channing (Boston: Heath, 1885), 130–31.

18. Joseph Featherstone, "Childhood, Modernity, and the Religion of Life" (unpublished manuscript, 1978).

19. Pestalozzi, *Christopher and Alice,* quoted in Anderson, *Pestalozzi,* 29, 32; idem, *How Gertrude Teaches Her Children,* 200.

20. Pestalozzi, "Letters to Greaves," in Anderson, *Pestalozzi,* 191–92.

21. Johann Heinrich Pestalozzi, "Letter on His Work at Stanz, 1799," in F. V. N. Painter, ed., *Great Pedagogical Essays: Plato to Spencer* (New York: American Book Co., 1905), 360.

22. Silber, *Pestalozzi,* 294, 301; Gerald Lee Gutek, *Joseph Neef and the Americanization of Pestalozzianism* (University: University of Alabama Press, 1978); Will S. Monroe, *History of the Pestalozzian Movement in the United States* (Syracuse: C. W. Bardeen, 1907; reprint, New York: Arno and New York Times, 1969), 29.

23. Edgeworth's *Memoirs,* quoted in Alice Paterson, *The Edgeworths: A Study of Late Eighteenth Century Education* (London: W. B. Clive, 1914), 20.

24. Maria Edgeworth, *Practical Education* (New York: George F. Hopkins and Brown and Stansbury, 1801), 1:vi.

25. See Marilyn Butler, *Maria Edgeworth: A Literary Biography* (Oxford: Oxford University Press, Clarendon, 1972), 147–49, 158. For more on Maria Edgeworth's life and writings,

see Michael Butler, *Maria Edgeworth and the Public Scene: Intellect, Fine Feeling and Landlordism in the Age of Reason* (London: Macmillan, 1969); and Harriet Ritvo, "The Diminishing Countryside: Studies in Georgic Fiction, 1800–1875" (Ph.D. diss., Harvard University, 1975).

26. Edgeworth, *Practical Education*, 32, 10, 21, 23–28.

27. Edgeworth, *Practical Education*, 1:147.

28. These quotations also appear in Paterson, *The Edgeworths*, 29–30, who also discusses their views on schooling versus home education.

29. Edgeworth, *Practical Education*, 2:113.

30. The Alsatian pastor J. H. Oberlin had started extrafamilial child-care programs before Owen began his infant schools, but Oberlin's programs lacked the utopian scale or influence of Owen's work. On Oberlin, see Robert R. Rusk, *A History of Infant Education* (London: University of London Press, 1933); Ilse Forest, *Preschool Education: A Historical and Critical Study* (New York: Macmillan, 1927); and David Salmon and Winifred Hindshaw, *Infant Schools: Their History and Theory* (London: Longmans, Green, 1904).

31. On Owen's life, see, among other sources, his autobiography, *The Life of Robert Owen, Written by Himself* (London: B. Bell and Sons, 1836; reprint, New York: Knopf, 1920); Frank Podmore, *Robert Owen: A Biography* (1906; reprint, New York: Augustus M. Kelley, 1968).

32. Robert Dale Owen, "An Outline of the System of Education at New Lanark," quoted in John F. C. Harrison, *Utopianism and Education: Robert Owen and the Owenites* (New York: Teachers College Press, 1968), 145–46.

33. Robert Owen, *Life of Robert Owen*, 193, quoted in Forest, *Preschool Education*, 56; Robert Dale Owen, "Outline of the System of Education at New Lanark," quoted in Harrison, *Utopianism and Education*, 147.

34. Jane Dale Owen, "The Principles of Natural Education," preface to Robert Owen, *Lectures on an Entire New State of Society* (London, 1830), quoted in Harrison, *Utopianism and Education*, 187.

Chapter 2. "Too Large an Undertaking for a Few Ladies"

1. For overviews and local studies of these complicated changes, see, in particular, Paul Johnson, *A Shopkeeper's Millennium: Society and Revivals in Rochester, New York, 1815–1837* (New York: Hill and Wang, 1978); Anthony W. C. Wallace, *Rockdale: The Growth of an American Village in the Early Industrial Revolution* (New York: Knopf, 1978); Carl N. Degler, *At Odds: Women and the Family in America from the Revolution to the Present* (New York: Oxford University Press, 1980); and Mary P. Ryan, *Cradle of the Middle Class: The Family in Oneida County, New York, 1790–1865* (Cambridge: Cambridge University Press, 1981).

2. Steven Mintz and Susan Kellogg, *Domestic Revolutions: A Social History of American Family Life* (New York: Free Press, 1988), 43–60. See also Christopher Lasch, *Haven in a Heartless World: The Family Besieged* (New York: Basic, 1977); Nancy F. Cott, *The Bonds of Womanhood* (New Haven: Yale University Press, 1977); and Ann Douglas, *The Feminization of American Culture* (New York: Avon, 1977). On changes in women's roles after the Revolution, see Mary Beth Norton, *Liberty's Daughters: The Revolutionary Experience of American Women, 1750–1800* (Boston: Little, Brown, 1980); Linda K. Kerber, *Women of the Republic: Intellect and Ideas in Revolutionary America*

(Chapel Hill: University of North Carolina Press, 1980); Barbara Welter, "The Cult of True Womanhood: 1820–1860," *American Quarterly* 18 (summer 1966): 151–74; Gerda Lerner, "The Lady and the Mill Girl: Changes in the Status of Women in the Age of Jackson," *Midcontinent American Studies Journal* 10 (spring 1969): 5–15; and Glenna Matthews, *"Just a Housewife": The Rise and Fall of Domesticity in America* (New York: Oxford University Press, 1987).

3. See Mary P. Ryan, *The Empire of the Mother: American Writing about Domesticity, 1830–1860* (New York: Institute for Research in History and Haworth, 1982); and Ronald J. Zboray, "Antebellum Reading and the Ironies of Technological Innovation," in Cathy N. Davidson, ed., *Reading in America* (Baltimore: Johns Hopkins University Press, 1989), 80–200.

4. See Ross W. Beales, "Anne Bradstreet and Her Children," and N. Ray Hiner, "Cotton Mather and His Children," in Barbara Finkelstein, ed., *Regulated Children, Liberated Children: Education in Psychohistorical Perspective* (New York: Psychohistory Press, 1979), 10–43. For other sources on children in colonial New England, see, in particular, Edmund S. Morgan, *The Puritan Family: Religion and Domestic Relations in Seventeenth-Century New England*, rev. ed. (New York: Harper and Row, Torchbook, 1966); John Demos, *A Little Commonwealth: Family Life in Plymouth Colony* (New York: Oxford University Press, 1970); and Ross W. Beales, Jr., "In Search of the Historical Child: Miniature Adulthood and Youth in Colonial New England," *American Quarterly* 27 (1975): 380–83.

5. See Gerald F. Moran and Maris A. Vinovskis, "The Great Care of Godly Parents: Early Childhood Education in Puritan New England," in Alice B. Smuts and John W. Hagen, eds., *History and Research in Child Development*, Monographs of the Society for Research in Child Development, vol. 50, nos. 4–5 (Chicago: University of Chicago Press, 1986), 24–37; and John F. Walzer, "A Period of Ambivalence: Eighteenth-Century American Childhood," in Lloyd de Mause, ed., *The History of Childhood* (New York: Psychohistory Press, 1974), 351–81.

6. Kett, "Curing the Disease of Precocity"; Burr quoted in Walzer, "A Period of Ambivalence," 366.

   In *Literacy in Colonial New England: An Enquiry into the Social Context of Literacy in the Early Modern West* (New York: Norton, 1974), Kenneth A. Lockridge bases his assertion that few women in colonial America could read on signatures and marks on wills and other legal documents. E. Jennifer Monaghan, however, contends that reading and writing should be viewed separately and that many more women could read than could write ("Literacy and Gender in Colonial New England," in Cathy N. Davidson, ed., *Reading in America* [Baltimore: Johns Hopkins University Press, 1989], 53–80). *Literacy in the United States: Readers and Reading Since 1880* (New Haven: Yale University Press, 1991), Carl F. Kaestle's review of literacy in America, confirms this hypothesis.

7. See Bernard Bailyn, *Education in the Forming of American Society: Needs and Opportunities for Study* (Chapel Hill: University of North Carolina Press, 1960), 10, 21, 25, 49; and Lawrence Cremin, *American Education: The Colonial Experience, 1607–1783* (New York: Harper and Row, 1970).

8. For descriptions of some of these early schools, see Robert F. Seybolt, *The Private Schools of Colonial Boston* (Cambridge: Harvard University Press, 1935).

9. See Alice Morse Earle, *Child Life in Colonial Days* (New York: Macmillan, 1899), 97–98.

10. Maris Vinovskis, "Trends in Massachusetts Education, 1826–1860," *History of Education Quarterly* 12 (winter 1972): 501–29; Carl F. Kaestle and Maris A. Vinovskis, *Education and Social Change in Nineteenth-Century Massachusetts* (Cambridge: Cambridge University Press, 1980), 62, 52. On the transition from dame schools to primary schools in Massachusetts, see Joseph M. Wightman, *Annals of the Boston Primary School Committee* (Boston: George Rand and Avery, City Printers, 1860); James Breeden, "Policy, Polity, and Politics: The Primary School Board of Boston, 1818–1855" (Ed.D. diss., Harvard Graduate School of Education, 1972); and William Weber, "Before Horace Mann: Elites and Boston Public Schools, 1800–1822" (Ed.D. diss., Harvard Graduate School of Education, 1974).

11. See Gerald Lee Gutek, *Joseph Neef and the Americanization of Pestalozzianism* (University: University of Alabama Press, 1978). On the early Pestalozzian movement in the United States see also Will S. Monroe, "Joseph Neef and Pestalozzianism in America," *Education* (March 1894); Gerald Lee Gutek, "An Examination of Neef's Theory of Education," *History of Education Quarterly* 9 (summer 1969): 153–62; and Gerald Lee Gutek, *Pestalozzi and Education* (New York: Random House, 1968). On Maclure, Fretageot, and Phiquepal, see Arthur Bestor, ed., *Education and Reform at New Harmony: Correspondence of William Maclure and Marie Duclos Fretageot, 1820–1833* (Indianapolis: Indiana Historical Society, 1948; reprint, Clifton, N.J.: Augustus M. Kelley, 1973).

12. For descriptions of New Harmony, see especially Frank Podmore, *Robert Owen: A Biography* (1906; reprint, New York: Augustus M. Kelley, 1968), 285–346; Arthur E. Bestor, *Backwoods Utopias: The Sectarian and Owenite Phases of Communitarian Socialism in America, 1662–1829* (Philadelphia: University of Pennsylvania Press, 1950); and Anne Taylor, *Visions of Harmony: A Study in Nineteenth-Century Millenarianism* (New York: Oxford University Press, 1987).

13. See John William Jenkins, "Infant Schools and the Development of Public Primary Schools in Selected American Cities Before the Civil War" (Ph.D. diss., University of Wisconsin, 1978); Alan Pence, "Infant Schools in North America, 1825–1840," in Sally Kilmer, ed., *Advances in Early Education and Day Care*, vol. 4 (Greenwich: JAI, 1986), 1–25; and Lucy F. Townsend, "The Teacher as a Moral Authority: The Infant School Society of New York City, 1827–1840," paper presented at the Annual Meeting of the History of Education Society, Atlanta, Georgia, November 1989.

14. A Friend to the Poor, *Infant Education; or, Remarks on the Importance of Educating the Infant Poor* (New York: J. Seymour, 1827). On Bethune's pedagogy, see Alan Reece Pence, "Preschool Programs of the Nineteenth Century: Towards a History of Preschool Child Care in America" (Ph.D. diss., University of Oregon, 1980), 62; and idem, "Infant Schools in North America," 12.

15. See Carl F. Kaestle, *Pillars of the Republic: Common Schools and American Society* (New York: Hill and Wang, 1983), for more on Carll, Graham, Vaux, and Carey and the establishment of infant and primary schools in Philadelphia.

16. ISSCB, *First Annual Report* (Boston: T. R. Marvin, Printer, 1829), 7.

17. "Infant Schools," *Ladies' Magazine* 4 (April 1832): 182; ISSCB, *Seventh Annual Report* (Boston: William D. Ticknor, 1835), 9.

18. ISSCB, *Sixth Annual Report* (Boston: William D. Ticknor, 1834), 5.

19. "Infant Education," *Ladies' Magazine* 2 (February 1829): 89.

20. See Jenkins, "Infant Schools and the Development of Public Primary Schools," 147, 149–50; and Dean May and Maris Vinovskis, "A Ray of Millennial Light: Early Education and Social Reform in the Infant School Movement in Massachusetts, 1826–1840," in Ta-

mara K. Hareven, ed., *Family and Kin in Urban Communities, 1700–1930* (New York: New Viewpoints, 1977), 73.

21. See Stanley K. Schultz, *The Culture Factory: Boston Public Schools, 1789–1860* (New York: Oxford University Press, 1973), 271–74, and Wightman, *Annals of the Boston Primary School Committee*, 124–25.

22. Ralph Waldo Emerson, *Nature* (1836), in Brooks Atkinson, ed., *The Selected Writings of Ralph Waldo Emerson* (New York: Modern Library, 1940), 39; Bronson Alcott, "Observation on the Phenomena of Life as Developed in the Progressive History of an Infant, During the First Years of Its Existence," quoted in Charles F. Strickland, "A Transcendentalist Father: The Child-Rearing Practices of Bronson Alcott," *Journal of Family History* 1 (1976): 8. See also Bruce Allen Ronda, "The Transcendental Child: Images and Concepts of the Child in American Transcendentalism (Ph.D. diss., Yale University, 1975).

23. For Alcott's life and educational work, see Odell Shepard, *Pedlar's Progress: The Life of Bronson Alcott* (Boston: Little, Brown, 1937); Dorothy McCuskey, *Bronson Alcott, Teacher* (New York: Macmillan, 1940); and Madelon Bedell, *The Alcotts: Biography of a Family* (New York: Clarkson N. Potter, 1980).

24. Bronson Alcott, "Infant Schools," *American Journal of Education* (1833): 296–302; idem, *Observations on the Principles and Methods of Infant Instruction* (Boston: Carter and Hendee, 1830), reprinted in Walter Harding, ed., *Essays on Education by Bronson Alcott* (Gainesville, Fla.: Scholar's Facsimiles and Reprints, 1960), 27, 4. For a detailed study of Alcott's educational philosophy, see Fordyce Richard Bennett, "Bronson Alcott: The Transcendental Reformer as Educator" (Ph.D. diss., University of Illinois, 1976). The best sources of information about Alcott's pedagogical ideas and methods are his extensive and quite extraordinary journals and diaries in the Alcott-Pratt collection at the Houghton Library at Harvard University.

25. Amariah Brigham, *Remarks on the Influence of Mental Cultivation and Mental Excitement upon Health*, 2nd ed. (Boston: Marsh, Capen, and Lyon, 1833), 36, 55; Lydia Sigourney, *Letters to Mothers* (Hartford: Hudson and Skinner, 1838), 147. For the influence of Brigham's book, see May and Vinovskis, "A Ray of Millenial Light," 84–85. On infant schools and precocity, see also Caroline Winterer, "'Avoiding a 'Hothouse System of Education': Nineteenth-Century Early Childhood Education from the Infant Schools to the Kindergartens," *History of Education Quarterly* 32 (fall 1992): 289–314.

26. *American Journal of Education* 3 (June 1828): 347.

27. Quoted in May and Vinovskis, "A Ray of Millennial Light," 82; ISSCB, *Seventh Annual Report*, 4.

28. ISSCB, *Seventh Annual Report*, 6, 7. As J. Leslie Dunstan notes, the men's society was in such dire financial straits in the mid-1830s that it considered seeking help from the women's society. The men's society might not have survived either had its fortunes not been revived in 1840 by a fortuitous bequest (*A Light to the City: One Hundred Fifty Years of the City Missionary Society of Boston* [Boston: Beacon, 1966], 74, 76). On the difficulties encountered by other antebellum female reformers, see Barbara J. Berg, *The Remembered Gate: Origins of American Feminism* (New York: Oxford University Press, 1978).

29. Some of the most popular books published before Beecher's *Treatise on Domestic Economy* (Boston: Marsh, Capen, Lyon, and Webb, 1841) included Lydia Maria Child, *The Mother's Book* (Boston: Carter and Hendee, 1830); John S. C. Abbott, *The Mother at Home* (Boston:

Crocker and Brewster, 1833); idem, *The Child at Home* (Boston: Crocker and Brewster, 1834); Theodore Dwight, *The Father's Book* (Springfield, Mass.: Merriam, 1834); John Hall, *On the Education of Children* (New York: J. P. Haven, 1835); William Alcott, *The Young Mother* (Boston: Light and Stearns, 1836); Sigourney, *Letters to Mothers*; Samuel Goodrich, *Fireside Education* (New York: Huntington, 1838); and Heman Humphrey, *Domestic Education* (Amherst: Adams, 1840).

30. See Bernard Wishy, *The Child and the Republic: The Dawn of Modern American Child Nurture* (Philadelphia: University of Pennsylvania Press, 1968), 24–33, 77–78.

31. For the realignment of family structure, see Ryan, *Empire of the Mother*, 1–18, 40–43. For discussion of American domestic advice literature generally, see, in particular, Kathryn Kish Sklar, *Catharine Beecher: A Study in American Domesticity* (New Haven: Yale University Press, 1973); and Matthews, *"Just a Housewife."*

32. Sigourney, *Letters to Mothers*, 45; Goodrich, *Fireside Education*, 150. See also Anne L. Kuhn, *The Mother's Role in Childhood Education: New England Concepts, 1830–1860* (New Haven: Yale University Press, 1947), 149–72.

33. Samuel Goodrich, *Fireside Education*, 6th ed. (London: William Smith, 1841), 81, quoted in Kuhn, *Mother's Role, 100.*

34. "A Mother," *Thoughts on Domestic Education, The Result of Experience* (Boston: Carter and Hendee, 1829), 26; Humphrey, *Domestic Education*, 75.

35. Jacob Abbott, *The Little Philosopher; or, The Infant School at Home* (Boston: Carter and Hendee, 1830), v–vii, quoted in Kuhn, *Mother's Role*, 103.

36. Lydia Maria Child, *The Mother's Book* (Boston: Carter and Hendee, 1830), 10, 11, 12.

37. Goodrich, *Fireside Education* (1838), 16.

38. Sigourney, *Letters to Mothers*, 103; William A. Alcott, "There Is No School Like the Family School," *Mother's Assistant* 3 (January 1843): 2; Charles Holden, "The Family School," *Mother's Assistant* 3 (November 1843): 248. All are quoted in Kuhn, *Mother's Role*, 106, 107.

39. See Strickland, "A Transcendentalist Father." See also Bedell, *The Alcotts*, and Alcott's journals in the Alcott-Pratt Collection in the Houghton Library at Harvard University.

40. Elizabeth Peabody, "Female Education in Massachusetts; Reminiscences of Subjects and Methods of Teaching. With a Letter from the Author, Relating to Her Mother, Mrs. Elizabeth P. Peabody, and Reminiscences about School Life and Teaching by Mary P. Mann," *Barnard's American Journal of Education* 30 (July 1880): 308. For Peabody's family background and early life, see Ruth M. Baylor, *Elizabeth Palmer Peabody: Kindergarten Pioneer* (Philadelphia: University of Pennsylvania Press, 1965); Hersha S. Fisher, "Elizabeth Peabody: Her Family and Its Influence" (qualifying paper, Harvard Graduate School of Education, 1978); idem, "The Education of Elizabeth Peabody" (Ed.D. diss., Harvard Graduate School of Education, 1980); and Bruce A. Ronda, ed., introduction to *Letters of Elizabeth Palmer Peabody: American Renaissance Woman* (Middletown, Conn.: Wesleyan University Press, 1984). On Peabody's relationship with Channing, see her *Reminiscences of William Ellery Channing, D.D.* (Boston: Roberts Brothers, 1880).

41. Elizabeth Peabody, "General Principles of Education," in *Record of a School, Exemplifying the General Principles of Spiritual Culture* (Boston: James Munroe, 1835), 181, 185. For detailed accounts of the Temple School imbroglio, see Josephine Roberts, "Elizabeth Peabody and the Temple School," *New England Quarterly* 18 (1945): 536–40; Martha Saxton, *Louisa May, A Modern Biography of Louisa May Alcott* (New York: Avon, 1977); and Bedell, *The Alcotts*.

42. Elizabeth Peabody, "Prospectus," *Family School* 1 (November 1, 1836).
43. Elizabeth Peabody, "The History of Goodness," *Family School* 1 (September 1, 1836): 6–7.
44. Peabody, "Prospectus," 15.

Chapter 3. *"Come, Let Us Live with Our Children"*

1. On Froebel's life, see the *Autobiography of Froebel*, trans. Emilie Michaelis and H. Keatley Moore (London: Swan Sonnenschein, 1886), also published as "Autobiography in Letter to the Duke of Meiningen," trans. Lucy Wheelock, in Henry Barnard, ed., *Kindergarten and Child Culture Papers: Papers on Froebel's Kindergarten, With Suggestions on Principles and Methods of Child Culture in Different Countries* (Hartford: Office of *Barnard's American Journal of Education*, 1890), 21–48. See also Robert B. Downs, *Friedrich Froebel* (Boston: Twayne, 1978); Denton J. Snider, *The Life of Frederick Froebel, Founder of the Kindergarten* (Chicago: Sigma, 1900); and Jessie White, *The Educational Ideas of Froebel* (London: University Tutorial Press, 1905).
2. Quoted in Snider, *Life of Friedrich Froebel*, 33. On the influence of Fichte on Froebel, see Ann Taylor Allen, "Spiritual Motherhood: German Feminists and the Kindergarten Movement, 1848–1911," *History of Education Quarterly* 22 (fall 1982): 321. On the influence of Schelling, see Snider, *Life of Friedrich Froebel*, 33–35.
3. Froebel, *Autobiography of Froebel*, 54, 55.
4. Froebel, *Autobiography of Froebel*, 97. See Downs, *Friedrich Froebel*, 22, 23, 26.
5. See Froebel, *Autobiography of Froebel*, 114, 115.
6. See Downs, *Friedrich Froebel*, 27–39; and H. Courthope Bowen, *Froebel and Education by Self Activity* (New York: Charles Scribner's Sons, 1893), 36, 37.
7. Johannes Barop, "Critical Moments in the Froebel Community," in *Autobiography of Froebel*, 137.
8. Froebel, *Froebel's Letters on the Kindergarten*, quoted in White, *Educational Ideas of Froebel*, 84–85, and in Downs, *Friedrich Froebel*, 42.
9. Friedrich Froebel, *The Education of Man*, trans. W. N. Hailmann (New York: D. Appleton, 1892), 31, 55.
10. Froebel, *Education of Man*, 1. On the religious nature of Froebel's thought, see William Torrey Harris, preface to *Education of Man*, ix; and Robert Ulich, *History of Educational Thought* (New York: American Book, 1945), 286, quoted in Evelyn Weber, *The Kindergarten: Its Encounter with Educational Thought in America* (New York: Teachers College Press, 1969), 1.
11. Froebel, *Education of Man*, 10, 30.
12. Bertha Maria von Marenholtz-Bulow, *Reminiscences of Friedrich Froebel*, trans. Mrs. Horace Mann (Boston: Lee and Shepard, 1892), 224, 228, quoted in Downs, *Friedrich Froebel*, 59. For Froebel's laws, see Froebel, *Education of Man*, 42.
13. See Friedrich Froebel, *Pedagogics of the Kindergarten*, trans. Josephine Jarvis (New York: D. Appleton, 1895), 31–69. See also Kate Douglas Wiggin and Nora Archibald Smith, *The Republic of Childhood, Volume I: Froebel's Gifts* (Boston: Houghton Mifflin, 1895), 10.
14. Wiggin and Smith, *Republic of Childhood*, 77, 91.
15. See Maria Kraus-Boelte and John Kraus, *Kindergarten Guide, an Illustrated Hand-book, Designed for the Self-Instruction of Kindergartners, Mothers, and Nurses* (New York: E. Steiger, 1877).

16. The German phrase is *"Kommt, lasst uns unsern Kindern leben."* Catherine M. Prelinger translates it as "Come, let us live *for* our children." See her *Charity, Challenge, and Change: Religious Dimensions of the Mid-Nineteenth-Century Women's Movement in Germany* (New York: Greenwood, 1987), 91.

17. Froebel, *Education of Man*, 54; Friedrich Froebel quoted in White, *Educational Ideas of Froebel*, 114; Friedrich Froebel quoted in Downs, *Friedrich Froebel*, 51.

18. See Downs, *Friedrich Froebel*, 51–52; Susan Blow, *The Songs and Music of Friedrich Froebel's Mother Play* (New York: D. Appleton, 1895). For teachers' estimations of the book, see Susan Blow's introduction to her translation, *Mottoes and Commentaries of Froebel's Mother Play* (New York: D. Appleton, 1895); and Lucy Wheelock, "My Life Story," Lucy Wheelock Collection, Archives, Wheelock College, Boston.

19. Susan Blow, "Froebel's Philosophy," introduction to *Mottoes and Commentaries of Froebel's Mother Play*, 39.

20. Froebel, *Education of Man*, 19; Froebel, *Pedagogics of the Kindergarten*, 270, quoted in Weber, *The Kindergarten*, 16.

21. See Froebel, *Education of Man*, 20. For discussion of Froebel's views in the context of German history and politics, see Ann Taylor Allen, "Gardens of Children, Gardens of God: Kindergartens and Day-Care Centers in Nineteenth-Century Germany," *Journal of Social History* 19 (spring 1986): 438; and idem, *Feminism and Motherhood in Germany, 1800–1914* (New Brunswick: Rutgers University Press, 1991).

22. Quoted in Marenholtz-Bulow, *Reminiscences of Friedrich Froebel*, 142; Friedrich Froebel, *Entwurf eines Planes zur Begründung und Ausführung eines Kindergartens* (Leipzig, 1849), translated and quoted in Allen "Spiritual Motherhood," 322.

23. Allen, *Feminism and Motherhood in Germany;* Seth Koven and Sonya Michel, "Womanly Duties: Maternalist Politics and the Origins of Welfare States in France, Germany, Great Britain, and the United States, 1880–1920," *American Historical Review* 95 (October 1990): 1076–1108.

24. Friedrich Froebel, "Appendix to Letter I to Madame Schmidt, in Gera, Blankenburg, near Rudolstadt, in the Thuringian Forest, 1st May, 1840," in *Froebel's Letters on the Kindergarten*, ed. Emilie Michaelis and H. Keatley Moore (London: Swan Sonnenschein, 1891), 156–57. See also Alexander Bruno Hanschmann, "Froebel, The Apostle of Women," in *The Kindergarten System, Its Origin and Development as Seen in the Life of Friedrich Froebel*, trans. Fanny Franks (London: Swan Sonnenschein, 1897), 188–210.

25. My understanding of the German kindergarten movement is based largely on the work of Ann Taylor Allen, especially her *Feminism and Motherhood in Germany*.

26. See Ann Taylor Allen, "'Let Us Live with Our Children': Kindergarten Movements in Germany and the United States, 1840–1914," *History of Education Quarterly* 28 (spring 1988): 26–27. For further discussion of German kindergartens and liberalism, see Edward Ellsworth, "The Froebelian Kindergarten Movement, 1850–1880: An International Crusade for Political and Social Progress" (special paper published for the Wheelock College Centennial, Boston, 1989). For a fuller description of the Hamburg training school, see Prelinger, *Charity, Challenge, and Change*, esp. 88–95; and Michael Steven Shapiro, *Child's Garden: The Kindergarten Movement from Froebel to Dewey* (University Park: Pennsylvania State University Press, 1983), 27–28.

27. See Marenholtz-Bulow, *Reminiscences of Friedrich Froebel*, 1, 3, 4. See also Henry Barnard, "Bertha von Marenholtz-Bulow and the Kindergarten Memoir," in *Kindergarten and Child*

Culture Papers: Papers on Froebel's Kindergarten, With Suggestions on Principles and Methods of Child Culture in Different Countries (Hartford: Office of *Barnard's American Journal of Education,* 1890), 149–50.

28. Bertha Maria von Marenholtz-Bulow, *The New Education by Work According to Froebel,* trans. Mary Mann (Camden, N.J.: Philotechnic Institute, 1876), 32; Bertha von Maren-holtz-Bulow, *Die Arbeit und die neue Erẑihung* (Berlin, 1864), 53, and *Froebel's Infant Gardens* (London, 1855), 86, quoted in Allen, "Spiritual Motherhood," 327.

29. See Allen, "Spiritual Motherhood," 328; and Shapiro, *Child's Garden,* 31. For a description of Marenholtz's kindergarten activities and publication, see Barnard, "Bertha von Mar-enholtz-Bulow and the Kindergarten," 151–60.

30. For detailed descriptions and discussion of Schrader-Breymann and the Pestalozzi-Froebel Haus, see Allen, *Feminism and Motherhood in Germany.*

31. On the spread of kindergartens internationally, see Ellsworth, "The Froebelian Kinder-garten Movement"; and Roberta Wollons, "The Black Forest in a Bamboo Garden: Mis-sionary Kindergartens in Japan, 1868–1912," *History of Education Quarterly* 33 (spring 1993): 1–36.

Chapter 4. "Paradise of Childhood"

1. Edward Wiebe, *The Paradise of Childhood: A Practical Guide to the Kindergarten* (Spring-field, Mass.: Milton Bradley, 1869).

2. Biographical sources on Margarethe Meyer Schurz include Joseph Schafer, ed., *Intimate Letters of Carl Schurẑ, 1841–1869* (Madison: State Historical Society of Wisconsin, 1928); Hannah Werwath Swart, *Margarethe Meyer Schurẑ: A Biography* (Watertown: Watertown Historical Society, 1967); Jonathan Messerli, "Margarethe Meyer Schurz," in *NAW,* 3:242–43; and Barbara Beatty, "Margarethe Meyer Schurz," in John A. Garraty, ed., *American National Biography* (New York: Oxford University Press, forthcoming).

3. See Sy Quam, *First Kindergarten in the United States* (Watertown: Watertown Historical Society, 1988).

4. See Elizabeth Jenkins, "Froebel's Disciples in America," *American-German Review* 3 (March 1937): 15–18; Edward W. Hocker, "The First American Kindergarten Teacher," *American-German Review* 8 (February 1942): 9–10; Nina C. Vandewalker, *The Kindergarten in American Education* (New York: Macmillan, 1908), 12–14; and John Kraus, "The Kin-dergarten (Its Use and Abuse) in America," in National Education Association, *Addresses and Proceedings,* 1877 (Salem, Ohio: Office of the National Teacher, 1877): 198.

5. Milton Bradley, "A Reminiscence of Miss Peabody," *Kindergarten News* 4 (February 1894), 39–40. See James J. Shea, *It's All in the Game* (New York: Putnam, 1960), 103–8, 110–11; and Milton Bradley, preface to Edward Wiebe, *The Paradise of Childhood: A Practical Guide to Kindergartners,* quarter-century edition (Springfield, Mass.: Milton Bradley, 1896).

6. Wiebe, *Paradise of Childhood,* 95.

7. On Douai, see Ann Taylor Allen, "'Let Us Live With Our Children': Kindergarten Movements in Germany and the United States, 1840–1914," *History of Education Quarterly* 28 (spring 1988): 38–39.

8. Matilda H. Kriege, *The Child, Its Nature and Relations: An Elucidation of Froebel's Prin-ciples of Education* (New York: E. Steiger, 1872), 145. On Kriege, see Michael Steven Shapiro, *Child's Garden: The Kindergarten Movement from Froebel to Dewey* (University Park: Pennsylvania State University Press, 1983), 31–32, 36–37.

9. Details on Hailmann's life are from Barbara Greenwood, "William Nicholas Hailmann, 1836–1920," in *PKA*, 245–62; and Vandewalker, *The Kindergarten in American Education,* 13, 17, 21–23.

10. William N. Hailmann, *Kindergarten Culture in the Family and Kindergarten* (Cincinnati: Van Antwerp, Bragg, 1873), vii, 102, 118–19.

11. See Robert J. Fridlington, "Maria Kraus-Boelte," *NAW*, 2:346–48. See also Maria Kraus-Boelte, "Experience of a Kindergartner," *Kindergarten Messenger* (January–March 1875); Anna K. Harvey, "Maria Kraus-Boelte," and Carolyn C. Meleny, "A Remembrance of Maria Kraus-Boelte," in *PKA*, 75–83 and 84–90.

12. Bertha Meyer, *Aids to Family Government; From the Cradle to the School, According to Froebel* (New York: M. L. Holbrook, 1879), 10, 11, 160, 164, 168. On the Ronges, see Edward Ellsworth, "The Froebelian Kindergarten Movement, 1850–1880: An International Crusade for Political and Social Progress" (special paper published for the Wheelock College Centennial, Boston, 1989), 5.

13. See Vandewalker, *The Kindergarten in American Education,* 14–16; Messerli, "Margarethe Meyer Schurz," 242.

14. Elizabeth Peabody, *Kindergarten Guide,* in Elizabeth Peabody and Mary Mann, *Moral Culture of Infancy and Kindergarten Guide* (Boston: T. O. H. P. Burnham, 1863), 14, 9; idem, *Guide to the Kindergarten and Intermediate Class* (New York: E. Steiger, 1877), 15, 36. See also Barbara Beatty, "Child Gardening," in Donald Warren, ed., *American Teachers: Histories of a Profession at Work* (New York: Macmillan, 1990). On Peabody's care to distinguish the kindergarten from the infant school movement, see Caroline Winterer, "Avoiding a 'Hothouse System of Education': Nineteenth-Century Early Childhood Education from the Infant Schools to the Kindergartens," *History of Education Quarterly* 32 (fall 1992): 289–314.

15. Peabody, *Guide to the Kindergarten and Intermediate Class,* 18, 21. See also ibid., 19, 20.

16. Elizabeth Peabody, "Our Reason for Being," *Kindergarten Messenger* 1 (May 1873): 2, 1.

17. The best source on the spread of the early private kindergarten movement is still Vandewalker, *The Kindergarten in American Education.* Elizabeth Peabody summarized the growth of the early Froebelian kindergarten movement in this country in an 1879 letter to Henry Barnard reprinted as the chapter "Froebel's Kindergarten" in Henry Barnard, *Kindergarten and Child Culture Papers: Papers on Froebel's Kindergarten, With Suggestions on Principles and Methods of Child Culture in Different Countries* (Hartford: Office of *Barnard's American Journal of Education,* 1890), 7–16.

18. Elizabeth Peabody, "Genuine Kindergarten," *Kindergarten Messenger* 3 (May 1874): 12–13.

19. See Elizabeth Peabody, "The American Froebel Society," *Kindergarten Messenger,* n.s., 1 (July–August 1877): 158–59.

20. Elizabeth Peabody, *Lectures in the Training Schools for Kindergartners* (Boston: Heath, 1893), 13. On women and the kindergarten and kindergarten teaching as a women's occupation, see Karen Wolk Feinstein, "Kindergartens, Feminism, and the Professionalization of Motherhood," *International Journal of Women's Studies* 3 (January–February 1980): 28–38; Barbara Beatty, "'A Vocation from On High': Preschool Teaching and Advocacy as a Career for Women in Nineteenth-Century Boston" (Ed.D. diss., Harvard Graduate School of Education, 1981); and Barbara Finkelstein, "The Revolt against Selfishness: Women and the Dilemmas of Professionalism in Early Childhood Education," in Bernard Spodek and Olivia Saracho, eds., *Professionalism in Early Childhood Education* (New York: Teachers College Press, 1988), 10–28.

21. See Barbara Beatty, "'A Vocation from On High': Kindergartning as an Occupation for American Women," in Joyce Antler and Sari Knopp Biklen, eds., *Changing Education: Women and Radicals and Conservators* (Albany: State University of New York Press, 1990).

22. Elizabeth Peabody, "Child Gardening as a Profession," *Kindergarten Messenger* 1 (July 1873); 2; idem, "Motherliness," *Kindergarten Messenger*, n.s., 1 (July–August 1877): 151; idem, *Lectures in the Training Schools for Kindergartners*, 88.

23. Peabody, *Lectures in the Training Schools for Kindergartners*, 13, 88.

24. Elizabeth Peabody, *Kindergarten Messenger*, n.s., 1 (May–June 1877): 96; idem, "Kindergarten Intelligence," *Kindergarten Messenger* 3 (June 1875): 132; and idem, *Lectures in the Training Schools for Kindergartners*, 19.

25. Elizabeth Peabody, *Kindergarten Messenger and the New Education* 2 (February 1878): 3. For descriptions of these changes in schools, teachers, and teaching, see, in particular, David B. Tyack, *The One Best System: A History of American Urban Education* (Cambridge: Harvard University Press, 1974); Paul H. Mattingly, *The Classless Profession: American Schoolmen in the Nineteenth Century* (New York: New York University Press, 1975); and David Tyack and Elizabeth Hansot, *Managers of Virtue: Public School Leadership in America, 1820–1980* (New York: Basic, 1982).

26. Elizabeth Peabody, "Report of the American Froebel Union," *Kindergarten Messenger and the New Education* 3 (October 1879): 9.

27. Elizabeth Peabody, "Report of the Sixth Meeting of the American Froebel Union," *Kindergarten Messenger and the New Education* 3 (January 1879): 2; Henry Barnard quoted in Peabody, "Report of the American Froebel Union," 9.

28. Extensive data on the backgrounds of kindergartners were collected from alumnae registers of the Garland School, held in the archives of Simmons College, and alumnae files and registers at Alumnae Office and Archives, Wheelock College, by the author and Margaret C. Dollar and analyzed by the author, supported in part by funds from the Andrew W. Mellon Foundation, given by Radcliffe College for research at the Schlesinger Library. On female voluntarism and women's associations, see, among others, Karen J. Blair, *The Clubwoman as Feminist: True Womanhood Redefined, 1868–1914* (New York: Holmes and Meier, 1980); and Theodora Penny Martin, *The Sound of Our Own Voices* (Boston: Beacon, 1987). For data on the social status of men teachers and administrators and on immigrant and working-class women teachers, see Lotus Delta Coffman, *The Social Composition of the Teaching Population* (New York: Columbia University, 1911); and Mattingly, *The Classless Profession*.

29. Sources on Blow's life include Laura Fisher, "Susan E. Blow," in *PKA*, 184–203; Agnes Snyder, *Dauntless Women in Early Childhood Education, 1857–1931* (Washington, D.C.: Association for Childhood Education International, 1972), 59–85; Dorothy Ross, "Susan E. Blow," in *NAW*, 181–83; Sorca M. O'Connor, "Susan E. Blow: A Retrospective Feminist Analysis," (paper, American Educational Research Association, April 1990); and Shapiro, *Child's Garden*, 50–57.

30. See Elizabeth Peabody to William Torrey Harris, August 25, 1870, typescript, Ruth M. Baylor Collection, Massachusetts Historical Society, Boston; original, William Torrey Harris Papers, Missouri Historical Society, St. Louis. For descriptions of some of Peabody and Harris's arguments, see Kurt F. Leidecker, *Yankee Teacher: The Life of William Torrey Harris* (New York: Philosophical Library, 1946), 297, 367. On Harris generally and on his involvement with the kindergarten in particular, see Harriet Neil, "William Torrey

Harris," in *PKA*, 167–83; Lawrence A. Cremin, *The Transformation of the School: Progressivism in American Education, 1876–1957* (New York: Vintage, 1964), 14–20; Selwyn K. Troen, *The Public and the Schools: Shaping the St. Louis School System, 1838–1920* (Columbia: University of Missouri Press, 1975), 99–115; and Shapiro, *Child's Garden,* 46–50.

31. See William T. Harris, "Report of the Superintendent," in *Seventeenth Annual Report of the Board of Directors of the St. Louis Public Schools for the Year Ending August 1871* (St. Louis, 1872), quoted in Robert H. Bremner, *Children and Youth in America: A Documentary History,* vol. 2., *1866–1932, Part 7 through 8* (Cambridge: Harvard University Press, 1971), 1454.

32. See William T. Harris, *Twenty-First Annual Report of the Board of Directors of the St. Louis Public Schools for the Year Ending August 1875* (St. Louis, 1876), in Bremner, *Children and Youth in America,* 455. Harris's report included Blow's, reprinted in Bremner, *Children and Youth in America,* 456. See also Sorca M. O'Connor, "Mothering in Public: Contrasts in Organizational Structure and Leadership in the Day Nursery and Kindergarten in St. Louis, 1886–1920" (paper, American Educational Research Association, April 1992).

33. "Rough draft by W. T. Harris for formation of the St. Louis Kindergarten Association, 1889," William Torrey Harris Papers, quoted in Troen, *The Public and the Schools,* 113; Harris, *Twenty-First Annual Report,* in Bremner, *Children and Youth in America,* 456.

34. St. Louis Board of Education, *Twenty-Fifth Annual Report of the Board of Directors of the Saint Louis Public Schools for the Year Ending August 1, 1879* (St. Louis, 1879), 95–96, quoted in Shapiro, *Child's Garden,* 55.

35. William T. Harris, "Report from a Department Sub-Committee on Kindergartens," *Journal of Social Science* 12 (1880): 8–11, reprinted in Bremner, *Children and Youth in America,* 458.

36. See Shapiro, *Child's Garden,* 60–61.

37. See Troen, *The Public and the Schools,* 107, 108, 110, 112, 113. As the Missouri Supreme Court decision attested, Americans in the 1870s and early 1880s were not yet ready to extend public education to children under six. In fact, the first public kindergarten in the United States had opened on September 26, 1870, in a primary school building on Somerset Street in Boston, and cost appears to have caused the ultimate demise of this class and to have prevented other public kindergartens from being started in Boston at this time. See *Annual Report of the School Committee of the City of Boston, 1871* (Boston, 1872), 207–208; and *Thirty-Fifth Semi-Annual Report of the Superintendent of Public Schools,* School Document No. 2, Boston, March 1879, 66, quoted in Douglas E. Lawson, "Corrective Note on the Early History of the American Kindergarten," *Educational Administration and Supervision* 25 (1939): 700, 702.

38. On the importance of fairs and expositions, see Lawrence A. Cremin, *American Education: The National Experience, 1783–1876* (New York: Harper and Row, 1980), 332–34. For more on the Centennial Kindergarten, see Shapiro, *Child's Garden,* 65–83.

39. Nina Vandewalker includes quotations from the *Philadelphia Ledger* describing the Centennial Kindergarten in her sketch of Burritt in *PKA,* 139. Press coverage included a series of woodcuts by Frank Leslie, which were reprinted in his *Frank Leslie's Illustrated Historical Register of the Centennial Exposition* (New York: Frank Leslie's Publishing House, 1877). See Shapiro, *Child's Garden,* 77.

40. Elizabeth Peabody, *New England Journal of Education* 3 (June 10, 1876): 285.

41. Kraus, "The Kindergarten," 205. For Peabody's resignation, see Elizabeth Peabody, "Valedictory of the Kindergarten Messenger," *New England Journal of Education* 3 (December 30, 1876): 297; and Shapiro, *Child's Garden*, 80–81.

42. On Bradley and Steiger, see Shea, *It's All in the Game;* David Wallace Adams and Victor Edmonds, "Making Your Move: The Educational Significance of the American Board Game, 1832–1904," *History of Education Quarterly* 17 (winter 1977): 359–83; and Shapiro, *Child's Garden*, 68–72.

43. Early alumnae records of Wheelock College in Boston frequently list home kindergartning as an occupation of graduates. On Anna Wright's interest in the kindergarten and her son's reaction, see Shapiro, *Child's Garden*, 68–78.

44. Inez and Marshall McClintock, *Toys in America* (Washington, D.C.: Public Affairs, 1961), 83–84, 147–160, 336, 350, 370. See Bernard Mergen, *Play and Playthings* (Westport, Conn.: Greenwood, 1982).

45. Peabody, "Froebel's Kindergarten," 15. See Shapiro, *Child's Garden*, 72–73.

46. See Vandewalker, *The Kindergarten in American Education*, 147–55.

47. Francis Hedge quoted in Elizabeth Peabody, "The Festival of Froebel's Birthday," *Kindergarten Messenger*, n.s., 1 (May–June 1877): 70.

48. "A Kindergartner," "Kindergarten Training in St. Louis," *New England Journal of Education* 5 (January 18, 1877): 33.

Chapter 5. Educating "Other Peoples' Children"

1. U.S. Department of the Interior, Bureau of Education, *Public and Private Kindergartens*, U.S. Bureau of Education, *Report* 1897–98 (Washington, D.C.: GPO, 1898), 2: 2537–79.

2. On Adler, see Michael Steven Shapiro, *Child's Garden: The Kindergarten Movement from Froebel to Dewey* (University Park: Pennsylvania State University Press, 1983), 86–87.

3. On Shaw's life, see *Pauline Agassiz Shaw: Tributes Paid Her Memory* (Boston: privately printed, 1917), Schlesinger Library, Radcliffe College; Charles W. Eliot, "A Tribute," and Laura Fisher, "Mrs. Shaw's Service to the Kindergarten," in *PKA*, 98–108; and Geoffrey Blodgett, "Pauline Agassiz Shaw," in *NAW*, 3:278–80.

4. See Fanny L. Johnson, "History of the Kindergarten Movement in Boston," *Kindergarten Review* 12 (April 1902): 474–81; Caroline D. Aborn, "Matilda H. Kriege, 1820–1899," and Margaret J. Stannard, "Mary J. Garland, 1834–1901," in *PKA*.

5. Francis W. Parker, "The Kindergarten of Boston," *Kindergarten Magazine* 1 (March 1889): 334–35. For a more detailed description of Shaw's North End kindergartens, see Marvin Lazerson, "Urban Reform and the Schools: Kindergartens in Massachusetts, 1870–1915," *History of Education Quarterly* 11 (summer 1971): 115–42.

6. See Johnson, "History of the Kindergarten Movement in Boston," 477. On Hall's life and work, see Dorothy Ross, *G. Stanley Hall: The Psychologist as Prophet* (Chicago: University of Chicago Press, 1972).

7. On Hall's genetic psychology, see Charles Everett Strickland, "The Child and the Race: The Doctrines of Recapitulation and Culture Epochs in the Rise of the Child-Centered Ideal in American Educational Thought, 1875–1900" (Ph.D. diss., University of Wisconsin, 1963).

8. See G. Stanley Hall, *The Contents of Children's Mind on Entering School* (New York: E. L. Kellogg, 1893), 13, 16, 22. The study was originally published in the *Princeton*

Review 11 (May 1883): 249–72, and then reprinted in *Pedagogical Seminary* 1 (June 1891): 139–73, and in Theodate Smith, ed., *Aspects of Child Life and Education* (Boston: Ginn, 1907), 1–52.

9. Hall, *Contents of Children's Mind*, 22–24.

10. Lucy Wheelock, "My Life Story," unpublished autobiography, Lucy Wheelock Collection, Archives, Wheelock College, 12, 14.

11. See G. Stanley Hall, "Psychological Education," *American Journal of Insanity* 53 (October 1896): 237. On the child study movement, see Leila Zenderland, "Education, Evangelism, and the Origins of Clinical Psychology: The Child Study Legacy," *Journal of the History of the Behavioral Sciences* 24 (April 1988): 152–65; and Alexander Siegel and Sheldon White, "The Child Study Movement: Early Growth and Development of the Symbolized Child," *Advances in Child Behavior and Development* 17 (1982): 233–85.

12. "Clark University Summer School," *Kindergarten Magazine* 12 (September 1899): 22; Wheelock, "My Life Story," 22. See Summer School records, boxes 1 and 2, Clark University Archives..

13. "Topical Syllabi for Educational Study. New Series, School Year 1895–6. XIII. Kindergarten," in *Topical Syllabi, 1894–99*, Clark University Archives. See also Sheldon H. White, "Child Study at Clark University: 1894–1904," *Journal of the History of the Behavioral Sciences* 26 (April 1990): 131–50.

14. G. Stanley Hall, "The Study of Children," *Report of the Commissioner of Education for the Year 1892–93*, 368–69, volume 5 of Hall's Collected Papers, Clark University Archives.

15. G. Stanley Hall, "Child Study in Summer Schools," *Regents Bulletin*, State University of New York, July 5–7, 1894, 333, 334, Clark University Archives.

16. Wheelock, "My Life Story," 13.

17. David Snedden, in Massachusetts Board of Education, *Annual Report 1913–1914* (Boston, 1914), 198, quoted in Robert Melvin Tank, "Young Children, Families, and Society in America since the 1820s: The Evolution of Health, Education, and Child Care Programs for Preschool Children" (Ph.D. diss. University of Michigan, 1980), 65.

18. See Marvin Lazerson, "If All the World Were Chicago: American Education in the Twentieth Century," *History of Education Quarterly* 24 (summer 1984): 165–80.

19. See biographical entries on Bryan by Patty Smith Hill in *PKA*, 223–30; and M. Charlotte Jammer in *NAW*, 1:263–64. See also Cora L. Stockham, "The Louisville Free Kindergarten," *Kindergarten Magazine* 1 (January 1889): 281–82; and J.B.O., "Anna E. Bryan," *Kindergarten News* 6 (April 1896): 115–17.

20. Louisville Free Kindergarten Association Report quoted in Stockham, "The Louisville Free Kindergarten," 281; Anna Bryan, "The Free Kindergarten as a Philanthropic Agent," Louisville Free Kindergarten Association, *Report for 1894–95*, 11, 12, Gutman Library, Harvard Graduate School of Education.

21. Bryan, "The Free Kindergarten," 13.

22. Anna Bryan, "The Letter Killeth," *Journal of Proceedings and Addresses* (National Education Association) (1890): 573, 574–75.

23. Cora L. Stockham, "A Glimpse of the Louisville Kindergartens," *Kindergarten Magazine* 2 (April 1890): 385, 386.

24. Patty Smith Hill, "The Free Kindergarten as the Basis of Education," Louisville Free Kindergarten Association, *Report for 1894–95* (Louisville: Louisville Free Kindergarten Association, 1895), 8.

25. See Elizabeth Dale Ross, *The Kindergarten Crusade: The Establishment of Preschool Education in the United States* (Athens: Ohio University Press, 1976), 76.

26. On Putnam, see Amalie Hofer, "Evolution of the Kindergarten Idea in Chicago," *Kindergarten Magazine* 5 (June 1893): 729–33; Bertha Payne Newell, "Alice H. Putnam," in *PKA*, 204–22; and Robert L. McCaul, "Alice H. Putnam," in *NAW*, 3:105–6.

27. See Newell, "Alice H. Putnam," 206. On female Progressives and domestic reform, see, in particular, Ellen Condliffe Lagemann, *A Generation of Women: Education in the Lives of Progressive Reformers* (Cambridge: Harvard University Press, 1979); and Ellen Fitzpatrick, *Endless Crusade: Women Social Scientists and Progressive Reform* (New York: Oxford University Press, 1990).

28. Putnam quoted in Newell, "Alice H. Putnam," 207–9.

29. Parker quoted in Newell, 210. On Parker, see Charles Francis Adams, Jr., *The New Departure in the Common Schools of Quincy* (Boston: Estes and Lauriat, 1881); Lawrence A. Cremin, *The Transformation of the School: Progressivism in American Education, 1876–1957* (New York: Vintage, 1964); and Michael Katz, "The 'New Departure' in Quincy, 1873–1881: The Nature of Nineteenth-Century Educational Reform," *New England Quarterly* (March 1967): 3–30.

30. On the kindergarten at Hull House, see Jane Addams, *Twenty Years at Hull House, with Autobiographical Notes* (New York: New American Library, 1960); Newell, "Alice Putnam," 213–14; Amalie Hofer, "The Social Settlement and the Kindergarten," *Kindergarten News* 5 (September 1895): 251–53; and Bertha Payne, "The Hull House Children's Building," *Kindergarten Magazine* 8 (February 1896): 391–97. There is some debate over whether kindergartners were as fully involved in the settlement movement as other settlement workers because, like Putnam, they did not always live in the settlement itself. Kindergartners in Boston's Elizabeth Peabody House did live in the settlement, however, as did other kindergartners in some other locations.

31. Dewey quoted in Payne, "The Hull House Children's Building," 397.

32. John Dewey, "Froebel's Educational Principles," *Elementary School Record* 1 (June 1900): 151. For detailed descriptions of the kindergarten at the University of Chicago Laboratory School, see Georgia P. Scates, "The Sub-Primary (Kindergarten) Department," *Elementary School Record* 1 (June 1900): 129–41; and Katherine Camp Mayhew and Anna Camp Edwards, *The Dewey School: The Laboratory School of the University of Chicago, 1896–1903* (New York: D. Appleton–Century, 1936), 56–73.

33. Dewey, "Froebel's Educational Principles," 147.

34. Sources on Harrison's life include her autobiography *Sketches Along Life's Road* (Boston: Stratford Co., 1930); McCaul, "Elizabeth Harrison," 147–50; Agnes Snyder, "Elizabeth Harrison (1849–1927) Bridging the Old and the New," in *Dauntless Women in Childhood Education, 1857–1931* (Washington, D.C.: Association for Childhood Education International, 1972), 127–66; and Ross, *Kindergarten Crusade*, 55–57.

35. "Miss Harrison and the Chicago Kindergarten College," *Kindergarten Magazine* 9 (May 1897): 740–42.

36. Susan E. Blow, "Kindergarten Education," in Nicholas Murray Butler, *Education in the United States* (New York: American Book Co., 1910), 43. See Ross, *Kindergarten Crusade*, 56.

37. Elizabeth Harrison, "The Scope and Results of Mothers' Classes," in National Education Association, *Addresses and Proceedings* (Washington, D.C.: NEA, 1903), 403.

38. "Miss Harrison and the Chicago Kindergarten College," 742.

39. Harrison, "Scope and Results of Mothers' Classes," 401.

40. Harrison, "Scope and Results of Mothers' Classes," 402; Elizabeth Harrison, "Hints for Mothers' Clubs," *Kindergarten Magazine* 2 (August 1889): 108.

41. Elizabeth Harrison, *A Study of Child Nature from the Kindergarten Standpoint*, 17th ed. (Chicago: Chicago Kindergarten College, 1895), 9, 11–12.

42. "The Chicago Conference of Mothers, An Epoch in the History of Education," *Kindergarten Magazine* 7 (November 1894): 211, 214, 217, 219, 220–21.

43. "The School of Psychology," *Kindergarten Review* 9 (May 1899): 607.

44. William Torrey Harris, "Two Kinds of Psychology," *Kindergarten Review* 9 (May 1899): 603–5.

45. See Janet Wilson James, "Emma Marwedel," *NAW*, 2:506–8. For more on Marwedel, see Fletcher H. Swift, *Emma Marwedel, 1818–1893: Pioneer of the Kindergarten in California* (Berkeley: University of California Publications in Education, 1931); and Earl Barnes, "Emma Marwedel," in *PKA*, 265–69.

46. Emma Marwedel, *Conscious Motherhood, or the Earliest Unfolding of the Child in the Cradle, Nursery, and Kindergarten* (Boston: Heath, 1889), 18, 24.

47. Biographical sources on Kate Douglas Wiggin include her autobiography, *My Garden of Memory* (Boston: Houghton Mifflin, 1923); Doyce B. Nunis, Jr., "Kate Douglas Wiggin," in *NAW*, 605–7; Nora Archibald Smith, "Kate Douglas Wiggin," and Lucy Wheelock, "A Tribute to Kate Douglas Wiggin," in *PKA*, 283–95 and 296–98; Nora Archibald Smith, *Kate Douglas Wiggin as Her Sister Knew Her* (Boston: Houghton Mifflin, 1925); Snyder, *Dauntless Women in Early Childhood Education*, 89–123; and Lois Rather, *Miss Kate: Kate Douglas Wiggin in San Francisco* (Oakland, Calif.: Rather, 1980). Wiggin's papers are held at the Bowdoin College Library in Brunswick, Maine.

48. Wiggin, *My Garden of Memory*, 107; Kate D. S. Wiggin, "The Free Kindergarten Work of the Pacific Coast," in *Superintendent's Report on the Work of the New Silver Street Kindergarten Society* (San Francisco: C. A. Murdock, 1883), 24–25. See *Annual Statement of the Silver Street Kindergarten Society for the Year Ending December 31st, 1885* (San Francisco: C. A. Murdock, 1886), 9; Joaquin Miller, "A Day in a Kindergarten," in *Sixth Annual Statement of the Silver Street Kindergarten Society for the Year Ending December 31, 1887* (San Francisco: C. A. Murdock, 1888), 22–23; *Annual Statement of the Silver Street Kindergarten Society for the Year Ending December 31st, 1891* (San Francisco: C. A. Murdock, 1892), 12. Silver Street records are held at the Bancroft Library at the University of California at Berkeley.

49. Wiggin, "Free Kindergarten Work of the Pacific Coast," 24–25; San Francisco Public Kindergarten Society, *Report for the Three Years Ending Sept. 1st, 1881*, 13, Bancroft Library, University of California, Berkeley.

50. San Francisco Public Kindergarten Society, *Report for the Three Years Ending Sept. 1st, 1881*, 14; Kate Douglas Wiggin, *The Story of Patsy* (Boston: Houghton Mifflin, 1895), 65–66.

51. Kate Douglas Wiggin, *Children's Rights: A Book of Nursery Logic* (Boston: Houghton Mifflin, 1894), 8.

52. On children's rights generally, see, among others, Hillary Rodham, "Children and the Law," and Victor L. Worsfold, "A Philosophical Justification for Children's Rights," in Rochelle Beck and Heather Bastow Weiss, eds., *The Rights of Children*, Harvard Educational Review Reprint Series, No. 9 (Cambridge: Harvard Educational Review, 1982),

1–28 and 29–48; Hillary Rodham, "Children's Rights: A Legal Perspective," in Patricia A. Vardin and Ilene N. Brody, eds., *Children's Rights: Contemporary Perspectives* (New York: Teachers College Press, 1979); Martha Minnow, "Rights for the Next Generation: A Feminist Approach to Children's Rights," *Harvard Women's Law Journal* 9 (1986): 1–24; and Michael Grossberg, "Children's Legal Rights? An Historical Look at a Legal Paradox," in Roberta Wollons, ed., *Children At-Risk* (Albany: State University of New York Press, 1992). For a fascinating nineteenth-century view of children's own sense of their rights, see Margaret Schallenberger, "A Study of Children's Rights, As Seen By Themselves," *Pedagogical Seminary* 3 (1894): 87–96.

53. For biographical information on Smith, see entries in *The National Cyclopaedia of American Biography*, B:161 and 26:400; and references throughout Wiggin's autobiography, *My Garden of Memory*.

54. Nora Archibald Smith, *The Children of the Future* (Boston and New York: Houghton, Mifflin and Company, 1898), 4, 34, 37, 45.

55. On Cooper and Hearst, see Anna K. Stovall, "Sarah B. Cooper, 1834–1896," in *PKA*, 270–79; Kathleen Jacklin, "Sarah Cooper," in *NAW*, 1:380–82; Rodman Wilson Paul, "Phoebe Apperson Hearst," *NAW*, 2:171–73; and Shapiro, *Child's Garden*, 93–95. The correspondence between Cooper and Hearst, which includes the poignant notes they exchanged right before Cooper's death, is in the Phoebe Apperson Hearst Papers at the Bancroft Library at the University of California, Berkeley.

56. See Susan M. Yohn, "An Education in the Validity of Pluralism: The Meeting Between Presbyterian Mission Teachers and Hispanic Catholics in New Mexico, 1870–1912," paper presented at the Annual Meeting of the Organization of American Historians, Washington, D.C., March 25, 1990, and personal correspondence, April 10, 1990; and Sylvia Hunt, "To Wed and to Teach: The Myth of the Single Teacher," paper presented at the Annual Meeting of the History of Education Society, Atlanta, Georgia, November 1990, and personal correspondence, November 7, 1990.

57. Thomas Charles, "Letter From New Mexico," *Kindergarten News* 5 (May 1895): 153; Lucie Calista Maley, "Benefit of the Kindergarten to the Indian Children," *Kindergarten Magazine* 10 (March 1898): 438–39. For more on Hailmann, see Barbara Greenwood, "William Nicholas Hailmann, 1836–1920," in *PKA*, 258.

Chapter 6. "The Land of Childhood"

1. *Report of the United States Commissioner of Education for 1897–98* (Washington, D.C.: United States Department of Education, 1899), 2:2537; United States Department of Commerce and Labor, Bureau of the Census, "Abstract of the Census with Supplement for Massachusetts," *Thirteenth Census of the United States, Taken in the Year 1910* (Washington, D.C.: GPO, 1913), 221, table 2.

2. See Fanny L. Johnson, "History of the Kindergarten Movement in Boston," *Kindergarten Review* 12 (April 1902): 478; "School Document No. 18," in *Annual Report of the School Committee of the City of Boston for the Year Ending in June of 1888* (Boston, 1889), 11.

3. Edwin P. Seaver, "The Introduction of the Kindergarten into Boston: How the Financial Difficulties Were Overcome," *United States Bureau of Education Report for 1890–91* (Washington, D.C.: GPO, 1892), 1046.

4. William Torrey Harris, "Story of the Kindergarten in St. Louis," *United States Bureau of Education Report, 1890–91* (Washington, D.C.: GPO, 1892), 1047.

5. Nina C. Vandewalker, "The Kindergarten in the Chicago School System," *Kindergarten Magazine* 9 (May 1897): 683; Edna Isabelle Matthews, "Chicago Public School Kindergartners Organize," *Kindergarten Magazine* 6 (February 1898): 411.

6. Matthews, "Chicago Public School Kindergartners Organize," 413, 411, 412. On the Federation of Chicago Teachers, see Marjorie Murphy, *Blackboard Unions: The AFT and the NEA, 1900–1980* (Ithaca: Cornell University Press, 1990); and Wayne J. Urban, *Why Teachers Organized* (Detroit: Wayne State University Press, 1982). On teachers' salaries, see James C. Boykin and Roberta King, *The Tangible Rewards of Teaching: A Detailed Statement of Salaries Paid to the Various Classes of Teachers and School Officers*, U.S. Bureau of Education Bulletin No. 15 (Washington, D.C.: GPO, 1914). On the social-class backgrounds of teachers, see John L. Rury, "Who Became Teachers? The Social Characteristics of Teachers in American History"; on economic incentives, see Susan B. Carter, "Incentives and Rewards to Teaching"; and on labor organizing among teachers, see Wayne J. Urban, "Teacher Activism," in Donald Warren, ed., *American Teachers: Histories of a Profession at Work* (New York: Macmillan, 1990), 9–48, 49–62, and 190–210, respectively.

7. See Jenny B. Merrill, "The Men Who Have Helped the Kindergarten in New York City," and James M. Bruce, "New York Kindergarten Association," *Kindergarten Magazine and Pedagogical Digest* 29 (April 1907): 546–47 and 574; and Mary H. Waterman, "The New York Kindergarten Association," *Kindergarten Review* 17 (April 1907): 461–67.

8. On enrollments in kindergartens in New York, see Jenny B. Merrill, "Twelve Hundred and Fifty Children in New York Public Kindergartens," *Kindergarten Magazine* 11 (October 1898): 106; E. Lyell Earle, "Some Problems of the Kindergarten Today: Are We Neglecting the Child of Kindergarten Age?" *Kindergarten-Primary Magazine* 21 (June 1909): 292–95 and Waterman, "The New York Kindergarten Association," 464.

9. Bruce, "New York Kindergarten Association," 576. For a fascinating study of ethnicity in New York public kindergartens from a child study perspective, see Earl Barnes, "Ideals of New York Kindergarten Children," *Kindergarten Magazine* 15 (October 1903): 86–100.

10. *The Kindergarten and Americanization*, U.S. Department of the Interior, Bureau of Education Kindergarten Circular No. 3 (Washington, D.C.: GPO, 1918), 3; S. E. Weber, *The Kindergarten as an Americanizer*, U.S. Department of the Interior, Bureau of Education Kindergarten Circular No. 5 (Washington, D.C.: GPO, 1919), 2, 4.

11. National Kindergarten Association, *Annual Report 1909–1911*, Gutman Library, Harvard Graduate School of Education, 3.

12. National Kindergarten Association, *Annual Report 1909–1911*, 34.

13. For a first-person account of the establishment of public kindergartens for black children in Washington, D.C., see Anna J. Murray, "A New Key to the Situation," *Southern Workman* 29 (September 1900): 503–7. For the San Francisco experience, see Golden Gate Kindergarten Association, "Report of Work, 1911–1915," Bancroft Library, University of California, Berkeley.

14. Marguerite Crespi Marsh, "Resume of National Kindergarten Propaganda," in *International Kindergarten Union Yearbooks 1915–1918*, 96, box I-6, Archives of the Association for Childhood Education International, Historical Manuscripts and Archives Department, University of Maryland College Park Libraries, College Park.

15. Josephine Silone Yates, "Kindergartens and Mothers' Clubs," *Colored American Magazine* 8 (1905): 308. See also Andrew Billingsley and Jeanne M. Giovannoni, *Children of the Storm: Black Children and American Child Welfare* (New York: Harcourt Brace Jovanovich,

1972). For statistics on the spread of public kindergartens in the South, see Nina C. Vandewalker, "Kindergarten Progress from 1919–20 to 1921–22," U.S. Department of the Interior, Bureau of Education Kindergarten Circular No. 16 (Washington, D.C.: GPO, 1924), 3–4.

16. "A Week in the Hampton Kindergarten," *Southern Workman* 36 (October 1907): 537–544. See Passie Fenton Ottley, "Kindergartens for Colored Children," *Southern Workman* 30 (February 1901): 103–4; and Alice Dugged Cary, "Kindergartens for Negro Children," *Southern Workman* 29 (August 1900): 492. For an overview, see Charles E. Cunningham and D. Keith Osborn, "A Historical Examination of Blacks in Early Childhood Education," *Young Children* 34 (March 1979): 20–29.

17. Murray, "A New Key," 504 (see also 503); Josephine Silone Yates, "Education and Genetic Psychology," *Colored American Magazine* 10 (1906): 293–97; Yates, "Kindergartens and Mothers' Clubs," 304–11. On Haydee Campbell, see the biographical essay in Monroe A. Majors, *Noted Negro Women* (Chicago: Donohue and Henneberry, 1893), 329; and Cunningham and Osborn, "Blacks in Early Childhood Education," 24. On the Louisville Free Kindergarten Association's training class for African-Americans, see Patty Smith Hill, "The Free Kindergarten as an Educational Need of the South," and Finie Murfree Burton, "The Louisville Free Kindergarten Association; Its History, Origin, and Work," both in Louisville Free Kindergarten Association, *Seventeenth Annual Report, 1904–05,* Gutman Library, Harvard Graduate School of Education, 17, 18.

18. Brochure, "Kindergarten Training Class at Chauncy-Hall School," 1894, Lucy Wheelock Collection, Archives, Wheelock College, Boston.

19. See Barbara Beatty, "'The Kind of Knowledge of Most Worth to Young Women': Post-Secondary Vocational Training for Teaching and Motherhood at the Wheelock School, 1888–1914," *History of Higher Education Annual* 6 (1986): 29–50.

20. Margaret Tillotson Edsall, Diary, Schlesinger Library, Radcliffe College, MC354, entries for February 20, May 10, and May 31, 1888. For other accounts of training, see Lucy Wheelock, "My Life Story," 76, Lucy Wheelock Collection, Archives, Wheelock College, Boston; Elizabeth Dale Ross, *The Kindergarten Crusade: The Establishment of Preschool Education in the United States* (Athens, Ohio: Ohio University Press, 1976), 52–66; and Michael Steven Shapiro, *Child's Garden: The Kindergarten Movement from Froebel to Dewey* (University Park: Pennsylvania State University Press, 1983), 38–40.

21. *Kindergartens in the United States: Statistics and Present Problems,* U.S. Department of the Interior, Bureau of Education Bulletin No. 6 (Washington, D.C.: GPO, 1914), 7; Vandewalker, "Kindergarten Progress"; "Statistical Summary of Education," *Biennial Survey of Education in the United States, 1956–58,* quoted in Neith Headley, *The Kindergarten: Its Place in the Program of Education* (New York: Center for Applied Research in Education, 1959), 11; and Nina C. Vandewalker, *Kindergarten Training Schools,* U.S. Department of the Interior, Bureau of Education Bulletin No. 5 (Washington, D.C.: GPO, 1916), 7.

22. Vandewalker, *Kindergarten Training in Schools,* 7–8.

23. California Kindergarten Training School, *Report of the Twelfth Year, 1892,* Bancroft Library, University of California, Berkeley.

24. Kate Douglas Wiggin, "Our Kindergartners," in Nora A. Smith, ed. *A History of Our Beginnings,* Froebel Society of the California Kindergarten Training School Tract No. 1, August 12, 1883, 6, 8, 10, Bancroft Library, University of California, Berkeley.

25. Nora Archibald Smith, "The Gentlemen," in *A History of Our Beginnings,* 15–16.

26. Sarah B. Cooper, "Woman's Work," in Smith, *A History of Our Beginnings,* 16–17.

27. Programs for graduation exercises of the California Kindergarten Training School for the classes of 1881 on, Bancroft Library, University of California, Berkeley.

28. E.E.M., "Kindergarten Lectures at Radcliffe," *Kindergarten Review* 8 (May 1898): 612–13.

29. Curricular Materials, Department of Pedagogy, and McKeag Biography File, Archives, Wellesley College. See Margarethe Muller, *Carla Wenckebach, Pioneer* (Boston: Ginn, 1908); and *Wellesley College Calendar*, 1988, 49. On the Brookline Training Class for College Graduates, see Samuel P. Dutton, "The Training of College Graduates for the Work of Teaching," *Education* 16 (May 1896): 524–26.

30. On Norton, Hanus, and interest in the kindergarten at Harvard, see Arthur O. Norton, Biography File, Archives, Wellesley College; and Arthur G. Powell, *The Uncertain Profession: Harvard and the Search for Educational Authority* (Cambridge: Harvard University Press, 1980). On Devereaux and the Page school, see Biography File and Anne L. Page Memorial School files, Archives, Wellesley College.

31. Lawrence A. Cremin, David A. Shannon, and Mary Evelyn Townsend, *A History of Teachers College, Columbia University* (New York: Columbia University Press, 1954); Geraldine Joncich Clifford and James W. Guthrie, *Ed School* (Chicago: University of Chicago Press, 1988); "Teachers' College—Kindergarten Department Columbia University," *Kindergarten Magazine* 19 (April 1907): 532–81.

32. See Shapiro, *Child's Garden*, 163–70.

33. Agnes Burke, Edith V. Conard, Alice Dalgliesh, Charlotte G. Garrison, Edna V. Hughes, Mary E. Rankin, and Alice Thorn, *A Conduct Curriculum for the Kindergarten and First Grade* (New York: Scribner's, 1923): 44–45, quoted in Evelyn Weber, *The Kindergarten: Its Encounter with Educational Thought in America* (New York: Teachers College Press, 1969), 131. On Thorndike, see Geraldine Joncich's detailed biography, *The Sane Positivist: A Biography of Edward L. Thorndike* (Middletown, Conn.: Wesleyan University Press, 1968).

34. Quoted in Beulah Amidon, "Forty Years in Kindergarten," *Survey Graphic* 23 (September 1934), 508–9.

35. For the classic critique, see William Heard Kilpatrick, *The Montessori System Examined* (Boston: Houghton Mifflin, 1914). See also Elizabeth Harrison, *The Montessori Method and the Kindergarten*, U.S. Department of the Interior, Bureau of Education Bulletin No. 28 (Washington, D.C.: GPO, 1914); and idem, *Sketches Along Life's Road* (Boston: Stratford Co., 1930), 182–96.

36. International Kindergarten Union, *The Kindergarten: Reports of the Committee of Nineteen on the Theory and Practice of the Kindergarten* (New York: Houghton Mifflin, 1913). See Shapiro, *Child's Garden*, 171–91; Weber, *The Kindergarten*; and Caroline T. Haven, "The International Kindergarten Union—Its Origin," and Annie E. Laws, "Its Past—What It Has Accomplished," *Kindergarten Magazine* 20 (June 1908): 331–33 and 333–35.

37. Julia Wade Abbot, *The Child and the Kindergarten*, U.S. Department of the Interior, Bureau of Education Kindergarten Circular No. 6 (Washington, D.C.: U.S. GPO, 1920), 23.

38. Frederick Burk and Caroline Frear Burk, *A Study of the Kindergarten Problem* (San Francisco: Whitaker and Ray, 1899), 81.

39. Samuel Chester Parker and Alice Temple, *Unified Kindergarten and First-Grade Teaching* (Boston: Ginn, 1925), 1, 2, 23–24, 569.

40. Polly Welts Kaufman, "Boston Women and City School Politics, 1872–1905: Nurturers and Protectors in Public Education" (Ph.D. diss., Boston University, 1978); Patricia A.

Schmuck, "Women School Employees in the United States," in Patricia A. Schmuck, ed., *Women Educators: Employees of Schools in Western Countries* (Albany: State University of New York Press, 1987), 91.

41. Augusta Larned, "Public School Lambs," *Kindergarten Magazine* 11 (June 1895): 744, 745, 747.

42. Almira M. Winchester, *Kindergarten Supervision in City Schools*, U.S. Department of the Interior, Bureau of Education Bulletin, 1918, No. 38 (Washington, D.C.: GPO, 1919), 23–30.

43. For comparisons of the administrative practices of male public school superintendents and principals and female kindergarten directors, see David Tyack and Elizabeth Hansot, *Managers of Virtue: Public School Leadership in America, 1820–1980* (New York: Basic, 1982). For some interpretations of these differences, see Michael W. Apple, "Work, Gender, and Teaching," *Teachers College Record* 84 (spring 1983): 611–28; Jean Anyon, "Intersections of Gender and Class: Accommodation and Resistance by Working-Class and Affluent Females to Contradictory Sex Role Ideologies," and Madeline Arnot, "A Feminist Perspective on the Relationship Between Family Life and School Life," in *Journal of Education* 166 (November 1, 1984): 25–110 and 5–24.

44. Winchester, *Kindergarten Supervision in City Schools*, 30, 46.

45. Winchester, *Kindergarten Supervision in City Schools*, 9–21.

46. Luella A. Palmer, *Adjustment Between Kindergarten and First Grade, Including a Study of Double Sessions in the Kindergarten*, U.S. Department of the Interior, Bureau of Education Bulletin No. 24 (Washington, D.C.: GPO, 1915), 21, 22–24. For documentation of superintendents' concerns about the cost of kindergartens, see Marvin Lazerson, "Urban Reform and the Schools: Kindergartens in Massachusetts, 1870–1915," *History of Education Quarterly* 11 (summer 1971): 130–35.

47. National Education Association report on teachers' salaries and salary trends, July 1923, 13, quoted in *Organizing Kindergartens in City School Systems*, U.S. Department of the Interior, Bureau of Education Kindergarten Circular No. 2 (Washington, D.C.: GPO, 1923), 3. See also Boykin and King, *The Tangible Rewards of Teaching*.

48. Palmer, *Adjustment Between Kindergarten and First grade*, 25. I gained the insight about kindergartners' awareness of the trade-off between class sizes and double sessions from talking with Rhoda Case Brown, Wheelock College Class of 1921, who taught kindergarten for thirty-five years in New London, Connecticut.

49. Patty Smith Hill, "The Future of the Kindergarten," *Teachers College Record* 10 (November 1909): 48–49; Laura Fisher, "The Kindergarten in the School," *Kindergarten Review* 10 (May 1900): 562.

50. E. E. M., "Kindergarten Lectures at Radcliffe," 613.

51. Palmer, *Adjustment Between Kindergarten and First Grade*, 5, 6, 7, 9.

52. Winchester, *Kindergarten Supervision in City Schools*, 23.

53. Quoted in Nina C. Vandewalker, "The Kindergarten Conference," in *University Record* 2 (May 7, 1897): 52–53.

54. Charles W. Eliot, "The Improvements Which the Kindergarten has Suggested in Higher Departments of Instruction," *Kindergarten Review* 12 (June 1902): 591, 593, 595, 596, 598.

55. Quoted in Vandewalker, "The Kindergarten Conference," 53. See Palmer, *Adjustment Between Kindergarten and First Grade;* Vandewalker, *Kindergarten Training Schools;* Waite, *The Kindergarten in Certain City School Surveys*, U.S. Department of the Interior, Office of Education Bulletin (Washington, D.C.: GPO, 1926); and Mary Dabney Davis, *Kinder-*

garten-Primary Education, U.S. Department of the Interior, Office of Education Bulletin (Washington, D.C.: GPO, 1930). Observational studies include Winifred E. Bain, *An Analytical Study of Teaching in Nursery School, Kindergarten, and First Grade* (New York: Bureau of Publications, Teachers College, Columbia University, 1928); and Grace Langdon, *Similarities and Differences in Teaching in Nursery School, Kindergarten, and First Grade* (New York: John Day, 1933).

56. *Kindergartens in the United States,* 11–12; Lazerson, "Urban Reform and the Schools," 136; Vandewalker, *The Kindergarten in American Education*, 254.

57. Vandewalker, *The Kindergarten in American Education*.

Chapter 7. *"A Place for Children in the Modern World"*

1. Ada Hart Arlitt, "The Contribution of the Nursery School to the Home," in Dorothy Canfield Fisher and Sidonie Matsner Gruenberg, eds., *Our Children: A Handbook for Parents* (New York: Viking, 1932), 107.

2. Steven L. Schlossman, "Philanthropy and the Gospel of Child Development," *History of Education Quarterly* 21 (fall 1981): 297.

3. Ibid., 278–79, 291.

4. On the history of British nursery schools, see Ilse Forest, *Preschool Education: A Historical and Critical Study* (New York: Macmillan, 1927); Education Enquiry Committee, *The Case for Nursery Schools* (London: George Philip and Son, 1929); and Nanette Whitbread, *The Evolution of the Nursery-Infant School: A History of Infant and Nursery Education in Britain, 1800–1970* (London: Routledge and Kegan Paul, 1972).

5. Margaret McMillan, "How I Became a Socialist," *Labour Leader*, July 11, 1912, quoted in Carolyn Steedman, *Childhood, Culture and Class in Britain: Margaret McMillan, 1860–1931* (New Brunswick: Rutgers University Press, 1990), 15.

6. Patty Smith Hill, foreword to Margaret McMillan, *The Nursery School* (New York: Dutton, 1921), ix–x. See Emma Stevinson, *The Open-Air Nursery School* (London: Dent, 1923).

7. John Watson, *Psychological Care of the Infant and Child* (New York: W. W. Norton, 1928), 5–6, 81, 87.

8. Caroline Pratt, *I Learn From Children: An Adventure in Progressive Education* (New York: Simon and Schuster, 1948), 14–15.

9. Joyce Antler, *Lucy Sprague Mitchell: The Making of a Modern Woman* (New Haven: Yale University Press, 1987), 218, 301.

10. Pratt, *I Learn From Children*, 58, 65; Caroline Pratt, "Pedagogy as a Creative Art," in Caroline Pratt and Jessie Stanton, *Before Books* (New York: Adelphi, 1926), 8, 9, 10; Caroline Pratt, foreword to Lucy Sprague Mitchell, *Here and Now Story Book* (New York: Dutton, 1921), xi.

11. Pratt, *I Learn From Children*, 203, 204, 168.

12. Some of my impression of Pratt's personality was gained from private discussion with Joyce Antler, who interviewed many of Pratt's former Bank Street colleagues.

13. For sources on Harriet Johnson, see Barbara Biber, Lucy S. Mitchell, Jessie Stanton, and Louise Woodcock, "Harriet Merrill Johnson," and "The Working Background of Harriet Johnson's Contribution to Education," in Harriet M. Johnson, *School Begins at Two*, ed. Barbara Biber (New York: New Republic, 1936); and Antler, *Lucy Sprague Mitchell*, 209–10 and 257. On female reformers in New York in the 1890s and early 1900s and the

Henry Street Settlement, see Ellen Condliffe Lagemann, *A Generation of Women: Education in the Lives of Progressive Reformers* (Cambridge: Harvard University Press, 1979), especially 67–68.

14. Lucy Sprague Mitchell, introduction to Harriet Johnson, *A Nursery School Experiment* (New York: Bureau of Educational Experiments, 1922), 3.

15. Harriet M. Johnson, *The Art of Block Building* (New York: John Day, 1933), 39–40. See also Elizabeth S. Hirsch, ed., *The Block Book* (Washington, D.C.: National Association for the Education of Young Children, 1974).

16. Harriet M. Johnson, *Children in the Nursery School* (New York: John Day Company, 1928), xv, 56, 60, 11. For rules against rough behavior, see ibid., 57. See also Harriet M. Johnson, *School Begins at Two*, ed. Barbara Biber (New York: New Republic, 1936).

17. Johnson, *Children in the Nursery School*, 92, 94, 97.

18. Johnson, *Children in the Nursery School*, 94, 97. On the history of Bank Street, see Antler, *Lucy Sprague Mitchell*.

19. Abigail Eliot, personal interview with Barbara Beatty, July 1, 1980, typescript in Abigail Adams Eliot Papers, Schlesinger Library, Radcliffe College; Abigail Eliot, "By the Skin of My Teeth," *Radcliffe Quarterly* 72 (September 1986): 27; Abigail Eliot, letter to Charles Eliot, January 27, 1920, Eliot Papers, Schlesinger Library.

20. Abigail Eliot, Letter to her mother from Deptford, September 13, 1921, Eliot Papers; "America's First Nursery Schools: An Interview with Abigail A. Eliot," in James L. Hymes, Jr., *Living History Interviews*, vol. 1, *Beginnings* (Carmel, Calif.: Hacienda, 1978), 10.

21. "America's First Nursery Schools," 11; Abigail Adams Eliot, Letters to Mrs. Henry G. Pearson, June 14, 1921, and July 20, 1921, Abigail Adams Eliot Papers, Schlesinger Library, Radcliffe College.

22. Abigail Eliot, Letter to Mrs. Henry G. Pearson, August 21, 1921, Eliot Papers, Schlesinger Library.

23. "America's First Nursery Schools," 11; Abigail Eliot, "Report of the Ruggles Street Nursery School and Training Center," in Samuel J. Braun and Esther P. Edwards, *History and Theory of Early Childhood Education* (Worthington, Ohio: Charles A. Jones Publishing Company, 1972), 152. For the entrance age, see "America's First Nursery Schools," 19.

24. Abigail Eliot, "Educating the Parent through the Nursery School," *Childhood Education* 3 (December 1926): 183.

25. Eliot, interview with Beatty, 8.

26. Tribute to Abigail Adams Eliot, vita, "Ruggles Street Nursery Training School, 1926," Eliot Papers, Schlesinger Library; Eliot-Pearson files, Archives, Wessell Library, Tufts University.

27. On Gesell's life and work, see Louise Bates Ames, *Arnold Gesell: Themes of His Work* (New York: Human Sciences, 1989); W. R. Miles, *Arnold Lucius Gesell, 1880–1961: A Biographical Memoir*, Biographical Memoirs, no. 37 (New York: Columbia University Press, 1964); Arnold Gesell, "Autobiography," in *A History of Psychology in Autobiography*, vol. 4 (Worcester, Mass.: Clark University Press, 1952), 123–42; and William Kessen, *The Child* (New York: Wiley, 1965).

28. See Roy Lubove, *The Professional Altruist: The Emergence of Social Work as a Career* (New York: Atheneum, 1977); Sol Cohen, "The Mental Hygiene Movement, the Development of Personality, and the School: The Medicalization of American Education,"

History of Education Quarterly 23 (summer 1983): 123–49; and Margo Horn, *Before It's Too Late: The Child Guidance Movement in the United States, 1922–1945* (Philadelphia: Temple University Press, 1989).

29. Arnold Gesell, *The Pre-School Child* (New York: Houghton Mifflin, 1923), 2, iv.

30. For information on kindergartners' views on coordination with primary grades, see "The Contribution of the Kindergarten to the Elementary School," Association for Childhood Education International Yearbook 1919–1922, ACEI Archives; IKU Committee on "Reading Readiness," 1929–30, "Points of View on the Problem of 'Reading Readiness,'" group 1, box 1, ACEI Archives.

31. Arnold Gesell, "The Guidance Nursery of the Yale Psycho-Clinic," in National Society for the Study of Education, *Twenty-Eighth Yearbook: Preschool and Parental Education* (Bloomington, Ill.: Public School Publishing Company, 1929), 168–69. See Ames, *Arnold Gesell,* 136–37.

32. Gesell, "The Guidance Nursery," 167.

33. Douglas Thom, *Habit Clinics for the Child of Preschool Age* (Washington, D.C.: Children's Bureau, 1924), 36, 60.

34. Douglas A. Thom, "The Need of Mental Hygiene for Teachers of Young Children," *Childhood Education* 7 (April 1931): 396; Grace Caldwell, "The Play School for Habit Training," in National Society for the Study of Education, *Twenty-Eighth Yearbook: Preschool and Parental Education* (Bloomington, Ill.: Public School Publishing Company, 1929), 210. See also Julia Grant, "New Habits for Old: Parent Education and the Nursery School Movement in Boston," paper presented at the Annual Meeting of the History of Education Society, Chicago, October 29, 1989.

35. National Society for the Study of Education, *Twenty-Eighth Yearbook: Preschool and Parental Education* (Bloomington, Ill.: Public School Publishing Company, 1929), 343–50.

36. Lucy Wheelock, *Talks to Mothers* (Boston: Houghton Mifflin, 1920), 2.

37. On the Child Study Association, see Roberta Wollons, "Women Educating Women: The Child Study Association as Women's Culture," in Joyce Antler and Sari Knopp Biklen, eds., *Changing Education: Women and Radicals and Conservators* (Albany: State University of New York Press, 1990), 51–68; Steven L. Schlossman, "Before Home Start: Notes toward a History of Parent Education in America, 1897–1929," *Harvard Educational Review* 46 (August 1976): 436–67; and Julia Grant, "Modernizing Motherhood: Child Study Clubs and the Parent Education Movement, 1915–1940" (Ph.D. diss., Boston University Graduate School, 1992).

38. See Alice Smuts, "Edna Noble White," in Barbara Sicherman and Carol Hurd Green, eds., *Notable American Women: The Modern Period* (Cambridge: Harvard University Press, 1980), 728–29; and Roderick Nash, "Lizzie Merrill Palmer," in *NAW,* 3:11–12.

39. "The Merrill-Palmer Nursery School," in National Society for the Study of Education, *Twenty-Eighth Yearbook,* 195, 197; Forest, *Preschool Education,* 297–299, 362.

40. Edna Noble White, *The Merrill-Palmer School: A Report of Twenty Years, 1920–1940* (Detroit: Merrill-Palmer School, 1940), 17. See idem, "The Nursery School: A Teacher of Parents," *Child Study* 4 (October 1926): 8, 43.

41. Forest, *Preschool Education,* 302. White also encouraged public school home economics departments to start parent education programs and nursery schools in which high school students worked as assistant teachers, a practice still common in many high schools today.

42. Helen T. Woolley, "The Real Function of the Nursery School," address delivered at the Parenthood Conference of the Child Study Association, October 1925, *Child Study* 3

(February 1927): 6. For more on Woolley, see Rosalind Rosenberg, *Beyond Separate Spheres: Intellectual Roots of Modern Feminism* (New Haven: Yale University Press, 1982), 62, 66; and Elizabeth Scarborough and Laurel Furumoto, *Untold Lives: The First Generation of American Women Psychologists* (New York: Columbia University Press, 1987), 199–201. Another prominent nursery educator, Barbara Greenwood, found "considerable variation in the trend of scores" and no significant results after extensive mental testing and retesting of children attending the laboratory nursery school at UCLA. See Barbara Greenwood, Charles W. Waddell, Eva Scantlebury, Elizabeth Pell, Helen B. Thompson, and William M. Happ, *A Six-Year Experiment with a Nursery School* (Los Angeles: University of California at Los Angeles, 1931), 105.

43. Woolley, "The Real Function of the Nursery School," 10–11.

44. Helen T. Woolley, "Agnes: A Dominant Personality in the Making," *Pedagogical Seminary and Journal of Genetic Psychology* (March 1926): 569, 578, 597.

45. Helen T. Woolley, "Peter: The Beginnings of the Juvenile Court Problem," *Pedagogical Seminary and Journal of Genetic Psychology* (December 1926), 28–29.

46. Helen T. Woolley, *David: A Study of the Experience of a Nursery School in Training a Child Adopted from an Institution,* Case Studies No. 2 (New York: Child Welfare League of America, 1925), 3–26.

47. Elizabeth Cleveland, *Training the Toddler* (Philadelphia: Lippincott, 1925), 3, 8.

48. Bird Baldwin, "Preschool Laboratories at the Iowa Child Welfare Research Station," in National Society for the Study of Education, *Twenty-Eighth Yearbook,* 212.

49. Hillis quoted in Dorothy Bradbury, *Pioneering in Child Welfare: A History of the Iowa Child Welfare Research Station, 1917–1933* (Iowa City: State University of Iowa, 1933), 7. See also Hamilton Cravens, *Before Head Start: The Iowa Station and America's Children* (Chapel Hill and London: University of North Carolina Press, 1993).

50. Bird T. Baldwin, "Measuring Childhood," ACEI Archives, n.d., 163–65, 162. See Bird T. Baldwin and Lorle I. Stecher, *The Psychology of the Preschool Child* (New York: Appleton, 1924). See also Robert R. Sears, *Your Ancients Revisited: A History of Child Development* (Chicago: University of Chicago Press, 1975), 16–17, 20.

51. Eva I. Grant, "The Effect of Certain Factors in the Home Environment Upon Child Behavior," and Louise C. Coast, "A Study of the Knowledge and Attitudes of Parents of Preschool Children," *University of Iowa Studies in Child Welfare* 17 (December 1, 1939): 63, 180. See Bradbury, *Pioneering in Child Welfare,* 58, 64; Dorothy Bradbury and Louise Propst, *Publications of the Iowa Child Welfare Research Station* (Iowa City: State University of Iowa, 1935); and National Society for the Study of Education, *Twenty-Eighth Yearbook,* 216.

52. Ruth Updegraff, *Practice in Preschool Education* (New York: McGraw-Hill, 1938), 3, 49. See also University of Iowa Child Welfare Research Station, *A Manual Of Preschool Practice* (Iowa City: State University of Iowa, 1934).

53. George D. Stoddard, "Educating the Very Young Child," in Dorothy Canfield Fisher and Sophie Matsner Gruenberg, *Our Children: A Handbook for Parents* (New York: Viking, 1932), 217, 223, 224. Like Baldwin, Stoddard, who had received his doctorate from the State University of Iowa in 1925, was deeply involved in the testing movement; indeed, tests that he developed as part of his doctoral work were used throughout the country as the "Iowa Placement Exams," precursors of the Iowa tests well known to American schoolchildren. For more on Stoddard, see Bradbury, *Pioneering in Child Welfare* and Cravens, *Before Head Start.* For nursery school schedules, see Mary Dabney Davis and

Rowna Hansen, *Nursery Schools, Their Development and Current Practices in the United States*, U.S. Department of the Interior, Office of Education Bulletin, 1932, No. 9 (Washington, D.C.: GPO, 1933), 38.

54. W. McKinley Menchan, "The Negro College Takes to the Nursery School," *School and Society* 36 (September 10, 1932): 339. See idem, *Introduction to Child Development and Parent Education* (New York: Vantage, 1969); and Ednora P. Cooper, "Hampton Institute's Preschool Group," *Southern Workman* (July 1934): 214–15.

55. On Howes's life and career, see Dolores Hayden, *The Grand Domestic Revolution: A History of Feminist Designs for American Homes, Neighborhoods, and Cities* (Cambridge, Mass.: MIT Press, 1981), 266–77; Barbara Miller Solomon, *In the Company of Educated Women: A History of Women's Higher Education in America* (New Haven: Yale University Press, 1985), 176–78; Nancy F. Cott, *Grounding of Modern Feminism* (New Haven: Yale University Press, 1987), 202–4; and Scarborough and Furumoto, *Untold Lives*, 73–90.

56. See Hayden, *The Grand Domestic Revolution*, for a discussion and description of early cooperative homemaking experiments and material feminism.

57. Ethel Puffer Howes, "The Mother's Basic Problem," *Child Study* 3 (January 1926), 1–2. See Ethel Puffer Howes and Dorothea Beach, *The Co-Operative Nursery School: What It Can Do for Parents* (Northampton, Mass.: Smith College, 1928).

58. Ethel Puffer Howes, "Progress of the Institute for the Co-ordination of Women's Interests," ICWI Collection, box 60, GW 1262, folder 26, Smith College Archives; Esther Stocks, "The Institute, Act IV, Scene 2," *Smith College Alumnae Quarterly* 20 (February 1929): 152, Smith College Archives. See Ethel Puffer Howes, "A 'Day Off' for Mothers" and "The Nursery School," *Woman's Home Companion*, May and December 1923, Smith College Archives. See also Esther H. Stocks, *A "Home Assistants" Experiment* (Northampton, Mass.: Smith College, 1928); Ethel Puffer Howes and Myra Reed Richardson, *How to Start a Cooperative Kitchen* and *How to Start a Cooperative Laundry* (New York: Crowell, 1923); Alice Peloubet Norton, *Cooked Food Supply Experiments in America;* and Dorothea Beach and Ethel P. Howes, *Cooked Food Supply Experiments in an Eastern College* (Northampton, Mass.: Smith College, 1928).

59. Ethel Puffer Howes, *How to Start a Cooperative Nursery* (New York: Crowell, 1923), 6; Ethel Puffer Howes and Dorothea Beach, *The Cooperative Nursery School* (Northampton, Mass.: Smith College, 1928), 13–16. See also Dorothea Beach, "Smith College Cooperative Nursery School," in National Society for the Study of Education, *The Twenty-Eighth Yearbook*, 217–23.

60. Howes and Beach, *Cooperative Nursery School*, 42; Mary Thayer Bixler, "The Affiliated Nursery School—The Parents' View," in Institute for the Coordination of Women's Interests, *The Nursery School as a Social Experiment* (Northampton, Mass.: Smith College, 1931), 29; Ethel Puffer Howes and Esther Stocks, "Co-operating Mothers," and "Keeping the Thread" (editorial), *Woman Citizen* (February 1927), box 60, GW 1262, file 17, ICWI Collection, Smith College Archives.

61. Howes and Beach, *Cooperative Nursery School*, 23–24.

62. Ethel Puffer Howes, "Continuity for Women," *Atlantic Monthly* 130 (December 1922): 738, quoted in Hayden, *The Grand Domestic Revolution*, 276; Lawrence K. Frank, Letter to President Thomas C. Mendenhall, May 7, 1963, Smith College Archives, quoted in Hayden, *The Grand Domestic Revolution*, 277. For the complicated series of misunderstandings that ended the Rockefeller funding, see C. Todd Stephenson, "Integrating the

Carol Kennicotts: Ethel Puffer Howes and the Institute for the Coordination of Women's Interests," *Journal of Women's History* 4 (Spring 1992): 89–113.

63. "The Nursery School of Wellesley College," *School and Society* 26 (October 8, 1927): 454; "At Wellesley Children Will Go to College Before They Go to School," *Christian Science Monitor*, September 9, 1927, Archives, Wellesley College, Wellesley, Mass.; "The Nursery School of Vassar College," *Detroit Educational Bulletin* 11, no. 10 (June 1928): 16, Archives, Vassar College, Poughkeepsie, N.Y.; *The Mildred R. Wimpfheimer Nursery School* (Poughkeepsie, N.Y.: Vassar College, 1928), 3, Archives, Vassar College, Poughkeepsie, N.Y. See also *The Wellesley Nursery School*, Archives, Wellesley College, Wellesley, Mass.

64. Eliot, interview with Beatty, 7; Eliot, "Educating the Parent," 185; "Parent Cooperative Nursery Schools: An Interview with Katharine Whiteside Taylor," in James L. Hymes, Jr., *Living History Interviews*, vol. 1, *Beginnings* (Carmel, Calif.: Hacienda, 1978), 41. See also Eliot, "Report of the Ruggles Street Nursery School," 155.

65. Katharine Whiteside Taylor, *Parent Cooperative Nursery Schools* (New York: Bureau of Publications, Teachers College, Columbia University, 1954), 4; "Confessions of a Coordinating Wife," *Smith Alumnae Quarterly*, February 1930, Smith College Archives.

66. E. Mae Raymond, "The Nursery School as an Integral Part of Education," *Teachers College Record* 27 (May 1926): 784, 785.

67. Raymond, "The Nursery School," 790; George Stoddard, "A Survey of Nursery School Costs," *Journal of Educational Research* 26 (September 1933): 354.

68. David Snedden, "Some Problems of Nursery School Education," *Teachers College Record* 28 (September 1926): 28.

69. Eunice Fuller Barnard, "Does the American Baby Need a School?" *New Republic*, August 11, 1926, 334.

70. National Society for the Study of Education, *Twenty-Eighth Yearbook*, 239–241; Davis and Hansen, *Nursery Schools, Their Development and Current Practices*, 1; Robert Melvin Tank, "Young Children, Families, and Society in America since the 1820s: The Evolution of Health, Education, and Child Care Programs for Preschool Children" (Ph.D. diss. University of Michigan, 1980), 294.

Chapter 9. Public Preschools

1. Molly Ladd-Taylor, *Raising a Baby the Government Way: Mothers' Letters to the Children's Bureau, 1915–1932* (New Brunswick: Rutgers University Press, 1986), 88–89. See Robyn Muncy, *Creating a Female Dominion in American Reform, 1890 to 1835* (New York: Oxford University Press, 1991), 38–65.

2. Ladd-Taylor, *Raising a Baby the Government Way;* Muncy, *Creating a Female Dominion,* 114–15, 152–53, 147.

3. White House Conference on Child Health and Protection, Committee on the Education and Training of the Infant and Preschool Child, *Nursery Education* (New York: Century, 1931), 136.

4. White House Conference, *Nursery Education,* 50, 52, 53; White House Conference on Child Health and Protection, *The Young Child in the Home* (New York: D. Appleton, 1936), 266, 267, 325–26, 332.

5. Mary Dabney Davis, *Kindergarten-Primary Education*, U.S. Department of the Interior, Office of Education Bulletin (Washington, D.C.: GPO, 1930), 3; David Tyack, Robert Lowe, Elizabeth Hansot, *Public Schools in Hard Times* (Cambridge: Harvard University Press, 1984), 40; Bess Goodykoontz, Mary Dabney Davis, and Mina Langvick, "Nursery Education," section from "Elementary Education," in *Biennial Survey of Education, 1928–1930*, U.S. Department of the Interior, Office of Education Bulletin No. 20, pt. 1 (Washington, D.C.: GPO, 1931), 59–120; Mary Dabney Davis, *Schools for Children Under Six*, U.S. Department of the Interior, Office of Education Bulletin No. 5 (Washington, D.C.: GPO, 1947, 29; Bess Goodykoontz, Mary Dabney Davis, and Hazel F. Gabbard, "Recent History and Present Status of Education for Young Children," in *The Forty-Sixth Yearbook of the National Society for the Study of Education*, vol. 2, *Early Childhood Education* (Chicago: University of Chicago Press, 1947), 44–49.

6. Patty Smith Hill, "The Kindergarten Child and the New Deal," pamphlet reprinted by Milton Bradley Company from *American Childhood Magazine*, n.d., n.p., ACEI Archives, University of Maryland; idem, "Shall the Youngest Suffer Most?" *The Parents' Magazine* (April 1932), ACEI Archives, University of Maryland, n.p.; White House Conference, *The Young Child in the Home*, 269–81.

7. Article in the Wellesley *Townsman* quoted in Matilda Remy, "The Closing of Kindergartens," *Childhood Education* (1933), 479.

8. Mary Dabney Davis, *Nursery Schools: Their Development and Current Practices in the United States*, U.S. Department of the Interior, Office of Education Bulletin, 1932, No. 9 (Washington, D.C.: GPO, 1933), 1.

9. Letter from Mrs. Alfred Alschuler, April 22, 1925, Chicago Women's Club Collection, Club Literary and Business Meetings, file, 1924–25, box 29, Chicago Historical Society; Rose M. Alschuler, "The Franklin School Nursery of the Chicago Public Schools," in National Society for the Study of Education, *Twenty-Eighth Yearbook* (Bloomington, Ill.: School Publishing Company, 1929), 157–58.

10. Alschuler, "Franklin School Nursery," 164. See Rose Alschuler, *Report of Nursery School Committee*, Chicago Women's Club Collection, Club Meetings 1925–1926, box 29.

11. Rose H. Alschuler, "A New Nursery School Set-Up," *Childhood Education* 5 (February 1929): 308, 307.

12. Rose H. Alschuler and associates, *Two to Six: Suggestions for Parents and Teachers of Young Children*, rev. ed. (New York: Morrow, 1937), 4, 103, 9, 12–13.

13. Davis, *Nursery Schools*, 67, 69. See Annie Judith Blanchard, "Correlation of the Early Elementary Grades in Grand Rapids," *Childhood Education* 4 (March 1928): 321.

14. National Association for the Education of Young Children Organizational History and Archives Committee, "NAEYC's First Half Century," *Young Children* (September 1976): 467. On Stolz, see Julia Grant, "Lois Meek Stolz," in Maxine Schwartz Seller, ed., *Women Educators in the United States, 1820–1993* (Westport: Greenwood, 1994), 472–79.

15. National Advisory Committee on Emergency Nursery Schools, *Emergency Nursery Schools during the First Year* (Washington, D.C.: National Advisory Committee on Emergency Nursery Schools, 1934), 8, quoted in Emily D. Cahan, *Past Caring: A History of U.S. Preschool Care and Education for the Poor, 1820–1965* (New York: National Center for Children in Poverty, Columbia University, 1989), 37–38.

16. NAEYC Organizational History and Archives Committee, "NAEYC's First Half Century," 463, 465. NANE decided not to join the new Association for Childhood Education that Patty Smith Hill's good friend Alice Temple was reorganizing from the International

Kindergarten Union. This split seems to have occurred in part because NANE identified itself with the more research-oriented child development institutes, most of which were headed by male psychologists, while the IKU was associated with primarily female teachers and teacher educators.

17. *Proceedings of the Second Conference of the National Association for Nursery Education* (New York: NANE, 1927), 8.

18. George D. Stoddard, "Conference Issues," in *Proceedings of the Fourth Conference of the National Nursery Association* (New York: NANE, 1931), 10.

19. Mary Dabney Davis, "Business Meetings," *Proceedings of the Sixth Conference of the National Association for Nursery Education* (New York: NANE, 1933), 90.

20. National Advisory Committee on Emergency Nursery Schools, *Emergency Nursery Schools during the Second Year, 1934–1935* (Washington, D.C.: National Advisory Committee on Emergency Nursery Schools, 1935).

21. Sonya Michel, "The Politics of Childhood: Federal Programs for Children from the WPA through Head Start," paper presented at annual meeting of the Organization of American Historians, Washington, D.C., March 9, 1990, 7–8; Robert Melvin Tank, "Young Children, Families, and Society in America since the 1820s: The Evolution of Health, Education, and Child Care Programs for Preschool Children" (Ph.D. diss. University of Michigan, 1980), 356.

22. Abigail Eliot, personal interview with Barbara Beatty, July 1, 1980, typescript in Abigail Adams Eliot Papers, Schlesinger Library, Radcliffe, 16.

23. Eliot, interview with Beatty, 18. Enrollment figures are from Grace Langdon, "The Facts about Emergency Nursery Schools," *Childhood Education* 11 (March 1935): 255; and Tank, "Young Children, Families, and Society in America," 356. See also Goodykoontz, Davis, and Gabbard, "Recent History and Present Status of Education for Young Children," 44; NAC, *Emergency Nursery Schools during the Second Year*, 21.

24. Langdon, "Facts about Emergency Nursery Schools," 257. See Dr. Grace Langdon, reports of field trips, WPA Collection, Dr. Grace Langdon files, National Archives, Washington, D.C.

25. Grace Langdon, "Report of Field Trip—Teacher Training Conference, Greensboro, NC, July 8–9, 1940," and "Regional Conference, Milwaukee, May, 1940," WPA Collection, Dr. Grace Langdon files, RG69, box 0422, National Archives, Washington, D.C. For teachers' previous experience, see NAC, *Emergency Nursery Schools during the Second Year*, 38.

26. NAC, *Emergency Nursery Schools during the Second Year*, 36–37; Eleanor Tilden Jefferson, Wheelock College class of 1923, interview with Barbara Beatty, May 29, 1993.

27. Dr. Grace Langdon, "Report of Field Trip, Wisconsin, April 22–29, 1940," 4–5, and "Conference of State WPA Nursery School Supervisors," WPA Collection, Dr. Grace Langdon files, RG69, box 0422, National Archives, Washington, D.C.; idem, "Field Trip Report, November 9–11, 1940," WPA Collection, Dr. Grace Langdon files, RG69, box 0422, National Archives, Washington, D.C.

28. Jessie Stanton, "Emergency Nursery Schools in New York City," *Childhood Education* 11 (November 1934): 79, 80.

29. Langdon, "Facts about Emergency Nursery Schools," 256. See NAC, *Emergency Nursery Schools during the Second Year*, 29, 23–24.

30. Dr. Grace Langdon, "Field Report, St. Louis, Missouri, February 24–29, 1940," 17, "Report of Field Trip, April 29–May 3, 1940," 4, and "Report of Field Trip, Wisconsin,

April 22–29, 1940," 11, WPA Collection, Dr. Grace Langdon files, RG69, box 0422, National Archives, Washington, D.C.

31. George Stoddard, "Emergency Nursery Schools on Trial," *Childhood Education* 11 (March 1935): 260, 261.

32. Dr. Grace Langdon, "Report of Field Trip, Wisconsin, April 22–29, 1940," 11, WPA Collection, Dr. Grace Langdon files, RG69, box 0422, National Archives, Washington, D.C. For the dinner in Kalamazoo, see Dr. Grace Langdon, "Field Trip Report: Regional Office, Region IV, February 19–24, 1940," WPA Collection, Dr. Grace Langdon files, RG69, box 0422, National Archives, Washington, D.C.

33. Langdon, "Facts about Emergency Nursery Schools," 46; Goodykoontz, Davis, and Gabbard, "Recent History and Present Status of Education for Young Children," 49–50, 61.

34. George Stoddard, "Nursery Schools in the Emergency Program," *School and Society* 40, (August 4, 1934): 149; idem, "The Tasks Which Await Us," *World Organization of Early Childhood Education*, Report on the Second World Conference held at UNESCO House, Paris, August 24–26, 1949, 12, quoted in Ruby Takanishi, "Federal Involvement in Early Education (1933–1973): The Need for Historical Perspectives," in Lilian Katz, ed., *Current Issues in Early Childhood Education* (Norwood, N.J.: Ablex, 1977), 1:155–56.

35. Abigail A. Eliot, "The Welfare of Young Children in the War Emergency," *Alpha Circle of the City of Boston Educational Service Quarterly* 8 (October 1942): n.p., Abigail Adams Eliot Papers, Schlesinger Library, Radcliffe College. On children during the war, see William M. Tuttle, Jr., "America's Home Front Children in World War II," in Glen H. Elder, Jr., John Modell, and Ross D. Parke, eds., *Children in Time and Place: Developmental and Historical Insights* (Cambridge: Cambridge University Press, 1993), 27–46.

36. Dorothy W. Baruch, *You, Your Children, and War* (New York: D. Appleton–Century, 1942), 204, 52, 59.

37. McNutt quoted in Tank, "Young Children, Families, and Society in America," 379, 380. See Steven Mintz and Susan Kellogg, *Domestic Revolutions: A Social History of American Family Life* (New York: Free Press, 1988), 161; "Dr. Eliot Urges 4-Hour Shift," *Boston Herald*, clipping, n.d., Abigail Eliot vertical file, Schlesinger Library, Radcliffe; and Michel, "The Politics of Childhood," 22.

38. Langdon quoted in Michel, "Politics of Childhood," 18. See ibid., 24, 30, 31; and Sonya Michel, "Children's Interests/Mothers' Rights: Women, Professionals, and the American Family, 1920–1945" (Ph.D. diss., Brown University, 1986), 356.

39. Richard Polenberg, *War and Society* (Philadelphia: Lippincott, 1972), 149.

40. Christine Heinig, "The Emergency Nursery Schools and the Wartime Child Care Centers: 1933–1946," in James L. Hymes, Jr., *Living History Interviews*, vol. 3, *Reaching Large Numbers of Children* (Carmel, Calif.: Hacienda, 1979), 24.

41. Rose H. Alschuler, ed. *Children's Centers* (New York: William Morrow, 1942), 14, 15.

42. Tank, "Young Children, Families, and Society in America," 375; Lois Meek Stolz, "The Kaiser Child Service Centers," in James L. Hymes, Jr., *Living History Interviews*, vol. 2, *Care of the Children of Working Mothers* (Carmel, Calif.: Hacienda, 1978), 27, 29.

43. Hymes quoted in Samuel J. Braun and Esther P. Edwards, *History and Theory of Early Childhood Education* (Worthington, Ohio: Charles A. Jones Publishing Company, 1972), 171; Hymes quoted in Stolz, "Kaiser Child Service Centers," 54. See also ibid., 42–43, 52.

44. Stolz, "Kaiser Child Service Centers," 49; "The Federal Government and a Child Care Program," November 5, 1943, Wayne Coy Papers, Franklin D. Roosevelt Library, Hyde

Park, New York, quoted in Polenberg, *War and Society*, 149. Fee information from Kellogg and Mintz, *Domestic Revolutions*, 163. Attendance statistics from Tank, "Young Children, Families, and Society in America," 387.

45. Eliot quoted in "Emotional Balance Held Great Need of Parents to Check Child Neuroses," *Boston Traveler*, January 21, 1947, Abigail Eliot vertical file, Schlesinger Library. See Cahan, *Past Caring*, 45; Gilbert Y. Steiner, *The Children's Cause* (Washington, D.C.: Brookings, 1976), 19; W. Norton Grubb and Marvin Lazerson, "Child Care, Government Financing, and the Public Schools: Lessons from the California Children's Centers," *School Review* 86 (November 1977): 5–37; and Elaine Tyler May, *Homeward Bound: American Families in the Cold War Era* (New York: Basic, 1988).

46. Abigail Eliot quoted in "Emotional Balance Held Great Need."

47. Joseph McVicker Hunt, *Intelligence and Experience* (New York: Ronald Press, 1961); Sheldon H. White, personal correspondence with author, May 24, 1994.

48. Benjamin Bloom, *Stability and Change in Human Characteristics* (New York: Wiley, 1964); White, personal correspondence.

49. Edward Zigler and Susan Muenchow, *Head Start: The Inside Story of America's Most Successful Educational Experiment* (New York: Basic, 1992), 16–17.

50. White, personal correspondence; Zigler and Muenchow, *Head Start*, 4–6.

This cognitive slant, encouraged by the increasingly influential research of Swiss psychologist Jean Piaget, was apparent in the early experimental preschool programs of Susan Gray and Rupert Klaus of George Peabody Teachers College in Nashville, Tennessee, which served as a model for Head Start. Gray's Early Training Project was a successful ten-week summer nursery school and weekly parent education program for sixty very poor black children and their mothers in Murfreesboro, Tennessee. Gray documented how she was able to raise the IQ scores of these educationally disadvantaged children through four-hour-a-day sessions consisting mostly of play and other typical nursery school activities in small groups of about five children to each teacher. Gray found that attending the summer preschool program also had a positive effect on children's younger siblings, though by the fourth grade most of these effects seemed to have disappeared. See Susan W. Gray, "Children from Three to Ten: The Early Training Project," in Sally Ryan, ed., *A Report on Longitudinal Evaluations of Preschool Programs*, DHEW Publication No. 76-30024 (Washington, D.C.: GPO, 1974), 61–68.

51. For a complete listing and brief biographies of the Head Start Planning Committee, see Joseph A. Califano, Jr., "Head Start, A Retrospective View: The Founders," in Edward Zigler and Jeanette Valentine, eds., *Project Head Start: A Legacy of the War on Poverty* (New York: Free Press, 1979), 43–134. See also Zigler and Muenchow, *Head Start*, 6–8.

52. See Zigler and Muenchow, *Head Start*, 9.

53. Polly Greenberg, *The Devil Has Slippery Shoes: A Biased Biography of the Child Development Group of Mississippi* (New York: Macmillan, 1969), 6, 132. See also Polly Greenberg, "Head Start—Part of a Multi-Pronged Anti-Poverty Effort for Young Children and Their Families . . . Before the Beginning: A Participant's View," *Young Children*, 45, 6 (September 1990): 40–52.

54. Greenberg, *The Devil Has Slippery Shoes*, 155, 171, 175–76. For Greenberg's list of good preschool programs, see ibid., 97. For Deutsch, see Martin Deutsch, Elizabeth Taleporos, and Jack Victor, "A Brief Synopsis of an Initial Enrichment Program in Early Childhood," in Sally Ryan, ed., *A Report on Longitudinal Evaluations of Preschool Programs*, DHEW Publication No. 76-30024 (Washington, D.C.: GPO, 1974), 49–60.

55. Greenberg, *The Devil Has Slippery Shoes*, 76–77.

56. Arthur R. Jensen, "How Much Can We Boost IQ and Scholastic Achievement?" *Harvard Educational Review* 39 (winter 1969): 1–123; Zigler and Muenchow, *Head Start*, 73–74; White, personal correspondence.

57. Zigler and Muenchow, *Head Start*, 44–45, 47. For other examples of concerns about Head Start, see Eveline Omwake, "Head Start—Measurable and Immeasurable," in Jerome Hellmuth, ed., *Disadvantaged Child* (New York: Brunner/Mazel, 1968), 2:531–44; and James S. Payne, *Head Start: A Tragicomedy with Epilogue* (New York: Behavioral Publications, 1973).

58. Stephen S. Baratz and Joan C. Baratz, "Early Childhood Intervention: The Social Science Base of Institutional Racism," reprinted in Robert H. Anderson and Harold G. Shane, *As the Twig Is Bent: Readings in Early Childhood Education* (Boston: Houghton Mifflin, 1971), 35, 50. See Urie Bronfenbrenner, "Is Early Intervention Effective?" DHEW Publication No. 76-30025 (Washington, D.C.: GPO, 1974).

59. Zigler and Muenchow, *Head Start*, 136, 146.

60. "Reasons Why Head Start Should Not Be Included in a Department of Education or Placed Under Educational Auspices in the Absence of Such a Department," Children's Defense Fund position paper, n.d., 2; Evelyn K. Moore, "Child Care in the Public Schools: Public Accountability and the Black Child," in Sharon L. Kagan and Edward Zigler, *Early Schooling: The National Debate* (New Haven: Yale University Press, 1987), 85. For more on the public school systems' history of segregation and alienation from the African-American community, see Sara Lawrence Lightfoot, *Worlds Apart: Relationships between Black Families and Schools* (New York: Basic, 1978).

61. Irving Lazar and R. B. Darlington, *Lasting Effects of Early Education*, Monographs of the Society for Research in Child Development 47 (Washington, D.C.: Society for Research in Child Development, 1982); John Berrueta-Clement, Lawrence Schweinhart, W. Steven Barnett, Anne Epstein, and David Weikart, *Changed Lives: The Effects of the Perry Preschool Program on Youths through Age 19*, Monographs of the High/Scope Educational Research Foundation 8 (Ypsilanti, Mich.: Highscope, 1984).

62. Zigler and Muenchow, *Head Start*, 207–9.

Conclusion

1. Fern Marx and Michelle Seligson, *The Public School Early Childhood Study: The State Survey* (New York: Bank Street College of Education, 1988); Anne Mitchell, Michelle Seligson, and Fern Marx, *Early Childhood Programs and the Public Schools* (Dover, Mass.: Auburn House, 1989); Sandra L. Robinson and Christopher Lyon, "Early Childhood Offerings in 1992: Will We Be Ready for 2000?" *Phi Delta Kappan* 76 (June 1994): 775–78.

2. David Elkind, *Miseducation: Preschoolers at Risk* (New York: Knopf, 1987). See also Samuel J. Meisels, "Four Myths about America's Kindergartens," *Education Week* 10 (May 8, 1991): 32. For modern studies of cultural differences in what parents want in preschool education and of the relationship of preschool education to cultural values, see Joseph Tobin, David Y. H. Wu, and Dana H. Davidson, *Preschool in Three Cultures: Japan, China, and the United States* (New Haven: Yale University Press, 1989), and Patricia P. Olmsted and David P. Weikart, eds., *Families Speak: Early Childhood Care and Education in Eleven Countries* (Ypsilanti, Mich.: High/Scope Press, 1994). For a popular compendium

of what Americans think preschools should teach and why they think preschools are important, see Robert Fulghum, *All I Really Need to Know I Learned in Kindergarten* (New York: Ivy, 1986).

3. See Susan D. Holloway and Bruce Fuller, "The Great Child-Care Experiment: What Are the Lessons for School Improvement?" *Educational Researcher* 21 (October 1992): 12–19. For an earlier study of issues relating to preschool quality and governance, see John I. Goodlad, M. Frances Klein, and Jerrold M. Novotny, *Early Schooling in the United States* (New York: McGraw-Hill, 1973). Two recent helpful discussions are W. Norton Grubb, "Choosing Wisely for Children: Policy Options for Early Childhood Programs," and Sharon L. Kagan, "Excellence in Early Childhood Education: Defining Characteristics of Next Decade Strategies," in Sharon Lynn Kagan, ed., *The Care and Education of America's Young Children*, Ninetieth Yearbook of the National Society for the Study of Education, vol. 1 (Chicago: University of Chicago Press, 1991), 214–36 and 237–58.

4. For samples of recent research on preschool purposes and practices, see Sue Bredekamp, ed., *Developmentally Appropriate Practice in Early Childhood Education Programs Serving Children from Birth through Age Eight* (Washington, D.C.: National Association for the Education of Young Children, 1987); Margaret V. Yonnemura, *A Teacher at Work: Professional Development and the Early Childhood Teacher* (New York: Teachers College Press, 1986); Center on Evaluation, Development, Research, Phi Delta Kappa, *Preschool Education* (Bloomington: Phi Delta Kappa, 1989); and idem, *Kindergarten Education* (Bloomington: Phi Delta Kappa, 1989); and David Elkind, ed., *Perspectives on Early Childhood Education: Growing with Young Children toward the Twenty-First Century* (Washington, D.C.: National Education Association, 1991).

5. Rebecca S. New and Bruce L. Mallory, "Introduction: The Ethic of Inclusion," and Sally Lubeck, "The Politics of Developmentally Appropriate Practice: Exploring Issues of Culture, Class, and Curriculum," in Bruce L. Mallory and Rebecca S. New, eds., *Diversity and Developmentally Appropriate Practices: Challenges for Early Childhood Education* (New York: Teachers College Press, 1994), 1–13, 17–43.

6. Sharon L. Kagan, "Readying Schools for Children: Polemics and Priorities," *Phi Delta Kappan* 76 (November 1994): 226–33 See Edward F. Zigler, "Formal Schooling for Four-Year-Olds? No," in Sharon L. Kagan and Edward Zigler, *Early Schooling: The National Debate* (New Haven: Yale University Press, 1987), 27–44; Jerold P. Bauch, ed., *Early Childhood Education in the Schools* (Washington, D.C.: National Education Association, 1986); and Edward F. Zigler and Mary E. Lang, *Child Care Choices: Balancing the Needs of Children, Families, and Society* (New York: Free Press, 1991).

7. Zigler and Lang, *Child Care Choices*, 199; Bettye M. Caldwell, "A Comprehensive Model for Integrating Child Care and Early Childhood Education," *Teachers College Record* 90 (spring 1989): 404–14.

8. George Stoddard, *Proceedings of the National Association for Nursery Education, Fifth Conference* (New York: NANE, 1933), 6.

Index